MODERN WORLD HISTORY
Combined Edition

INTERNATIONAL RELATIONS 1919–1989 | Tony McAleavy

BRITISH HISTORY 1906–1918 | Paul Grey and Rosemarie Little

GERMANY 1919–1945 | Paul Grey and Rosemarie Little

CAMBRIDGE
UNIVERSITY PRESS

PUBLISHED BY THE PRESS SYNDICATE OF THE UNIVERSITY OF CAMBRIDGE
The Pitt Building, Trumpington Street, Cambridge, United Kingdom

CAMBRIDGE UNIVERSITY PRESS
The Edinburgh Building, Cambridge CB2 2RU, UK
40 West 20th Street, New York, NY 10011–4211, USA
477 Williamstown Road, Port Melbourne, VIC 3207, Australia
Ruiz de Alarcón 13, 28014 Madrid, Spain
Dock House, The Waterfront, Cape Town 8001, South Africa

http://www.cambridge.org

First published 2001
Fourth printing 2004

Printed in the United Kingdom at the University Press, Cambridge

Typeset in Monotype Octavian and FF Meta

A catalogue record for this book is available from the British Library

ISBN 0 521 00384 9 paperback

Produced by Gecko Limited, Bicester, Oxon

Picture Research by Marilyn Rawlings, Sandie Huskinson-Rolfe of PHOTOSEEKERS.

ACKNOWLEDGEMENTS
We are grateful to the following for permission to reproduce photographs:
'Photo – AKG, London': pp. 56, 62 (inset), 67, 89, 106, 148, 154, 166–167 (background), 173, 221*b*, 222–223, 231, 238
(background), 254*l*, 255, 256, 259*l*, 261, 263, 265*r*, 267, 268, 269 (background); theartarchive: pp. 45, 52, 95, 99, 240,
253*l*; Bayerische Staatsbibliothek: p. 233; Bildarchiv Preussischer Kulturbesitz: pp. 236*l*, 239, 243, 262; Black Star
(photo: Gordon/Cranbourne): p. 136; *A Bloomsbury Family*, 1907 by Sir William Orpen (1878–1931), Scottish
National Gallery of Modern Art, Edinburgh, UK/Bridgeman Art Library, London: p. 172, *The Old Room in Slumland*
(b/w photo), Private Collection/BAL: p. 174, Private Collection/BAL: p. 179, *The Polling Station*, c.1912
(woodblock) by Sir William Nicholson (1872–1949), Private Collection/The Stapleton Collection/BAL: p. 189,
Women's Suffrage poster, Private Collection/BAL: p. 192 left, *Suffragette Propaganda Poster by E.J. Harding Andrews*,
Emily J. Harding (fl.1910), Fawcett Library, London, UK/BAL: p. 192 right, Poster published by the National
Women's Social and Political Union, printed by David Allen & Sons Ltd, 1913, British Library, London, UK/BAL:
193 bottom; Camera Press Limited: pp. 113, 118, 122, 127, 131, 141, 145, 147, 153, 155, 156, 157, 158, 160, 163, 249*br*;
David Low/Evening Standard: Centre for the Study of Cartoons and Caricature, University of Kent, Canterbury:
pp. 55, 63 (inset), 69, 73, 258; Deutsche Bücherei, Leipzig: p. 235*b*; Mary Evans Picture Library: pp. 171 top &
bottom, 185, 187 top, 198, 199 bottom, 212 (detail), 213, 215 (bottom), 216; Hulton Archive: pp. 16, 20, 26, 35, 38, 40,
50, 57, 77, 83, 111, 114*l*, 120–121 (background and inset), 197, 203, 209, 210, 234, 244; Robert Hunt Library: p. 70;
Illustrated London News Picture Library: pp. 15, 27; The Imperial War Museum, London: pp. 8, 9, 18, 34, 37, 68, 81,
86–87 (background), 91, 242, 266; David King Collection: pp. 10, 11, 32, 78, 79, 107, 110, 114*r*, 132*t*; The Kobal
Collection: p. 236*tr* (Universal), p.236*br* (Decla-Bioscope); by courtesy of The National Portrait Gallery, London:
p. 72; Peter Newark's Historical Pictures: pp. 13, 39, 42, 47, 48, 54, 74, 86 (inset), 94*l* and *r*, 98, 101, 112, 117, 125, 135,
139, 176, 177*l*, 186, 193*t*, 199*t*, 200*t*, 205, 206, 207, 215*t*, 217*bl*, 251, 257; Popperfoto: pp. 33, 46, 49, 62–63
(background), 75, 87 (inset), 97, 102, 109, 133, 142 (inset), 142–143 (background), 143 (inset), 149, 150–151, 165, 167
(inset), 187*b*, 195, 200*b*, 217*tl*, 218, 269 (inset), 235*t*, 249*tr*, 254*r*; "reproduced with permission of Punch Ltd": pp. 4,
14, 31, 177*r*, 217*r*; Rex Features/Sipa: p. 90; Süddeutscher Verlag Bilderdienst: pp. 24, 36, 44, 53, 59, 60, 71, 126, 140,
247, 250; Syndication International: p. 211; Timepix/Mansell Collection/Rex: p. 22; Associated Press/Topham: pp.
85, 132*b*, 138, 159, 161, 164, Topham Picturepoint: pp. 43, 130, 144, 225, 228, 241, 245*b*, 248 (background), 249*t* and *bl*,
265*l*; Ullstein Bilderdienst: pp. 6, 64, 82, 221*t*, 245*t*, 246, 269 (inset); Roger Viollet, Paris: p. 51; Visual Arts Library,
London, Berlin, Nationalgalerie: p. 237; Wiener Library: p. 76 (© Bundesarchiv): p. 232, 259, 260.

Every effort has been made to reach copyright holders. The publishers would be glad to hear from anyone whose
rights they have unwittingly infringed.

Cover illustration: British Library, London, UK/Bridgeman Art Library, London: left, A propaganda poster for the
Hitler Youth, courtesy of Bundesarchiv, Koblenz: center, The Imperial War Museum, London:
background and right.

Contents

The origins of the First World War

In the late summer of 1914 the most powerful countries in Europe went to war. By the time the fighting stopped, four years later, millions of people had been killed. Why did this disastrous war start? In 1919, the countries on the winning side met together and said that the war had been Germany's fault.

Was the war the fault of the German government?

Historians have identified a number of long-term and short-term causes of the war.

LONG-TERM CAUSE 1
THE RISE OF GERMANY

Until the middle of the nineteenth century Germany was divided into many separate states. The most important of these German states was a kingdom called Prussia. In the 1860s the leaders of Prussia wanted to unite Germany. France was unhappy about this and went to war against Prussia from 1870 to 1871. France was beaten and the victorious Prussian government was able to set up a new German Empire. This was a massive new state that included most German-speaking people. Wilhelm I, King of Prussia, was declared to be the emperor or Kaiser of Germany. His chief minister, Bismarck, became the powerful Chancellor of Germany.

Between 1871 and 1914 the economy of the new German state went from strength to strength. This was based on an amazing industrial revolution and by 1914 the output of German factories had overtaken the output of British factories. Chancellor Bismarck was very skilful. After 1871 he stopped the German government from getting involved in any more wars. France was the sworn enemy of Germany but Bismarck made sure that France remained isolated. As long as he was in charge of German foreign policy there was no danger of Germany going to war against Russia or Britain. This all changed when Germany got a new Kaiser – Wilhelm II – and Bismarck lost the chancellorship.

LONG-TERM CAUSE 2
THE NEW KAISER AND WORLD POWER

Now that Germany was the equal of Britain in terms of wealth and industry, some German people felt that their country should have a worldwide empire like Britain. One German who believed this was the new ruler of Germany, Kaiser Wilhelm II, who came to power in 1888. He made Bismarck retire in 1890. Wilhelm wanted a new, more aggressive approach to the rest of the world. He ended the friendly relationship that Bismarck had encouraged between Germany and Russia. As a result of his attitude other countries began to see Germany as a threat.

SOURCE A

L'ENFANT TERRIBLE!

CHORUS IN THE STERN. "DON'T GO ON LIKE THAT—OR YOU'LL UPSET US ALL!!"

A Punch cartoon suggests that the new Kaiser 'rocked the boat' with his aggressive foreign policy. Figures representing Russia, Britain, France and Austria-Hungary cower at the stern of the boat.

LONG-TERM CAUSE 3
THE ARMS RACE

After 1897 the German government started building up an enormous navy that could challenge the might of the British navy. The Germans knew that a worldwide empire would have to be defended by a worldwide navy.

The German government passed a law in 1900 ordering the building of a huge new fleet of 41 battleships and 60 cruisers. The British responded energetically to this threat by increasing the size of their navy. They introduced a new type of powerful battleship called a 'Dreadnought' in 1906. The Germans responded by building similar ships of their own. The British went on to order even more substantial battleships called 'Super Dreadnoughts'.

Other countries also took part in this arms race. The French increased their forces and by 1914 had an army of nearly 4 million soldiers. The Russians spent a fortune on military railways that were clearly designed to take troops to fight Germany and Austria-Hungary. Russian spending on its army was huge. People in Germany feared that this mighty force would one day flatten Berlin.

LONG-TERM CAUSE 4
THE TWO ALLIANCES

Germany signed a treaty of alliance with Austria-Hungary in 1879. The two states remained allies in the decades that followed. At first the only likely enemy of this alliance was France. However, Wilhelm's clumsy policy encouraged Russia to join forces with France. In 1892 France and Russia agreed to an alliance: if either country was attacked by Germany, the other state would go to war against the Germans.

The government of Britain began to look around for allies at the turn of the century. British politicians thought about an alliance with Germany against France and Russia. However, German policy under the Kaiser was so badly managed that Britain felt forced to look to France and Russia. Britain established friendly relations with France in 1904 and Russia in 1907. The link was not an official alliance but an 'entente' or understanding that the countries would try to work together. People talked of the Triple Entente: an anti-German grouping of France, Russia and Britain.

EUROPE, 1914 – THE TWO HOSTILE ALLIANCES

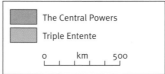

The Central Powers

Triple Entente

0   km   500

>> Activity

Look at the information on these two pages about four long-term causes of the First World War. For each cause explain in your own words:

a how it made war more likely;

b whether it shows that the German government was to blame.

The crisis in Europe: summer 1914

By January 1914 the situation in Europe was tense. Between January and August a number of short-term causes led to the outbreak of war.

>> **Activity**

1 Look at the information on page 7 about three short-term causes of the war. For each cause try to work out:

    a how it led to war;

    b whether it shows that Germany was to blame for the outbreak of war.

2 Using the information from pages 4–7 explain how far Germany was responsible for causing the First World War.

SOURCE B

The Archduke Franz Ferdinand and his wife leaving the townhall at Sarajevo shortly before they were assassinated by a Serb nationalist.

SHORT-TERM CAUSE 1
THE KILLING IN SARAJEVO

The city of Sarajevo in Bosnia was the centre of world attention in June 1914. Bosnia was part of Austria-Hungary but many of its people were Serbs who wanted to be ruled by the neighbouring state of Serbia. On 28 June 1914 a Serb called Gavrilo Princip shot dead the Archduke Franz Ferdinand, heir to the throne of Austria-Hungary, and his wife.

The killing of the Archduke was linked to a bitter dispute between Austria-Hungary and the state of Serbia. Austria-Hungary was looking for an excuse for a war against Serbia.

Austria-Hungary blamed Serbia for the murder and got ready to attack.

The system of alliances led to several other countries becoming involved in the outbreak of war between Austria-Hungary and Serbia. While Austria-Hungary was allied to Germany, Serbia was closely linked to Russia. The government of Austria-Hungary looked to Germany for help. Serbia expected Russian help. The Russians, in turn, hoped for support from France and Britain. In this way, the killing at Sarajevo made possible a wider war which would involve all the powerful countries of Europe.

SHORT-TERM CAUSE 2
THE GERMAN DECISION FOR WAR

In 1913 there had been another argument between Austria-Hungary and Serbia and Russia about how land taken from Turkey should be divided. This nearly led to war between the two alliances. It had not because the German government refused to support Austria-Hungary.

A year later the German policy changed. On 5 July 1914 the Kaiser gave his full backing for an Austrian attack on Serbia. Austria-Hungary would not have risked war without help from their more powerful ally. The German government knew that there was a good chance that Russia would go to war on the side of Serbia, and that the result would be a general war.

SOURCE C

The Austro-Hungarian ambassador to Berlin reported a discussion with the Kaiser on 5 July.

The Kaiser told me that we might rely upon Germany's full support. It was Kaiser Wilhelm's opinion that action must not be delayed. Should war break out between Austria-Hungary and Russia, Germany would stand at our side. Kaiser Wilhelm would regret it if we do not make use of the present situation, which is all in our favour.

In the following weeks of crisis the German government did more than offer support. It urged Austria-Hungary to make sure that war broke out. When Britain and Russia tried to get Austria-Hungary to negotiate, Germany told her ally to ignore these attempts to stop the war.

SHORT-TERM CAUSE 3
CONFUSION ABOUT THE BRITISH POSITION

The Germans were not sure whether the British would fight. If the British had made clear their determination to fight, the German leaders might have thought again about the war. The position of the British Foreign Secretary, Sir Edward Grey, was not complicated. Although Britain had links with France and Russia there was no official alliance. Legally, Britain was not bound to go war on the side of France and Russia.

As the crisis developed, senior civil servants urged Grey to say that Britain would definitely side with France and Russia. They hoped that an announcement like this would frighten the Germans into stepping back from war. Grey disagreed.

He wanted to try to avoid war by negotiating. Talks continued right up to 3 August when Germany attacked France via Belgium. At this point Britain stopped talking and, a day later, went to war.

SOURCE D

The Russian Foreign Minister, Sergei Sazonov, blamed Britain for not threatening war.

In 1914 Sir Edward Grey should have made a clear statement that Britain would stand by France and Russia. I insistently asked him to do this but he refused. He could have saved humanity from that terrible catastrophe.

The First World War

On 28 July Austria-Hungary declared war on Serbia. By 4 August Germany and Austria-Hungary (the Central Powers) were at war with Russia, France and Britain (the Allies). Generals in all countries were desperate to mobilise their troops; that is, to get them moving towards the frontier with the enemy. Rapid mobilisation reduced the time available for discussion and negotiation to virtually nothing.

Helft uns siegen!

zeichnet die Kriegsanleihe

Stalemate in the West

Each side expected the war to be short-lived. The German plan was for a quick knock-out blow against France. This nearly worked. The German army swept through Belgium and northern France. The German advance was finally stopped by the French army on the River Marne, not far from Paris . The Germans were driven back a little and a front-line was established. This front-line did not change very much for the following three years.

Attempts to break the stalemate led to enormous casualties. In 1916 the Germans tried to break through at the Battle of Verdun. They failed but in the fighting that went on between February and July there were about a million casualties. In the same year the British attacked on the River Somme. On the first day of the Battle of the Somme, 60,000 British troops were killed but the outcome was indecisive. In 1917 Britain once again tried to break through the German lines at a place called Passchendaele; there were half a million casualties. The result of this enormous suffering was that the British line moved forward only four miles.

Once the fighting had led to stalemate, the leaders had no idea how to end the war without losing face. Both sides looked for new allies to break the deadlock. Italy and Romania joined the Allied side and Bulgaria joined with the Central Powers. These new combatants did not end the war; quite the opposite. Each new player wanted some of the profits of war and was ready to fight until it got a 'fair share'.

A German poster from the First World War showing a heroic image of a frontline soldier. The poster was advertising a scheme to raise money for the German war effort.

The horror of the fighting is vividly conveyed in this painting, Gassed, *by the British artist, John Singer Sargent. It shows a line of British soldiers blinded in a German gas attack.*

The naval war and the Americans

There was no decisive victory in the war at sea. The only major naval battle took place in the North Sea in 1916 at the Battle of Jutland. Neither the British nor the German fleet was destroyed but afterwards the German fleet retired to port and did not venture out for the rest of the war. Unable to destroy the British navy, Germany turned to submarine warfare. The German submarines were known as U-boats. They attacked British shipping in order to try to cut off vital supplies.

The U-boat campaign helped to bring America into the war on the side of Britain and France. By 1917 U-boats were trying to sink any ship that might be trading with Britain. This involved attacks on American ships. The American government responded by declaring war on Germany in April 1917. The power and wealth of the USA greatly strengthened the position of the Allies.

While the USA entered the war on the Western Front, Russia was being defeated in the east. The war had been going badly for the Russians for some time. Revolution in Russia in 1917 led to a collapse of the Russian war effort and withdrawal from the war. Faced with total defeat, the new communist rulers of Russia agreed to all the German demands and signed the Treaty of Brest-Litovsk in March 1918. Under this peace treaty Germany dealt very harshly with Russia, taking control of huge areas of Russian territory.

German defeat and the armistice

Meanwhile, on the Western Front it took time for the American army to make a full contribution to the fighting. In March 1918 the Germans launched their last major offensive in the west. They tried to smash through to Paris before American reinforcements arrived in great force. After some successes the German attack petered out. By August 1918 the American reinforcements were in place and the allied forces were ready for a huge counter-attack. With the help of tanks the Allies made a decisive breakthrough. The German generals decided that they were about to be defeated and the German government asked the American President Wilson for peace. There was an agreement to stop fighting on 11 November 1918. This agreement was called the Armistice.

Discussion points

> Why were casualties so high on the Western Front?

> Why had Russia left the war by January 1918?

> How did the USA come to join the war? What difference did this make?

The Russian Revolution

Russia before communism

In 1917 Russia had been ruled for many years by Tsar Nicholas II. He was an autocrat; this meant that there were no limits to his power. The great majority of Russians were extremely poor peasants living in the countryside. A small but growing number of people lived in towns and worked in mines and factories.

In 1904–1905 Russia fought a war against Japan and lost. Defeat led to an attempted revolution in Russia in 1905. Tsar Nicholas only retained control by promising reforms. He set up a parliament for Russia called the 'duma'. This had little real power and it proved to be a great disappointment. Russia took part in the First World War and fought against Germany and Austria-Hungary. The war was a disaster for Russia and by 1917 many Russians were ready for another revolution.

WHY DID SOME RUSSIANS WANT A CHANGE OF GOVERNMENT IN 1917?

> The gap between rich and poor was enormous. Peasants and factory workers wanted a fairer deal.

> Ordinary people had no political power. They were angry that the Tsar could do what he liked and disappointed that the duma had no real power.

> Russians did very badly in the First World War. Russian armies were defeated by Germany.

> The war put a great strain on the Russian economy. Prices went up and food was scarce.

The storming of the Winter Palace in Petrograd by Bolshevik forces in November 1917. The Soviet artist created a romantic version of what happened. In fact, very little fighting took place and only six people were killed.

The two revolutions of 1917

Revolution first broke out in St Petersburg (known at the time as Petrograd) in March 1917. Shortages of bread led to strikes and riots in the city. Law and order broke down. The army mutinied and refused to help . Tsar Nicholas admitted defeat and abdicated on 15 March.

The Soviets and the Bolsheviks

Although the Tsar was no longer in charge, there was confusion about who would replace him. The duma set up a so-called 'provisional government'. Workers and soldiers in Petrograd established a governing committee or 'soviet'. Soon soviets were set up in other large towns. Both the provisional government and the soviets claimed to be in charge.

Among the revolutionaries was a group of communists known as Bolsheviks. The Bolshevik leader, Lenin, returned from exile to Petrograd in April 1917. Lenin and the Bolsheviks wanted to overthrow the provisional government. His slogan was 'All power to the soviets!' One of Lenin's most important colleagues was Leon Trotsky. He played a key role in the organisation of the Petrograd soviet. On the 6–7 November Bolshevik fighters, known as Red Guards, seized power in Petrograd. Soviets all over Russia followed the lead from Petrograd and took control of their local area. The Bolshevik revolution had begun.

The Treaty of Brest-Litovsk

At first, Lenin was convinced that the revolution would soon spread to the rest of the world. There was no need for a foreign policy because non-communist states were doomed. This belief encouraged him to make peace with Germany in 1918. Russia lost huge areas of territory under the treaty of Brest-Litovsk. Lenin was not concerned because he thought the settlement would soon be swept aside by a world revolution.

The civil war

The Bolshevik take-over was opposed by many Russians. In May 1918 fighting broke out between the Red Guards and anti-communist forces known as the 'Whites'. This was the start of a vicious civil war. In areas such as the Ukraine, Georgia and Siberia independent White governments were set up. The British, French, Americans and Japanese also sent forces to fight the Bolsheviks. The Bolshevik leader, Leon Trotsky, organised the Red Army very effectively. The Whites were divided among themselves and the foreign armies began to withdraw in 1919. By 1920 the civil war was over and the Bolsheviks had won,

World revolution?

Immediately after the Russian Revolution communists in other countries tried to copy the Russian example. Lenin encouraged this; he thought that without communist revolutions in other countries, revolutionary Russia would be destroyed. In 1919 an organisation known as Comintern (the Communist International) was set up by the Bolsheviks to encourage revolutionaries in other countries. There were many followers of communism in Germany. Communists briefly took power in Hungary but were overthrown in July 1919.

Lenin died in 1924. By this time there was no immediate prospect of a world revolution. Stalin took control of the Soviet Union and Trotsky went into exile in 1927. The new Soviet leader did little to encourage revolution abroad. Instead, he concentrated on transforming the Soviet Union into a powerful industrial country. However, all over the world, governments remained afraid of the spread of communist ideas.

An early Soviet poster celebrating Mayday and calling for workers of the whole world to rise up in revolution. A red flag, with its pole in Russia, encircles the globe. The anticipated world revolution did not occur.

Discussion points

> Why did many Russians want a new government in 1917?

> What part did Lenin play in the revolution?

> How successful were communists at spreading the revolution outside Russia?

Paris 1919

Britain, France and the USA won the First World War. In 1919 their leaders met together in Paris to decide on the future of Europe and the world. These leaders were known as the Big Three.

What were the motives of the Big Three in 1919?

PROBLEMS FOR THE WINNERS

The leaders of the victorious countries faced a number of complex problems:

> Germany had nearly defeated Britain, Russia and France single-handed. How could the winners make sure that Germany could not fight another war in the future?

> Communists had seized power in Russia. Communists wanted to destroy all other capitalist governments by workers' revolution.

> Central and Eastern Europe were in chaos. The royal families of Germany and Austria-Hungary had abdicated before the peace conference.

> The British and the French governments had entered into a number of secret treaties during the war. They had promised Japan special treatment in Asia. Under the Treaty of London of 1915 Italy had agreed to join the allies in return for the promise of gains from Austria-Hungary. Japan and Italy now expected to be given their rewards.

> Nationalists in Eastern Europe had set up new governments even before the war had officially ended. By early November 1918 there were new states in Yugoslavia, Poland and Czechoslovakia.

> The end of the war came more quickly than the allies had expected. The victorious allies had given little thought to the arrangements for the peace. When they did begin discussing the peace it became clear that the winners had very different views about the future.

Woodrow Wilson,
US President

David Lloyd George,
British Prime Minister

Georges Clemenceau,
French Prime Minister

Differences between the Big Three

Perhaps the biggest problem faced at the peace conferences was the fact that the winning countries had very different views about what should happen next. The key players were the so-called Big Three. (The term 'the Big Four' is used when Italy is also included.) The differences between the Allies were hidden while the war was fought. The French and the British did not agree with many of Wilson's views. However, they had been desperate to make sure that the USA supported the war. During the war, they kept quiet in public, for fear that disagreement would limit the American war effort. Once the fighting had stopped the French and the British started to disagree with the Americans.

>> Activity

'Writing the peace treaties was never going to be easy.' Do you agree with this statement? Use the information in the table to support your answer.

A 'just peace' or reparations?

The American President Wilson was a very religious man. His aim was a just peace. He believed that God wanted him to make the world a better place. He disliked his allies in Britain and France. Wilson believed that politics was a simple matter of right and wrong. The European leaders were more concerned about selfish national interest than doing good. Wilson thought that Europeans had caused the war and it was America's mission to stop this happening again. In 1919 Wilson said, 'I do not mean any disrespect to any other great people when I say that America is the hope of the world. And if she does not justify that hope the results are unthinkable.' He thought that the old style of politics could be swept away if a new world organisation was set up called the League of Nations.

Wilson was a great believer in the idea of self-determination. This meant that each nation should have the right to decide for itself how it should be governed. Living far away in America, Wilson did not appreciate how difficult self-determination was in much of Eastern Europe. If Czechs and Germans and Slovaks lived together in an area, who had the right of self-determination? The opposite of self-determination was imperialism: the control of many nations by one powerful empire. The British and the French were imperialists. Their governments were very suspicious of talk of self-determination.

Britain and France wanted reparations from Germany. This was the payment of compensation for the damage caused in the war. Wilson was much less concerned about reparations. Britain and France had built up huge debts to pay for the war; they saw reparations as a way of getting rid of these debts. The USA did not have enormous war debts. Indeed, America was owed much of the money borrowed by Britain and France.

SOURCE A

Anti-German propaganda. An American recruitment poster of 1917 suggests that the German army was extremely brutal and must be stopped. After the war there was an argument about how far Germany should be punished for its actions.

The Fourteen Points

Woodrow Wilson made his own idealistic aims clear a year before the Paris conference. Speaking in January 1918, long before the war ended, President Wilson stated what he wanted as Fourteen Points.

SOURCE B

A summary of the Fourteen Points:

1 There should be no secret deals or treaties between states.

2 Countries should be free to send ships anywhere in the world without interference.

3 There should be free trade between countries.

4 The level of armaments should be reduced in each country.

5 The future of colonies should be reviewed and the wishes of local people taken into consideration.

6 Other countries should leave Russian territory.

7 The Germans should leave Belgium.

8 Alsace and Lorraine should be returned to France.

9 The Italian borders should be adjusted to bring Italian speakers into Italy as far as possible.

10 The different peoples of Austria-Hungary should be given their freedom.

11 Invading armies should leave the Balkan states.

12 Non-Turkish people in the Turkish Empire should be free to have their own governments.

13 An independent Poland should be set up. Poland should have access to the sea.

14 A League of Nations should be set up to preserve the future peace of the world.

>> How can you tell from the Fourteen Points that Wilson believed in the idea of self-determination?

SOURCE C

In January 1918 Wilson explained the thinking behind the Fourteen Points.

One principle runs through the whole program. It is the principle of justice to all peoples and all nationalities, whether they be strong or weak. Without this principle there can be no international justice. For this principle, the people of the United States are ready to devote their lives, their honor, and everything that they possess.

SOURCE D

Wilson knew that he disagreed with the French and the British. As early as 1917 he wrote a private note that said:

England and France have not the same views with respect to peace that we have by any means. When the war is over we can force them to our way of thinking because by that time they will, among other things, be financially in our hands.

SOURCE E

A HOME FROM HOME.

A British Punch *cartoon shows Wilson striding purposefully from America to Europe. His boots are decorated with the numbers 1–14: a reference to Wilson's famous Fourteen Points.*

The response of the European allies

The British and the French leaders did not agree with all the Fourteen Points. The French leader, Clemenceau, asked why Wilson needed as many as 14 when God had made do with only 10 commandments. The Fourteen Points attacked many ideas that the French and British held dear. They were also annoyed at what the Fourteen Points did not say. Wilson said nothing about the future of Germany and ways of making Germany pay reparations for starting the war.

SOURCE G

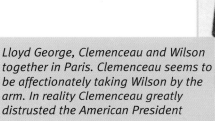

Lloyd George, Clemenceau and Wilson together in Paris. Clemenceau seems to be affectionately taking Wilson by the arm. In reality Clemenceau greatly distrusted the American President

SOURCE F

When the war was virtually over, on 29 October 1918, Clemenceau met Lloyd George. Now that the fighting had finished they could begin to express their disagreements with Wilson. According to one account, they discussed how far they agreed with the Fourteen Points.

Clemenceau: Have you ever been asked whether you accept the Fourteen Points? I have never been asked.

Lloyd George: I have never been asked either. We cannot accept the second point under any conditions; it means the power of the blockade goes. Germany has been broken almost as much by the blockade as by military methods. If this power is to be handed over to the League of Nations and Great Britain were fighting for her life, no League of Nations would prevent her from defending herself.

>> Activity

Britain and France did not like all of the Fourteen Points. Look at this list of British and French policies:

> They had made secret treaties before and during the war.

> They had powerful navies: the British Navy was the strongest in the world. These forces were sometimes used to stop the free movement of ships at sea.

> Both Britain and France ruled great empires that they wished to keep, regardless of the feelings of the local people.

Look back at Wilson's Fourteen Points. Which particular points do you think the British and the French governments disliked?

15

Clemenceau and a harsh peace

The French leader at Paris was Georges Clemenceau. His nickname was 'the tiger'. He was aware that most French people wanted revenge for the devastation of the war. The level of destruction was like no previous war and much of the bloodshed and destruction had taken place in France.

France had suffered greatly during the First World War. A quarter of all French men aged 18–27 had been killed. Another 4 million had been wounded. Much of north-eastern France had been devastated. The French government had borrowed huge sums of money to fight the war and was faced with an enormous debt. The French wanted Germany to pay for all these losses. They also wanted revenge for the defeat in the war of 1870–71 and the loss of Alsace-Lorraine.

Ideally the French wanted to break up Germany into a number of small, weak states. Failing this, Clemenceau called for Germany to lose the Rhineland, Saarland, Upper Silesia, Danzig and East Prussia. These areas included much of Germany's coal and heavy industry.

The French leaders disagreed very strongly with the USA over the question of compensation or reparations. The position of the USA was very different to France and Britain. For the two European countries, particularly France, the war had been an economic catastrophe. The USA had not suffered economically during the war and had no demands for substantial reparations.

SOURCE H

The Ruins of Corbie Abbey *by H.S. Power. The abbey, in Corbie near Amiens, was ruined during the First World War. Scenes of such destruction were common in France.*

Focus

Look at the statements on this page made by people present at the peace talks. What can we learn from these quotations about the French attitude at the peace conference?

SOURCE I

One eye-witness at the peace conference was a famous British economist called John Maynard Keynes. Keynes later wrote a description of the French leader, Clemenceau.

His approach was simple. He believed that Germans could understand nothing except intimidation. Germans have no honour, pride or mercy. You cannot negotiate with a German; you must dictate to him.

Politics was about power. Some lip-service was needed to the 'ideals' of foolish Americans and hypocritical Englishmen. It would be stupid to take too seriously Wilson's ideas about the League of Nations and self-determination.

SOURCE J

Mark well what I am telling you. In six months, in a year, five years, ten years, when they like, as they like, the Germans will invade us again.

We were attacked. We are victorious. We represent right, and might is ours. This might must be used in the service of the right.
Clemenceau, 1919

SOURCE K

André Tardieu, one of the French negotiators at Paris in 1919, was keen to take a hard line towards Germany.

France, like Britain and the United States, needs a zone of safety. Britain and America are naval powers and they create their zone of safety with their fleets and the destruction of the German fleet. France is unprotected by the ocean and must create its zone of safety by the occupation of the Rhineland area. To ask us to give up occupation of the Rhineland is like asking England and the United States to sink their fleets of battleships.

France has a unique experience of Germany. No one has suffered as she has. When dealing with Germany, it is France which must be heard.

Lloyd George and a compromise peace

Lloyd George was the British Prime Minister. He occupied the middle ground between France and the USA. Like Clemenceau he had to listen to public opinion at home. This had been influenced by a press campaign demanding harsh treatment for Germany. He was not personally anxious to punish the Germans severely. He was afraid that if Germany was too weak this would give France too much power in Europe.

The chief concern of Lloyd George was to make sure that the British Empire did not suffer as a result of the settlement. There was an early difference of opinion between Wilson and Lloyd George over the future of the former German colonies. Wilson hated imperialism and he wanted the colonies to be looked after by the new League of Nations until they became independent. Lloyd George wanted them divided up between the winning powers. Lloyd George wanted to make sure that South Africa, Australia and New Zealand were rewarded with nearby German territories. Both Britain and France also wanted a share of the former Turkish lands of the Middle East.

The British government team was suspicious of France. Traditionally, France had been an enemy of Britain. The British did not want a Europe dominated by France, any more than they wanted a German-controlled Europe. This was another reason for making sure that Germany was not too harshly treated. Lloyd George was also worried that a weak Germany would be unable to stop the spread of communism.

SOURCE L

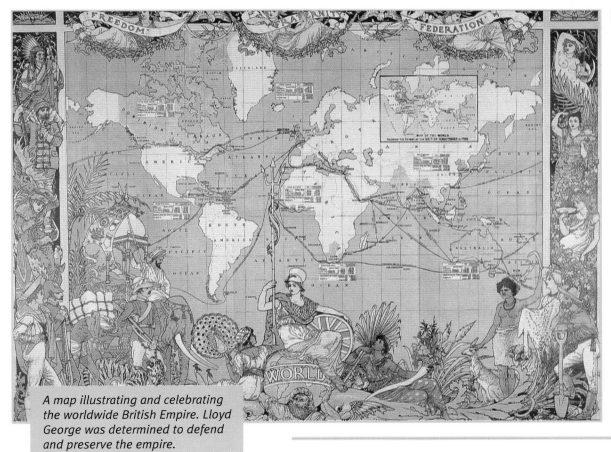

A map illustrating and celebrating the worldwide British Empire. Lloyd George was determined to defend and preserve the empire.

>> Activity

Look back at pages 12–17. Explain in your own words:

a what each of the Big Three wanted at the Paris peace talks;

b how far the Big Three disagreed with each other.

The Treaty of Versailles

During the early months of 1919 the Big Three argued in Paris about the peace settlement. In June 1919 they finally agreed about how Germany should be treated. This settlement was called the Treaty of Versailles.

How far did the Big Three get what they wanted?

The League and self-determination

The peace talks began in January 1919. President Wilson wanted the Conference to set up the League of Nations as one of its first tasks. Britain and France agreed. The rules of the League of Nations were drawn up. These rules were known as the League Covenant. The Covenant was included in the Treaty of Versailles and in all the other peace treaties.

Wilson believed very strongly in self-determination for all peoples. Groups from all over the world made their way to Paris to argue that they should be allowed to set up their own nation-states. People ruled over by the French and British Empires demanded independence. The French and the British were unhappy at this. Wilson gave way to pressure from his allies. The idea of self-determination was not applied to the world empires of France and Britain. People such as Irish and Vietnamese nationalists, who had gone to Paris hoping for independence, left disappointed.

The mandates

Britain and France wanted control of German and Turkish colonies. The USA wanted these to be run by the League. Finally, a compromise was accepted. The colonies were divided up among the winning powers, but they agreed to look after these territories on behalf of the League of Nations. These lands were to be known as 'mandates' of the League of Nations. Through the mandates, Britain and France added considerably to their world-wide empires. The German colonies in Africa were divided among Britain, France and South Africa.

SOURCE A

A contemporary painting by William Orpen shows the German delegates signing the Treaty of Versailles. On the opposite side of the table sit Wilson, Lloyd George and Clemenceau, flanked by their assistants.

SOURCE B

A member of the French delegation at Paris later recalled disagreements among the Big Three.

Then discussions began. Calm and unruffled on most points, bitter and stormy on three of the most important to France: the left bank of the Rhine, the Saar Valley and question of reparations. These three points took up long sittings and led to fierce debates. Mr Lloyd George would arrive at the meeting looking glum and announce, 'They will not sign.' He recommended to his allies a policy of extreme moderation.

André Tardieu, 1921

German loss of territory

In northern Europe new states were set up in Poland, Lithuania, Estonia and Latvia. Germany had annexed the three Baltic states from Russia a year earlier. In keeping with the idea of self-determination these small states now became independent. Clemenceau was particularly keen to ensure that Poland was large and powerful. He hoped that a strong Poland would weaken the future position of Germany. The new Poland took territory from Germany, Russia and Austria-Hungary. Former German land in West Prussia, Posen and part of Upper Silesia was given to Poland. As a result there was a barrier or corridor of Polish territory that divided most of Germany from the German lands of East Prussia. This Polish Corridor was necessary if Poland was

to have access to the sea in line with Wilson's Fourteen Points. The French wanted the largely German-speaking port of Danzig to be given to Poland. Lloyd George disagreed. Instead Danzig was turned into a 'free city'; this meant that it was not part of any state but was controlled by the League of Nations.

Each of the Big Three agreed that Alsace and Lorraine should be returned to France. Wilson had mentioned the return of Alsace-Lorraine in his Fourteen Points. The French also wanted to annex the nearby coal-rich district of the Saarland. Neither Wilson nor Lloyd George was prepared to give the Saarland to France. Instead it was decided that the area should be run by the League of Nations for 15 years, but during this time the French would have control of its coal-mines. Clemenceau had also wanted the large and wealthy Rhineland area of Germany to be permanently divided from the rest of the German state. A separate Rhineland would weaken Germany and form a barrier between Germany and France. The British and the Americans argued that this would be a mistake. The Germans would be so angry that afterwards they would demand revenge. Clemenceau eventually compromised. The Big Three agreed that no German soldiers should be allowed into the Rhineland and that it should be occupied by allied troops for 15 years.

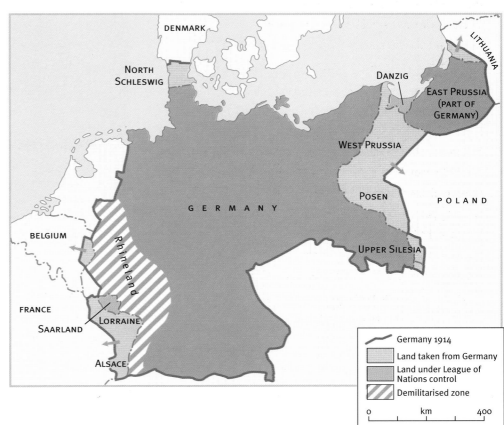

VERSAILLES AND THE TREATMENT OF GERMANY

German losses in Belgium and Denmark

Alsace-Lorraine and the Polish Corridor were the largest losses of German territory. In addition, Germany lost the small districts of Eupen, Moresnet and Malmédy to Belgium. The treaty ordered that there should be a plebiscite or vote in North Schleswig to see whether the local people wanted to stay in Germany or join Denmark. The result of the plebiscite was that North Schleswig became part of Denmark.

The French were successful in arguing that there should be strict limits on the armed forces of Germany. The treaty banned Germany from using tanks and armoured cars. There was to be no German airforce. The German army was limited to a mere 100,000 men. The German navy was to be limited to six battleships and there were to be no German submarines.

War guilt and reparations

The treaty made it clear that Germany was guilty of causing the First World War. This was stated in Clause 231 of the treaty. The idea of war guilt was used to justify the payment of reparations.

SOURCE C

Extracts from the Versailles Treaty:

Clause 231   The Allied governments affirm and Germany accepts the responsibility of Germany and her allies for causing all the loss and damage to which the allied governments and their nationals have been subjected as a consequence of the war imposed upon them by the aggression of Germany and her allies.

Clause 232   The Allied governments require and Germany undertakes that she will make compensation for all damage done to the civilian population of the Allied powers.

While the Americans agreed to go along with French ideas about war guilt, they differed wildly in their view of the right level of compensation. The French wanted Germany to pay an enormous $200 billion in reparations, the British argued for $120 billion and the American view was that the right figure was $22 billion. In the end the conference failed to agree and set up a Reparations Commission to look into the matter of the level of payment after the Treaty was signed.

SOURCE D

The French view of German guilt was reflected in the Allied statement to the German delegation June 1919.

In the view of the Allied Powers the war which began on August 1 1914, was the greatest crime against humanity and the freedom of peoples that any nation calling itself civilised has ever committed. Germany's responsibility is not confined to having planned and started the war. She is no less responsible for the savage and inhuman manner in which it was conducted. The conduct of Germany is almost unexampled in human history. No less than seven million dead lie buried in Europe because Germany saw fit to go to war. There must be Justice for the dead. There must be Justice for the people who now stagger under war debts. There must be Justice for those millions whose homes and lands German savagery has spoiled and destroyed.

SOURCE E

The treaty insisted that Germany should be largely disarmed. Here a German tank is dismantled in order to comply with the treaty.

Why did Wilson accept the treaty?

The American leader was unhappy with much of the treaty. Many British leaders were also concerned that the treaty was too hard on Germany. They went along with it because they thought the problems of the treaty could be sorted out at a later date. Wilson put much faith in the League of Nations. He thought that this organisation would be able to solve any arguments between countries.

SOURCE F

On 14 February 1919 Wilson wrote to his wife expressing his delight that the French and British had agreed to the setting up of the League of Nations.

This is our first real step forward. For I now realise, more than ever before, that once established, the League can arbitrate and correct mistakes which are in the treaty.

THE 14 POINTS AND THE PEACE TREATIES COMPARED

Achieved in full

7   Germany to leave Belgium

8   Alsace-Lorraine to be returned to France

10 Independence for the peoples of Austria– Hungary

13 Independence for Poland

Partially achieved

9   Italian borders to be settled

11 Invading armies to leave Balkans

14 An effective League of Nations to keep the peace

Not achieved

1   A ban on secret treaties between states

2   Free movement of ships anywhere in the world

3   Free trade between countries without import taxes

4   General disarmament

5   Greater independence for colonies

6   Non-interference in Russia

12 Independence for the non-Turkish people of the Turkish Empire.

>> Activity

Look back at what the Big Three wanted to achieve at the Paris peace talks. Read the information in this unit and work out how far Wilson and Clemenceau were successful in getting what they wanted.

The other peace treaties

Tómaš Masaryk, the first President of the Czechoslovak state created from the lands of the former Austria-Hungary.

The Paris peace conference was not simply concerned with Germany. The Big Three also made important decisions about the future of Austria-Hungary, Bulgaria and the Turkish Ottoman Empire. All these states had been on the losing side during the First World War. The plans for these territories were stated in a series of treaties signed between 1919 and 1923. All of the treaties included reference to the League of Nations as the organisation which would solve future problems between states. All of the defeated countries were initially ordered to pay reparations.

SAINT-GERMAIN: THE TREATY WITH AUSTRIA 1919

The peace settlement dealt with the two parts of Austria-Hungary in separate peace treaties. The agreement with Austria was known as the Treaty of St Germain and was signed in September 1919.

Terms of the treaty

Austria lost the South Tyrol and Istria to Italy and huge areas of land to three new states: Czechoslovakia, Poland and Yugoslavia.

The lands given to Czechoslovakia included some of Austria's wealthiest territories and over 3 million German speakers were placed in the new state.

Austria was reduced to a small mountainous country of 6.5 million people. A third of the population lived in the great city of Vienna.

Austria was forbidden from ever seeking unification or 'Anschluss' with Germany.

The Austrian army was limited to 30,000 men.

NEUILLY: THE TREATY WITH BULGARIA 1919

Bulgaria had also fought on the losing side. The Treaty of Neuilly was signed in November 1919.

Terms of the treaty

Land was taken from Bulgaria and given to Greece, Yugoslavia and Romania.

The Bulgarian army was restricted to no more than 20,000 men.

TRIANON: THE TREATY WITH HUNGARY 1920

While the peace talks were taking place, Hungarian communists seized power in Budapest led by Béla Kun. The signing of a peace treaty was delayed until Béla Kun had been overthrown and a right-wing government took over. The new ruler of Hungary, Admiral Horthy, was forced to sign the Treaty of Trianon in March 1920. The idea of self-determination led to the carving up of the old Hungary.

Terms of the treaty

Two thirds of Hungarian territory was given to Czechoslovakia, Yugoslavia and Romania.

The population of Hungary was reduced by these changes from 18 million to 7 million people.

The Hungarian army was limited to 35,000.

SÈVRES: THE TREATY WITH TURKEY 1920

The Ottoman family had ruled over a powerful Turkish Empire for many centuries. The Ottoman Empire had been in decline in the years before the First World War. The Turks fought on the losing side in the war.

Terms of the treaty

Turkey lost nearly all its land in Europe to Greece.

The lands of the Turkish Empire in the Arab Middle East were confiscated: France took charge in Syria and Britain took control in Palestine, Jordan and Iraq.

Turkey was to pay reparations.

LAUSANNE: REVISING THE TURKISH TREATY 1923

Many Turkish people were outraged by the treaty. A general known as Atatürk led a revolution and overthrew the Ottoman family in 1921. Once in power Ataturk used his armies to overturn the Treaty of Sèvres by force. As a result a new agreement, the Treaty of Lausanne, was signed in 1923.

Terms of the treaty

Turkey regained much of the land lost to Greece.

No reparations were to be paid.

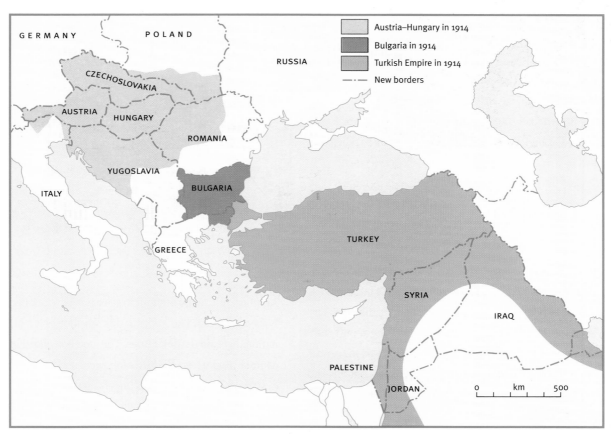

THE DISMEMBERMENT OF AUSTRIA–HUNGARY AND TURKEY

Discussion points

> What evidence is there that the winners tried to punish the losers through these treaties?

> How do you think the people of these countries reacted to news of these treaties?

Aftermath: the immediate

The peace treaties of 1919–23 created a new Europe. As the treaties were carried out, many problems emerged. There was political turmoil across central and Eastern Europe.

What was the immediate impact of the treaties?

The Weimar Republic

Defeat and the peace treaty brought chaos to Germany. In 1919 a new government was set up in the town of Weimar, and it became known as the Weimar Republic. The new government was attacked on all sides. Between 1919 and 1923 there were repeated attempts by both left-wing and right-wing militants to overthrow the new Weimar Republic. In January 1919 communist revolutionaries, called Spartacists, tried to stage a revolution in Berlin. In April communists tried to seize power in Munich. Both of these rebellions were smashed by armed and violent groups of ex-servicemen known as 'Freikorps' (Free Corps). In 1920 a Freikorps force attempted to seize Berlin. The army sympathised with the Freikorps and refused to fight them. This attempt at a right-wing revolution was eventually stopped by a strike by left-wing workers.

Attempts to pay the reparations bill after 1921 added to Germany's economic problems and helped to cause a huge level of inflation. At the same time a new political crisis created economic problems. The French invaded the Ruhr area in January 1923, on the grounds that the Germans were not paying their reparations. This was the centre of German industry. Germans responded with strikes – but this had the effect of doing more damage to Germany than to France.

The economic situation went out of control in 1923; inflation made banknotes virtually worthless. This was known as hyper-inflation. Pensioners lost their life savings. On 20 November 1923 one American dollar was worth 4 billion German marks.

SOURCE A

Hyper-inflation in Germany, 1923. A child plays with huge, worthless bundles of banknotes.

Another right-wing attempt to seize power was launched in November 1923. The leader of this rebellion was a militant nationalist called Adolf Hitler. The rebellion ended in fiasco in Munich after a few of Hitler's followers had been shot. Hitler was dealt with leniently and was imprisoned for a short time. By this time the economy of Germany had begun to recover and it seemed that stability was beginning to return to the country.

>> Activity

Describe in your own words how the Treaty of Versailles led to chaos in Germany.

consequences
of the treaties

TROUBLE IN EASTERN EUROPE
Anger in Hungary

The peace treaties created great bitterness and instability in Hungary. As in Germany, left-wing and right-wing militants tried to seize power. In 1919 the communist Béla Kun briefly set up a Soviet-style government. He was overthrown and Admiral Horthy, a right wing military dictator, came to power. He remained in charge until the Second World War. Under Horthy there was no democracy in Hungary.

Hungarians were horrified by the terms of the Trianon Treaty. Before the First World War Hungarians had controlled a huge, multi-national empire in Eastern Europe. In 1920 Hungary lost two-thirds of its pre-war territory. The lost land was given to Romania, Yugoslavia and Czechoslovakia. In each of these countries there was a Hungarian minority. After 1920 Hungarian foreign policy was completely dominated by a wish to 'get back' the lost lands. As a result, Romania, Czechoslovakia and Yugoslavia felt threatened. The governments of these three countries formed an alliance in order to protect themselves from the threat of a Hungarian invasion. This became known as the Little Entente.

Ethnic tension in Czechoslovakia

Czechoslovakia was the only new state in Eastern Europe that allowed free speech and democracy. There was great tension between different ethnic groups. The Czechs of the western part of the country were wealthier than the Slovaks of the east. Slovaks complained that they were treated as second-class citizens. Only 65 per cent of the population were Czechs or Slovaks. There were over 3 million Germans, known as the Sudeten Germans, and in many border areas the Germans were in a majority. Like the Slovaks, some Sudeten Germans said that they were not treated fairly by the Czechs.

War and revolution in Poland

Poland, with 30 million people, was by far the largest of the states set up by the treaties. The new Polish state was immediately involved in a series of brief wars with most of its neighbours. The Poles were not content with the borders set up in the peace treaties. Between 1918 and 1921 Poland fought against Germany, Czechoslovakia, Lithuania and the Soviet Union. These wars showed how difficult it was to impose the terms of the peace treaties. In 1920 the Poles defied the treaties and took control of the Lithuanian city of Vilna. By 1921 Poland had conquered a huge area of Belarus and Ukraine from the Soviet Union.

Polish politics were chaotic in the early 1920s. It seemed impossible to form a stable government and the country was close to civil war. The chaos came to an end in May 1926 when Marshal Pilsudski seized power and ended democracy in Poland.

>> Activity

How successful were the treaties in the new states of Hungary, Czechoslovakia and Poland? Describe in your own words the consequences of the peace treaties in each of these countries.

A harsh treaty?

The Germans were horrified at what they saw as the harshness of the peace treaty. They had hoped for milder terms in line with the Fourteen Points. There has been a lively argument since 1919 about the fairness of the Treaty of Versailles.

Was the Treaty of Versailles fair?

Germans had difficulty coming to terms with defeat. They had been proud of their army and were surprised and upset when Germany was defeated. Some said that people inside Germany — Jews, socialists and communists — had deliberately organised the surrender. They talked about the 'stab in the back'. The politicians who signed the armistice were called the 'November criminals'. Those Germans who felt that their country had been betrayed were appalled by the treaty. The section of the Versailles Treaty that most angered people in Germany was Clause 231 describing German 'war guilt'. They felt that it was wrong to put the entire blame for the war on their country. The payment of reparations was also deeply resented.

The Big Three had not allowed Germany to negotiate the treaty. The Germans were simply given the treaty and forced to sign it. This lack of discussion and consultation angered Germans who called it a 'diktat': a dictated peace.

The loss of German land was a severe blow. The fact that East Prussia was now separated by the Polish Corridor seemed unfair. Germans also resented bitterly the loss of their colonies in Africa.

SOURCE A

Count Brockdorff, the leader of the German delegation at Paris, set the tone for the national response to the treaty on 7 May 1919.

We are told that we should acknowledge that we alone are guilty of having caused the war. I would be a liar if I agreed to this. We are not trying to avoid all responsibility for this World War. However, we emphatically deny that the German people should be seen as the only guilty party. Over fifty years the imperialism of all European states has poisoned the international situation.

SOURCE B

Adolf Hitler was an obscure German corporal at the end of the war. In 1925 he expressed a common German view of the Treaty.

What I would like to do with the Treaty of Versailles! Each one of the points of that treaty is branded in the minds and hearts of the German people and sixty million men and women find their souls aflame with a feeling of rage and shame. A torrent of fire bursts forth as from a furnace, and a will of steel is forged from it, with the common cry – 'We will have weapons again!'

SOURCE C

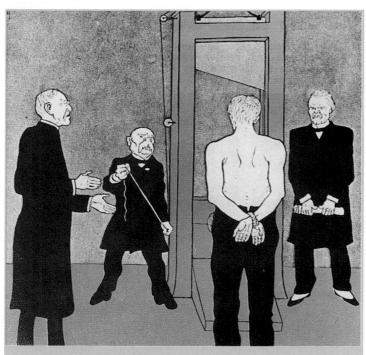

A German cartoonist sums up the common German view of the treaty. Wilson and Lloyd George look on as Clemenceau prepares to guillotine a figure representing Germany.

Conflicting interpretations

Some of the people on the winning side also thought that Versailles was quite wrong. One non-German critic of the Versailles Treaty was John Maynard Keynes. He had been a British official at Paris and later he became a very famous economist. Keynes left the Conference early, disgusted at the treatment of Germany. In 1920 he wrote a famous attack on the Treaty of Versailles. His book, *The Economic Consequences of the Peace*, was widely read. Many people in Britain, the USA and Germany agreed with Keynes.

SOURCE E

John Maynard Keynes writing in 1920:

In my own opinion, it is not possible to lay the entire responsibility for the war on any single nation. By aiming at the destruction of the economic life of Germany this treaty threatens the health and prosperity of the Allies themselves. By making impossible demands it leaves Europe more unsettled than it found it.

SOURCE D

PEACE AND FUTURE CANNON FODDER

THE TIGER: "Curious! I seem to hear a child weeping!"

Between 1920 and 1939 many writers and politicians in Britain and the USA agreed with the view of Keynes. As a result politicians, particularly in the British government, were ready to make concessions to Germany to try to improve on a flawed treaty. Since 1950 most historians have disagreed with Keynes and have taken a more sympathetic view of the treaty.

SOURCE F

A modern historian, Sally Marks, summed up her view of the Versailles Treaty in 1976.

The Versailles Treaty was severe, but it is amazing that it was not more so. Thanks to Wilson's insistence, Germany lost remarkably little territory, considering how thoroughly she had lost the war. True the colonies were gone, but the European losses were relatively modest. The real difficulty was not that the Treaty was exceptionally severe but that the Germans thought it was, and in time persuaded others that it was.

A cartoon produced in 1919 by the British artist, Will Dyson, predicts that the treaty was flawed and would lead to another world war. As the leaders of France, the USA, Italy and Britain leave the peace conference they notice a small child crying because he will have to fight in a future war. Prophetically, the cartoonist suggests that the next war might happen in 1940.

>> Activity

Keynes thought the treaty was unfair. Marks thought that it was fair.

1. Look at the points in the table. Work out which points fit in with the argument of Keynes and which ones fit in with the more recent view of Sally Marks.

2. Using these points and your wider knowledge explain whether you think that the Treaty of Versailles was unfair.

SOURCE G

Clemenceau, Wilson and Lloyd George at the peace conference.
> *Was their treatment of Germany fair?*

ASSESSING THE TERMS OF THE TREATY

> It was wrong to put the sole blame for the war on Germany. Other countries had been aggressive in the years leading up to 1914. One of the causes of the war was imperialism; many countries, including Britain and France, had tried to build up world empires.

> The settlement removed only limited amounts of land from Germany. In places like Alsace-Lorraine and the Polish Corridor most people were not German-speakers and saw themselves as French or Polish.

> The treaty was unfair because it punished the people of Germany instead of the rulers of Germany. Reparations hurt ordinary Germans who were not guilty.

> German statements about the Fourteen Points were hypocritical. When Wilson described them in a speech in January 1918 the Germans made no reply. They only took the Fourteen Points seriously much later in the year when they had been beaten and were looking for the best possible terms. When Wilson was talking about the need for a just peace the Germans were busy defeating the Russians and imposing a brutal peace treaty on them. When they were winning, the Germans ignored fairness; when they were losing they demanded it.

> Germany was tricked because her government had been offered justice and fairness by Wilson when he made his speech about the Fourteen Points. When the Germans stopped fighting they expected to be dealt with under Wilson's terms. There was nothing about war guilt and reparations in the Fourteen Points.

> The treaty aimed to destroy the economy of Germany. This was a mistake that would do no-one any good. People throughout Europe would lose out if there were no successful German factories and businesses.

> The basic strength of the German economy was not destroyed by the Treaty of Versailles. Germany soon recovered its position as the most successful economy in Europe. In 1925 Germany was producing twice as much steel as Britain.

> The German Army was reduced in size but the leaders of the German Army were not removed. The army remained a powerful force in German society. The generals were ready and able to re-build German armed forces when the time was right.

The peace treaties of 1919–23

THE BIG THREE

The winners gathered in Paris in 1919 to decide on the future of Europe. The leaders of the victorious countries each had different objectives:

> **Woodrow Wilson, the US President,** wanted a fair peace. During the war he had called for a fair settlement in his famous Fourteen Points speech (January 1918). The USA had suffered much less than its allies in loss of life and economic damage. He accepted that Germany must be punished but he did not want this to be too harsh. He believed in self-determination – that every nation should have its own government.

> **Clemenceau, the French Premier,** called for harsh treatment of Germany. Much of the war had been fought in France and the level of damage was enormous. His aim was to weaken Germany so much that it would never again try to dominate Europe.

> **Lloyd George, the British Prime Minister,** wanted a middle ground between the French and American positions. He was more interested in the British Empire than events in Europe.

THE TREATY OF VERSAILLES 1919

This dealt with the future of Germany.

Germany was forced to disarm. The army was limited to 100,000. Tanks were banned and the navy was limited to six warships. German troops were banned from the Rhineland area, bordering France.

The territory of Germany was reduced. Alsace-Lorraine was returned to France. Poland gained West Prussia, Posen and part of Upper Silesia; Danzig was to be controlled by the League of Nations. A 'corridor' of Polish territory separated East Prussia from the rest of Germany. Small territories were given to Belgium, Denmark and Lithuania. The coal-rich Saarland was put under League of Nations control for 15 years and the coal mines were handed over to France for this period. Germany was forbidden from ever uniting with Austria. German colonies were confiscated.

Germany was ordered to pay huge compensation or 'reparations' to the winning powers. These payments were justified on the grounds that Germany was guilty of starting the war. A war guilt clause was included in this treaty.

THE OTHER PEACE TREATIES

Other treaties signed at the end of the First World War

> The Treaty of St Germain 1919 with Austria

> The Treaty of Neuilly 1919 with Bulgaria

> The Treaty of Trianon 1920 with Hungary

> The Treaty of Sèvres 1920 with Turkey. This was revised in 1923 and replaced by the Treaty of Lausanne.

Setting up the League of Nations

After the First World War a new organisation called the League of Nations was set up to solve arguments between countries in a peaceful way. The League was not a success and did not bring peace to the world.

Why was the League unable to ensure world peace?

The organisation of the League

The setting up of the League of Nations was written into the Treaty of Versailles and all the other treaties that were signed at the end of the war. The rules of the League, known as the League Covenant, formed part of each peace treaty. The League officially began its work in January 1920 when the Treaty of Versailles came into effect. Geneva was chosen for the League headquarters because it was in Switzerland, which had a long tradition of neutrality. Some officials worked permanently for the League in Geneva. They were known as the Secretariat.

The League set up a number of commissions and committees to deal with particular issues and problems. The most important commissions were those which dealt with disarmament and the running of the 'mandates' (the former German and Turkish colonies). The committees included the Health Organisation which campaigned to improve the health of people, particularly in poorer countries, and the International Labour Organisation which tried to improve conditions for working people.

The peace treaties not only set up the League but also established a group called the conference of ambassadors. The conference was supposed to have oversight of the way the peace treaties were put into effect. There was some uncertainty about which issues should be decided by the League and which should be sorted out by the conference of ambassadors.

All member states sent representatives to the League Assembly. This body met at least once a year. The League Assembly had no real power. Power in the League lay with a much smaller body known as the League Council. This was dominated by a few rich countries who were permanent members of the Council: Britain, France, Italy and Japan. In theory, decisions by the Council would be carried out by all member-states. Council decisions had to be unanimous: that is, all Council members had to agree. This rule made it difficult for the Council to take action if there was any disagreement among its members.

A European club?

Many non-Europeans were very unhappy with the way the Covenant gave power to the European countries of Britain, France and Italy. At the first meeting of the Assembly, non-Europeans criticised the rules of the League. The representatives from Argentina were particularly critical. They argued for a democratic League, with the Council elected by all the countries of the Assembly. These ideas were rejected and the Argentine delegation walked out.

Some non-European countries were worried that the League would be dominated by white people. The Japanese asked that the League should promise to oppose racial discrimination. The Americans and the British rejected this proposal. The Covenant took a very patronising view of people living in colonies. It considered that more 'civilised' states should have the job of looking after those 'peoples not yet able to stand by themselves under the strenuous conditions of the modern world'.

SOURCE A

Newton Rowell of Canada spoke at the first League Assembly in 1920 and was unhappy at the way some European countries had so much power on the League Council.

You may say that we should have confidence in the European statesmen and leaders. Perhaps we should, but it was European statesmanship, European ambition that drowned the world with blood and for which we are still suffering and will suffer for generations.

America says 'no' to the League

At first it was envisaged that the USA would be a member of the Council, but in the end America failed to join the League. Woodrow Wilson was a Democrat. The majority in the US Senate belonged to another party – the Republicans – and many of them disliked Wilson. There was a strong tradition of 'isolationism' in the USA: a belief that America should not get involved in international politics. Wilson was very stubborn and he failed to compromise or to persuade his opponents to support the League. In March 1920 the US Senate stopped the USA from joining the League. The absence of the USA greatly weakened the authority of the new League of Nations.

>> Activity

1 Explain the role of the following bodies within the League of Nations:

  a the Secretariat

  b the Assembly

  c the Council

  d Commissions and Mandates

2 Why were some non-European countries unhappy at the way the League of Nations was set up?

3 Why do you think the American decision not to join the League was a big blow to the organisation?

SOURCE B

THE GAP IN THE BRIDGE.

A British Punch *cartoon comments on the American refusal to participate in the League of Nations.*

> *How does the cartoonist suggest that American absence was a great blow to the structure of the League?*

Absent friends?

Forty-five states were founder-members of the League of Nations. These were all either victorious or neutral in the First World War. The defeated nations were not allowed to join immediately. As a result Germany, Austria and Hungary saw the League as a club for their enemies. The founders were frightened of the spread of communism, and the new Soviet Union was also not invited to join. Lacking American, German and Russian membership, the League could not really claim to be the voice of world opinion.

Tension between Britain and France

In the absence of other powerful countries, the League was dominated by Britain and France. These two countries had different views of how the League should work. The French wanted to make the League into a military alliance, with strict obligations on members to support each other. This was a result of the French obsession with the dangers of an attack on France by Germany. The British saw the League as a much looser, less formal organisation. The British resisted French demands for a stronger League. The British were finding it difficult to defend their own empire and had no wish to get involved unnecessarily in military conflicts anywhere else in the world.

SOURCE C

The British were very suspicious of the French. In 1919 George Saunders, a British official, criticised the French.

At the back of all this is the French scheme to suck Germany and everybody else dry and to establish French military and political control of the League of Nations. The French see the League of Nations as an organisation for the restoration of France to a supreme position in Europe and her maintenance in that position.

SOURCE D

In 1920 Marcel Cachin, a French politician, commented on the League without the USA.

The defeat suffered by Wilsonism in the United States strikes at the very existence of the League of Nations. America's place will remain empty at Geneva, and the two countries that dominate, France and Great Britain, are divided on almost every one of the topics to be discussed.

SOURCE E

A Soviet poster celebrating the work of the Communist International. This organisation was set up by Lenin to encourage world revolution. Fear of communism led to the exclusion of the Soviet Union from the League.

The French turn to direct action

By 1923 the French were unhappy at the League's inability to ensure Germany kept to the terms of the Treaty of Versailles. They were determined to make Germany pay reparations. The Reparations Commission announced in 1921 that Germany should pay £6,600 million over 42 years. The Germans, however, made only a small payment in 1922 and then stopped paying. The French were angry and took matters into their own hands.

The occupation of the Ruhr

On 11 January 1923 French and Belgian soldiers invaded the German industrial area of the Ruhr. This area was the heartland of the German economy. The occupation of the Ruhr did not work out well for France. The British and the Americans disapproved of the use of force. The people of the Ruhr refused to co-operate with the invaders and went on strike. Within a few months the French had to admit that direct action had not worked.

SOURCE F

French soldiers occupying the Ruhr set up a machine gun position in the centre of Frankfurt.

Collective security

Although the USA did not join the League, the ideas of Woodrow Wilson were central to its work. Wilson said that the League would provide 'collective security'. This meant that if a member state of the League was attacked, all other countries of the League would act together to stop the aggression. Collective security could make use of four possible weapons:

Discussion points

In practice collective security did not work very well in the 1920s and collapsed completely in the 1930s. Why do you think collective security often failed in reality?

1 The pressure of world public opinion

2 The use of trade sanctions

3 Reducing the armaments of all countries to a minimum level

4 The use of force

World public opinion

Wilson believed in the power of public opinion. He felt that if ordinary people were allowed to speak out politicians would never go to war. Wilson claimed that if the League of Nations had existed in 1914 politicians would not have dared to start the First World War.

Looking back, the ideas of Wilson seem very naive. His talk of the power of world public opinion was based on a number of mistakes:

> In democracies like the USA people felt free to disagree with their government and could express a public opinion. Many other countries were not democratic and in these countries there was no such thing as a voice of public opinion.

> There was no evidence that ordinary people preferred peace and justice to war and injustice. Aggressive governments often had widespread support among the public.

> World public opinion did not always speak with one clear voice. What people wanted in France, for example, at the end of the war was very different from what most Americans wanted.

> Democratic government had to pay attention to public opinion in their country. Powerful undemocratic governments could ignore public opinion at home and abroad.

SOURCE G

Men and women employed in a munitions factory during the First World War. The League was committed to ensuring that nations would not need to make weapons of mass destruction.

Disarmament

The League was committed to disarmament: getting rid of weapons. Woodrow Wilson saw the arms race before 1914 as one of the causes of the First World War. The Covenant said that all members of the League should disarm.

SOURCE H

The Covenant of the League of Nations committed all members to disarmament.

Article 8 The members of the League recognize that the maintenance of peace requires the reduction of national armaments to the lowest point consistent with national safety and the enforcement by common action of international obligations.

The problem with this talk of disarmament was that it was so vague. The Covenant said that countries could keep a minimum level of arms needed for self-defence: it was not at all clear what this level was. A Disarmament Commission was set up to persuade countries to get rid of their weapons. The Commission had no way of forcing countries to disarm or checking that they had disarmed.

The use of sanctions and force

Perhaps the most important part of the Covenant were those articles that stated how the League would respond to future aggression. These ideas were found in Articles 11 and 16 of the Covenant: Article 11 said that the League of Nations would take action to stop war; Article 16 said that an attack on one member state would be seen as an attack on all League members. The League Council would decide on the appropriate punishment to use against the offending state.

The League had no army of its own. Instead, the idea was that all countries could act to help any other country if it was attacked. This turned out to be completely unrealistic. Every member state would first of all stop trade with an an aggressive country, and if this failed every country would supply soldiers for a joint war against the aggressive country. This assumed that goverments would be remarkably generous and would risk the money and lives of their own people in order to sort out a quarrel between two other countries. The threat of trade sanctions was weakened by the absence of the USA from the League. Members of the League knew that if they stopped trading, the USA could simply fill the gap.

SOURCE I

The full Assembly of the League in session, Geneva 1923.
> How far could the League enforce its decisions?

The Geneva Protocol

From the beginning, people were aware that the League was weak. The French, terrified as they were by the idea of a strong Germany, tried to give real military power to the League. However, Britain blocked moves in the early 1920s to improve the arrangements for the use of force. In 1923 a 'draft treaty of mutual assistance' was discussed. This was meant to make the threat of force more practical by saying that the League would only ask members to send troops to nearby conflicts. In 1924 a document called the Geneva Protocol was discussed. The Protocol set out clear rules for the peaceful arbitration of disputes. If countries did not follow these rules the League was entitled to use trade sanctions and force. The British government was not keen to get involved in other peoples' arguments. Britain was able to throw out the draft treaty. The British leader, Ramsay MacDonald, initially supported the Geneva Protocol. He fell from power in 1924 and the new government rejected the Protocol. Attempts to strengthen the military power of the League had come to nothing.

>> Activity

Use information from this unit to explain why collective security was unlikely to be successful.

Critics of the League

Focus

People in many countries disapproved of the League of Nations. Look at the following sources from four countries. What different criticisms did these people have of the League?

SOURCE J

An American called Lewis P. Showalter wrote an attack on the idea of the League in 1919. Showalter was an isolationist. The isolationists were successful in keeping the USA out of the League in 1920.

If there were twenty nations in the League we could control one-twentieth of our own affairs. If the Japanese would choose to send Japanese workmen over here to crowd out our workmen from our factories, mills etc., we could not say no. If the Japanese choose to come over here, seize upon our farms and homes, or take them by taxation, you could not say no, as you had signed your death warrant when you went into the League.

SOURCE K

An early Soviet view of the League as a club for fat Western capitalists. The slogan on the flag says 'Capitalists of the world unite'.

SOURCE L

William Hughes, the Australian Prime Minister, attacked proposals for the League in 1918.

I object altogether to President Wilson's scheme of a League of Nations. Where does it end? I don't know. He wants some sort of world-state, in fact a Utopia, in which all the nations would have to surrender some of their self-governing rights. There is to be an international police and there is to be a navy and an army, and so on, for this purpose. But it will not bear examination for ten minutes. It is a very obvious thing that no country will allow for a moment its vital interests to be decided by anyone but itself. Those who shout loudest for international arbitration will stand most rigidly on their own rights when a vital right is threatened. Let us ask ourselves if Great Britain would agree to interference by any council of nations as regards the size of her navy. Certainly not!

SOURCE M

Adolf Hitler speaking in 1928 expressed a common German view of the League:

Our people must be delivered from the hopeless confusion of international convictions and educated consciously and systematically to fanatical Nationalism. Belief in reconciliation, understanding, world peace, the League of Nations and international solidarity – we destroy these ideas. There is only one right in the world and that right is one's own strength.

The achievements of the League

The commissions and committees of the League did some good work. Refugees from conflicts were given vital help. A famous Norwegian explorer, Fridjof Nansen, worked for the League on the problems of prisoners of war stranded in Russia and he helped half a million men to return safely home. The International Labour Organisation (ILO) was led by an energetic and effective French man called Albert Thomas. Under his guidance the ILO encouraged many countries to improve working conditions for ordinary workers. The ILO is still in existence today and continues to campaign for workers' rights. The Health Organisation organised work on health matters, particularly in poorer countries. It worked successfully to reduce the number of cases of leprosy. Like the ILO the Health Organisation continues its work today as part of the United Nations Organisation (today it is known as the World Health Organisation).

SOURCE N

Prisoners at the end of the First World War. The League did valuable work helping such men to return home.

THE LEAGUE IN ACTION

> In 1920 the League dealt successfully with a dispute between Sweden and Finland. Both countries claimed control of the Åland Islands. The League decided that the islands should be given to Finland and this decision was accepted by Sweden.

> Throughout the 1920s the League administered the Saarland area of Germany and the Baltic city of Danzig with great fairness.

> The League was unable to find a solution to an argument between Poland and Lithuania over the town of Vilna. Poland had seized the town in 1920 in defiance of the peace treaties and the League was unable to persuade Poland to leave.

> In 1922 the League successfully organised a rescue plan for the Austrian economy.

> In 1923 Italy invaded the Greek island of Corfu. The League could not agree on what action to take. France did not want to annoy the Italian government and blocked firm League action. A settlement was eventually reached between Greece and Italy but the League took no part in negotiating this deal.

> Greece and Bulgaria came close to all-out war in 1925. The League took prompt action and ruled that Greece was at fault. Both sides stopped fighting and Greece agreed to pay compensation.

>> Activity

The League was not a complete failure. In the 1920s it had a mixture of success and failure. It had some sucess in dealing with disputes between smaller countries. Look at the table: The League in action. What evidence is there of a mixture of success and failure?

Reparations: the Dawes and the Young Plans

In early 1923, France had invaded the Ruhr area to make Germany pay reparations. Sending soldiers into the Ruhr solved nothing. The use of force did not make the Germans pay up. In November 1923 France was forced to agree to take part in a review of the reparations organised by an American banker, Charles Dawes. The Dawes Plan was agreed in April 1924.

THE TERMS OF THE DAWES PLAN

> There was to be a 2 year freeze on the payment of reparations.

> The level of German payments was scaled down.

> The USA offered huge loans to Germany.

> The French agreed to get their forces out of the Ruhr.

The consequences of the Dawes Plan

During the following five years the Germans paid a reparations bill of about $1 billion, and received American loans of about $2 billion. Germany did well out of the Dawes Plan. Much of the money from the American loans was spent on building new German factories. The French had wanted reparations in order to make Germany weak. The Dawes Plan helped Germany to become even stronger. As a result of the occupation of the Ruhr the Treaty of Versailles had been significantly altered in Germany's favour.

The Young Plan: 1929

The German government continued to complain at the level of reparations. The question of reparations was reviewed in 1929 by a committee led by an American called Owen Young. The committee produced the Young Plan. This considerably reduced the amount of reparations. The Young Plan was a considerable achievement for the German Foreign Minister, Stresemann. However, it did not bring peace and harmony to Germany. Extreme nationalists objected to the payment of any reparations and bitterly denounced the Young Plan.

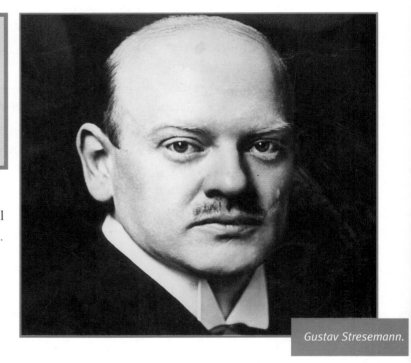

Gustav Stresemann.

After 1929 the Great Depression led to a great rise in unemployment in Germany and reparations effectively came to an end. In 1932 the participants in the Young Plan met to agree a conclusion to the sorry story of reparations. After a three-year freeze Germany was supposed to make a final payment. This payment was never made.

Discussion points

> How successful were French attempts to make Germany pay reparations?

> What was agreed in the Dawes and Young Plans? Who gained from these Plans?

> Why did the payment of reparations finally end?

The spirit of Locarno

In the 1920s there was much discussion and debate among the most powerful countries of the world. A number of international treaties were signed.

Did the agreements of the 1920s make the world a safer place?

Discussions in Washington 1921–2

The USA had refused to support the League of Nations. America ignored the League and organised conferences of its own in Washington in 1921 and 1922. The conferences concentrated on trying to limit tension in the Pacific Ocean between Japan and the USA. This was precisely the sort of dispute that the League was intended to sort out. The Washington Conferences showed the world the limits of the authority of the League. The Washington Treaty was signed in February 1922. The USA and Britain agreed to have navies of equal size. The Japanese navy was limited to three fifths of the size of each of the American and the British navies. The proportions of the navies were, therefore, set at 5:5:3.

SOURCE A

An American warship in the early 1920s. To comply with the Washington Treaty of 1922 the United States had to scuttle 30 warships, Britain destroyed 19 and Japan 17. France and Italy also agreed to limit the size of their navies. The League had no involvement in the Washington conferences.

The outcasts club together: Rapallo 1922

The British Prime Minister, Lloyd George, organised an international conference in Genoa in 1922. He wanted to find a solution to the argument between Germany and France over the payment of reparations and the level of German disarmament. The conference was a disastrous failure: the Americans refused to attend and the French and the Germans continued to disagree about reparations and disarmament.

Germany and Soviet Russia had not been invited to join the League of Nations. While the main conference was taking place at Genoa, the German delegation had discussions with the Soviets at the nearby town of Rapallo. A treaty was signed on 16 April between Germany and the Soviets. It became known as the Treaty of Rapallo. The two governments agreed to establish friendly relations, and secretly agreed to co-operate on military planning. News of the treaty and rumours of the secret military deal shocked the French government. The deal between Germany and the Soviet Union enabled Germany to get hold of most of the weapons banned under the Treaty of Versailles. As a result, the Treaty of Rapallo was a blow to the authority of the League of Nations.

>> Activity

1 Explain in your own words what was agreed in the Treaty of Rapallo and the Treaty of Washington.

2 For each treaty explain whether you think it made the League of Nations more or less powerful.

Locarno: 1925

After the failure of the occupation of the Ruhr, France looked for compromise with Germany. This search for compromise continued in 1925 when a major conference took place at Locarno, Switzerland. The key players at Locarno were the Foreign Ministers of France, Britain and Germany: Aristide Briand, Austen Chamberlain and Gustav Stresemann. The talks produced treaties that were greeted with wild enthusiasm. Many people saw Locarno as an end to the bitterness of the war and the start of a new period of peace in Europe. The three leaders won the Nobel Peace Prize for their work at Locarno.

SOURCE C

A German newspaper described the scenes at Locarno.

When the delegates arrived in their cars they passed through dense crowds. When the document had been signed, the Belgian, Rollin, went to the window, opened it and held the pact aloft. Loud cheers and prolonged applause arose from the street. Then came the speeches of Stresemann, Briand, Chamberlain, and finally, Mussolini. Soon afterwards the delegates left the building. The crowd shouted its approval, especially at the German delegates. Chamberlain, sitting in his car held a copy of the pact in his hand and received the cheers of the crowd.

Berliner Tageblatt, 1925

SOURCE B

The signing of the main Locarno Treaty, 1925. Stresemann can be seen signing on behalf of Germany. Despite the enthusiasm of people at the time, Locarno did not bring permanent peace to Europe.

THE TERMS OF THE LOCARNO TREATIES

> Under the main Locarno treaty Germany, France and Belgium agreed to accept their existing borders with each other as set up by the Versailles Treaty.

> Britain and Italy agreed to 'guarantee' the main agreement; this meant that Britain and Italy promised to take action if any of the three countries attacked each other.

> The main agreement and the guarantee did not apply to the eastern borders of Germany as laid down by the Versailles Treaty.

> Germany agreed to join the League of Nations.

> In separate treaties signed at Locarno, France promised to defend Belgium, Poland and Czechoslovakia if any of these countries was attacked by Germany.

In September 1926 the German delegates took their place at the League's Assembly Hall in Geneva. People saw this as a very historic and hopeful moment. They felt that the scars of the First World War were beginning to heal. The French leader, Briand, gave the Germans an enthusiatic welcome in his speech to the Assembly, saying, 'Away with rifles, machine guns and cannon! Make way for arbitration, conciliation and peace!' Locarno was seen as a symbol of a new period of peace and stability. Some talked enthusiastically about the 'spirit of Locarno'.

A minority of people were much more suspicious of the Locarno settlement. Behind his back, civil servants at the British Foreign Office made up a rhyme that expressed their view of the British Foreign Secretary:

'Good Sir Austen at Locarno,
Fell into a heap of guano.'

SOURCE D

Recent interpretations of Locarno have also been critical.

The League of Nations' commitment to collective security was devalued by Locarno. For, if collective security was in fact reliable, Locarno was unnecessary. If Locarno was necessary, the League of Nations was, by definition, inadequate to ensure the security of even its principal founding members. Locarno, hailed in 1925 as turning the corner towards permanent peace, in fact marked the beginning of the end of the Versailles international order.

H. Kissinger, 1994

>> Activity

Look at the following information about the effect of the Locarno settlement on Germany and France. Explain in your own words whether you think the Locarno treaties made the world a safer place.

LOCARNO: THE IMPACT ON GERMANY

> The main Locarno agreement said nothing about German frontiers in the east, and this encouraged German hopes to overturn this part of the 1919 settlement. Poland and Czechoslovakia were not allowed to take part in the main discussions and their representatives were invited to join only at the end in order to be told what the larger powers had decided.

> Each state saw the treaty differently. For Germany Locarno was the beginning of change to the Versailles Treaty.

> The Locarno settlement was a great triumph for the German Foreign Minister, Stresemann. After Locarno large amounts of American money were invested in Germany and this helped the Germans to improve their factories. Stresemann was not content with Locarno. He continued to ask for further concessions.

SOURCE E

Stresemann, the German Foreign Minister, expressed his real motives in a confidential letter written shortly before Locarno in September 1925.

In my view the foreign policy of Germany has for the short-term future three main objectives: First, a solution to the Rhine question favourable to Germany, and peace, without which Germany will not be able to regain its strength. Second, protection for the ten to twelve million Germans living under the foreign yoke. Third, the alteration of our eastern frontiers, so that we recover Danzig and the Polish Corridor. In the more distant future the reuniting of Austria with Germany.

French attitudes after Locarno

LOCARNO: THE IMPACT ON FRANCE

> The power of France to intervene in Germany was weakened by Locarno. The section forbidding invasion stopped France from repeating the 1923 occupation of the Ruhr.

> The French leaders continued to feel threatened and insecure after Locarno. They knew that sooner or later Allied troops would have to leave the Rhineland and that this would strengthen the German threat. This feeling of insecurity was expressed in the decision in 1927 to build the Maginot Line. Between 1929 and 1939 the French government spent a vast amount of money on the building of a huge line of fortifications along the border with Germany. This was the brainchild of a politician called André Maginot, and it was named after him.

SOURCE F

French pessimism was reflected in the building of the Maginot Line. It is also clear from this statement from a former French Prime Minister.

History eternally repeats itself. We have not finished with Germany. Any understanding with her is impossible, and England, whether she likes it or not, will be compelled to march with us at the moment of danger in order to defend herself.

Georges Clemenceau, 1928

SOURCE H

A French army recruitment poster shows troops stationed on the Maginot Line. The building of the Line was evidence of French insecurity.

SOURCE G

A modern historian has summed up French fears after Locarno.

The French position remained as brittle as ever. There was no firm entente with Britain. In 1928 the RAF drew up plans for a 'Locarno' war against France should she ever violate German territory. The Eastern alliances were a poor substitute. Germany, revived economically and secretly re-arming, had said nothing about her eastern frontier at Locarno. The French knew that when Germany was strong enough French security would once again be in the melting-pot.

R. Overy, *The Road to War*, 1989

>> Activity

French anxiety after Locarno led to yet another international agreement: the Kellogg–Briand Pact of 1928. Look at the following information about the Pact and answer these questions:

1 What was the Kellogg–Briand Pact?

2 How did the Pact show French anxiety about the future?

3 Why was the Pact virtually worthless?

The Kellogg–Briand Pact

In April 1927 Briand suggested that France and the USA should sign a pact promising never to go war against each other. This proposed agreement was meaningless because there was absolutely no possibility of war between America and France. However, Briand saw it as a way of symbolising the friendship between the two countries. The American government could see little value in the pact. The American Secretary of State was called Frank Kellogg. He eventually suggested that instead of an American–French agreement, all countries should be invited to sign an agreement not to go to war. On 29 August 1928 government leaders of 15 powerful countries gathered together to sign the Pact of Paris. This soon became known as the Kellogg–Briand Pact. It said that each participating country would not use warfare in order to get what it wanted. In the months that followed most countries in the world agreed to the Kellogg–Briand Pact. The Pact was worthless as it put no real obligations or restrictions on countries. Japan and Italy both signed the Pact but before very long they used war to get what they wanted and the Kellogg–Briand Pact was shown to be completely irrelevant.

SOURCE I

Aristide Briand. He was anxious to strengthen the position of France but the Kellogg–Briand Pact was of little practical value.

SOURCE J

The so-called Kellogg–Briand Pact was signed on 27 August 1928.

The High Contracting Parties solemnly declare that they condemn recourse to war for the solution of international controversies, and renounce it as an instrument of international policy in their relations with one another. The settlement or solution of all disputes or conflicts shall never be sought except by pacific means.

SOURCE K

Not everyone was impressed by the Pact. Stalin's comments about the Pact were dismissive.

They talk about pacifism. They speak about peace among European states. Briand and Austen Chamberlain are embracing each other. All this is nonsense. Every time that states make arrangements for new wars they sign treaties and call them treaties of peace.

Stalin, 1928

The rise of Hitler

Early life

Adolf Hitler was born in 1889 in Austria. On leaving school Hitler tried and failed to get a place in an art college. Unemployed and very unhappy, he lived in poverty in Vienna and Munich in the years before the First World War. His life was transformed by the outbreak of war. Hitler joined the German army and, for the first time, there was a sense of purpose to his life. For most of the war Hitler had a dangerous job as a messenger at the Front and he was awarded medals for bravery. He was horrified in 1918 when Germany lost the war. Like many Germans he felt that the Versailles Treaty of 1919 was very hard on Germany.

Although he hated communism, Hitler was impressed by the way communists were ready to use violence to get what they wanted. In November 1922 he said:

> 'The communists teach 'If you will not be my brother, I will bash your skull in.' Our motto shall be 'If you will not be a German, I will bash your skull in.' We cannot succeed without a struggle. We have to fight with ideas but, if necessary, also with our fists.'

After the war Hitler began his political life in the Bavarian city of Munich. In 1919 he joined and took over a tiny group called the German Workers' Party. Hitler was lazy but he was a brilliant public speaker. He appealed to the many ex-servicemen who were unhappy about Germany after the war. Slowly membership grew and in 1920 Hitler changed the name of the organisation to the National Socialist German Workers' Party (the term 'Nazi' is a shortened version of the German words 'National Sozialistisch' meaning national socialist). His followers deliberately got into fights with socialists and communists. In 1921 these Nazi street-fighters were organised into a private army called the 'Sturmabteilung' (the Storm Section or the Storm Troop) — the SA. They were also known as the brownshirts because of their distinctive uniforms.

A German crowd in Munich celebrating the outbreak of war in 1914. In it Adolf Hitler can be seen ringed.

November 1923: Hitler tries to seize power

Germany went through a great crisis in 1923. A French army occupied the industrial Ruhr area because Germany had not paid the reparations required as part of the Versailles Treaty. Germans went on strike as a protest against the French occupation and this led to many economic problems. The value of the German currency collapsed. People lost their life savings. Hitler decided that the time was right for a revolution.

On 8 November 1923 Hitler tried to use the SA to seize control of Bavaria. He planned to march to Berlin and force a Nazi government on the whole of Germany. This was a dismal failure. The event became known as the 'Beer Hall Putsch', because it began when Hitler used force to take over a meeting in a Munich beer hall. The next day, 9 November, the Nazi forces marched from the beer cellar and were stopped by armed police. The police opened fire, 16 Nazis were killed and the rest, including Hitler, then ran away. The revolution was over. Two days later Hitler was arrested.

After the Beer Hall Putsch Hitler was put on trial for treason. He made skilful use of the trial to win publicity and sympathy from German nationalists. He was treated leniently by the court; he was sentenced to five years in prison but he only served nine months. Hitler learnt a lot from his failed revolution. Afterwards he decided to concentrate on using legal means to get power.

Mein Kampf: 1925

While in prison Hitler wrote a book explaining his beliefs. This was called *Mein Kampf* or 'My Struggle' and was published in 1925. This book stated Hitler's basic ideas:

> The Treaty of Versailles was an unjust attack on the German nation and must be overturned.

> The leaders of the Weimar Republic were traitors because they had accepted the Treaty of Versailles.

> The Jewish people were the cause of many of Germany's problems. Jews were sub-human and were always trying to wreck Germany.

> Russian communism was wicked. Its leaders were Jews who wanted to destroy Germany.

> The German people needed more space or 'Lebensraum' (living space). This space should be taken from Russians and other non-German people of Eastern Europe.

The lean years

The Nazi Party was not very successful between 1925 and 1930. When Hitler came out of prison the German economy was beginning to recover. With jobs and more money people were less attracted to extremist nationalists like Hitler. The economic recovery, however, came to a very sudden end in 1930 as a result of the worldwide Depression. A return of unemployment and hard times caused a great upsurge in support for Hitler. Hitler finally took power in 1933. He was to remain Chancellor of Germany until his suicide in 1945 at the end of the Second World War.

This 1920s National Socialist German Workers' Party poster appealed to workers to vote for Hitler, the frontline soldier (Frontsoldaten).

Discussion points

> What was Hitler like as a person?

> Why do you think that Hitler's ideas were attractive to some Germans?

> Why did Hitler find it difficult to get support in the years 1925–30?

The Depression

One of the many Americans who was financially ruined as a result of the Wall Street Crash tries to sell his car for a very low price.

24 October 1929 was a fateful day in the history of the world. This was the day of the Wall Street Crash. The value of shares on the American stock market collapsed. People tried frantically to sell their shares before the prices fell even further. In one day no fewer than 13 million shares were sold. This was the start of an economic crisis that devastated the whole world.

What were the political consequences of the Depression?

THE ECONOMIC IMPACT OF THE DEPRESSION

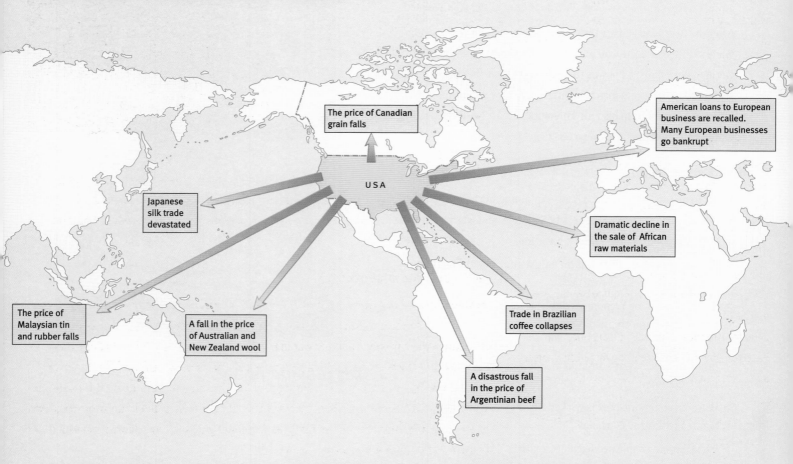

The price of Canadian grain falls

American loans to European business are recalled. Many European businesses go bankrupt

USA

Japanese silk trade devastated

Dramatic decline in the sale of African raw materials

The price of Malaysian tin and rubber falls

A fall in the price of Australian and New Zealand wool

Trade in Brazilian coffee collapses

A disastrous fall in the price of Argentinian beef

The depression began with the Wall Street Crash. This was a collapse of confidence among American investors. After Wall Street there was a dramatic slump in the USA. This had catastrophic results for the world economy. The world economy depended on the USA.

After Wall Street there was a worldwide economic crisis. Governments turned to protectionism: they imposed high import taxes to protect their own industries. This resulted in a further decline in world trade and widespread unemployment.

and international politics

The Depression and the USA

In the years before 1929 the American economy had grown at a dramatic rate. The USA was by far the most important manufacturing country in the world. On the eve of the Depression, the USA was producing 4.5 million cars a year, while Germany, Britain and France made less than half a million cars between them. Taken together, Britain, France, Germany, Italy, Japan and the USSR produced fewer manufacturing goods than the USA did by itself.

The national income of the USA fell by nearly a half between 1929 and 1932. American factories, which had become so successful, suddenly fell silent. Exports of cars fell from $541 million in 1929 to $76 million in 1932. Farmers were also badly hit: wheat exports fell from $200 million to a mere $5 million in 1932.

Isolationism

American foreign policy had been isolationist before the Depression. The US government became even more isolationist after 1929. Politicians were more interested in rebuilding the American economy.

In 1932 a new President was elected: F. D. Roosevelt. Under Roosevelt policy became even more isolationist. Roosevelt called for a New Deal for America. This New Deal policy was based on government spending on public projects and government help for businesses and farmers. Roosevelt needed the support of extreme isolationists in the US Congress to get support for his New Deal.

SOURCE B

Poverty in the USA during the Depression. A queue of poor black people wait for government handouts beneath a poster celebrating the wealth of some white Americans.

SOURCE C

Roosevelt made this statement shortly after becoming President in January 1933.

Our international relations, though vastly important, are secondary to the establishment of a sound national economy. I favour the practical policy of putting first things first.

America and the dictators

Lacking support from Washington, the leaders of France and Britain were encouraged to be cautious towards the dictators. Many American politicians said that America should be neutral if there was ever another war in Europe. This encouraged Hitler to think that Germany could be aggressive without much risk of war with the wealthy USA. American reluctance to get involved was seen during the crisis over Abyssinia in 1935. Mussolini was criticised by the US government for invading this African country but nothing practical was done to stop him. American companies greatly helped Mussolini by allowing a massive increase in the sale of American oil to Italy.

The Depression and Germany

In Europe the impact of the Depression was at its greatest in Germany. By 1932 German factories were only producing about 60 per cent of the output of 1928. By 1932 one out of every three of the working population was unemployed. The slump hurt farmers as well as factory workers. The income of German farmers fell by about half between 1928 and 1932. The result was massive discontent.

Democratic government was already in trouble before the Depression started. On both the left and the right, some German politicians had been unhappy for years with democracy. In addition, many senior army officers and civil servants disliked the rule of parliament. The Depression added a new sense of crisis to German politics. As early as 1930 emergency powers were given to the president that limited the power of the parliament or Reichstag.

Hitler's luck

The Depression was a tremendous piece of good luck for Adolf Hitler. Before the Depression his Nazi Party was very small. There were elections in Germany in 1928 and the Nazis won only 12 seats in parliament. Hitler's breakthrough came in September 1930 when the party won 107 seats and became the second largest party in Germany. At the same time, there was an increase in support for the communist party. As people lost their faith in democracy they turned to the two parties that wished to destroy parliament. Although deadly enemies, both Nazis and communists agreed that democracy was weak and worthless.

As unemployment rose in Germany there was an increase in street violence between gangs of Nazis and communists. The Nazis made further progress in the elections of July 1932 when they won 230 seats and became the largest party in the Reichstag. Hitler's appeal was based on the problems of the Depression; most of his supporters were impressed by the way his propaganda called for 'Work and Bread'.

SOURCE D

A Nazi election poster showing a heroic image of a German farmer. The poster promises voters 'Work, Freedom and Bread'.

Hitler takes over

Hitler was now in a powerful position. There were further elections in November 1932. The Nazis lost a little ground but remained the single largest party. Although he did not win an outright majority, Hitler was able to do deals with other parties and he became the Chancellor of Germany on 30 January 1933. After elections in March 1933 Hitler took complete control. Democracy came to an end on 23 March 1933 when the Reichstag passed the so-called 'Enabling Law'. This gave Hitler the power to introduce future laws without the agreement of the Reichstag. Hitler was now the dictator of Germany.

SOURCE E

Hitler's appeal to the German people was very straightforward. He could offer them a simple explanation for all their problems. This is an extract from a proclamation he made on 1 February 1933, the day after he became Chancellor:

More than fourteen years have passed since the unhappy day when the German people, blinded by the promises of enemies at home and abroad, lost everything. Since that day of treachery, God has withheld his blessing from our people. Arguments and hatred spread among us. Within four years, unemployment must be finally overcome.

SOURCE F

One historian has assessed the results of the Depression for Germany.

Without the Depression Hitler would not have come to power. Mass unemployment reinforced all the resentments against Versailles and the Weimar democracy that had been smouldering since 1919. Overnight the National Socialists were transformed into a major political party; their representation in the Reichstag rose from 12 deputies in 1928 to 107 in 1930.

Anthony Adamthwaite, *The Making of the Second World War*, 1977

German rearmament

Hitler's rise to power did not lead to immediate war between Germany and other states. However, in October 1933 Hitler showed his contempt for the Versailles settlement by withdrawing Germany from the League of Nations. At the same time he withdrew Germany from the Disarmament Conference that had been meeting at Geneva since 1932. In the following two years he concentrated on strengthening his position in Germany and rearming Germany.

In February 1933, days after he came to power, Hitler instructed the German general, von Fritsch, to end German disarmament and to 'create an army of the greatest possible strength'. This was a breach of the Treaty of Versailles. Germany began a remarkable increase in its level of weaponry that was to gather momentum during the mid-1930s. By July 1933 tanks were being produced. By 1934 Germany was making aircraft and warships. The airforce did particularly well from the first days of rearmament. The production of military aircraft rose from 36 planes in 1932 to 1,938 planes in 1934 and 5,112 planes in 1936. In 1935 Hitler introduced conscription and began to increase massively the number of German soldiers. The limits on German power in the Treaty of Versailles had been completely overturned.

SOURCE G

Hitler surveys a massive Nazi rally. Once in power he committed Germany to rearmament.

The Depression and Britain

In Britain the Depression wrecked traditional manufacturing industries. The production of textiles fell by two thirds. Shipbuilding collapsed: in 1933 British yards were producing only 7 per cent of the amount produced in 1914. Between 1929 and 1932 iron and steel production halved.

At the time London was the most important financial centre in the world and the pound was a key currency in international trade. In 1931 the value of the pound was reduced and it was no longer linked to the price of gold. These changes were a blow to British pride and further evidence that Britain was losing its place as a great power. At the time of the Wall Street Crash, Britain was ruled by a Labour government. The crisis undermined the position of the government and led to a split in the Labour Party. The Prime Minister, Ramsay MacDonald, left the Labour Party and set up a coalition government with largely Conservative support.

Caution and cuts in defence

After the Depression, British leaders became very worried about the British Empire. They were not convinced that Britain was rich enough to defend its far-flung Empire. Above all, the government became convinced that they could not afford to fight two wars at the same time – one against Japan to defend the Empire in Asia and another to stop the rise of German power in Europe. Since the Empire was the first priority, the financial crisis encouraged the British government to take a very cautious approach to Germany.

Ramsay MacDonald responded to the Depression by cutting public spending. The result was a dramatic reduction in spending on defence in the early 1930s. It was not until 1936 that British spending on defence began to rise again. This further weakened Britain's ability to stand up to Hitler. Full-scale rearmament did not occur until 1938.

Cuts in defence spending coincided with a huge increase in German spending on weapons. By 1936 the German air force was close to overtaking in size that of Britain. British generals and admirals became very pessimistic about how well Britain could do in a war.

SOURCE H

Poverty in Britain in the 1930s. An unemployed man stands on a street corner in Wigan, northern England.

The Depression and France

The Depression took longer to have an impact on France because the French economy depended less on international trade. However, when the slump did start in France it had a very damaging effect. After 1933 French industry went through a great crisis. As late as 1938 France had still failed to restore the level of national income to that of the 1920s.

As in Britain, the slump had an impact on defence. With a huge debt for money borrowed during the First World War and war pensions the French government could not give its armed forces adequate weapons. The production of new aircraft fell and compared very badly with output in Germany. In one year, 1937, the French built 370 military aircraft while the Germans built 5,606.

The economic problems added to the bitter social divisions that existed in France. Unemployment trebled between 1931 and 1935. The membership of the French Communist Party rose dramatically at the same time. The Communist Party began to do very well in elections. The crisis also led to a great surge in extreme right-wing political support. A right-wing demonstration in Paris during February 1934 turned into a riot in which 14 people were killed. The deep divisions between left and right in France between 1933 and 1936 stopped the French government from standing up to Hitler.

SOURCE I

Unemployed French workers protesting in Paris, 1930. Their banner calls for 'Work or Bread'. The Depression in France heightened tensions between left- and right-wing extremists.

SOURCE J

The Nazi leader, Goebbels, speaking in April 1940, looked back to the early 1930s as a time when France failed to take firm action against Germany.

In 1933 the French Prime Minister should have said: 'Hitler cannot be tolerated. Either he disappears or we march!' But they didn't do it. They left us alone and they let us slip through the danger zone, and we were able to sail around all dangerous reefs. And when we were done, and well armed, better than they, then they started the war.

>> Activity

Look back at pages 46–51. Explain in your own words the link between the Depression and the following problems:

a The USA became more isolationist and did little to stop Hitler and Mussolini

b The extremist Nazi Party came to power in Germany

c The British government became less willing to fight a war in Europe.

d France became a weak and bitterly divided country.

Crisis in Manchuria

The authority of the League of Nations collapsed in the 1930s. Japan invaded the north Chinese province of Manchuria in 1931. Japan was criticised by the League but little was done in practice to drive the Japanese out of Manchuria.

Why did the League fail to stop Japan?

The rise of Japan

In 1853, after centuries of isolation, the peace of Japan was disturbed by the arrival of the American navy in Tokyo Bay. The arrival of the wealthy, well-armed Westerners was a great shock to people in Japan. They were both impressed and worried by their American visitors. In 1868 a group of angry 'samurai' or warrior nobles seized control of the government. They were determined to change Japan so that, unlike many other Asian lands, their country would not be taken over by Westerners. To resist Western armies the Japanese government was determined to make Japan as rich and powerful as Britain or America. In the late nineteenth century the Japanese government built up a strong economy and established a well-educated workforce. As a result the Japanese were able to build armaments as powerful as those of America and Europe.

Victory over Russia

The push for modernisation was so successful that in 1904 Japan was able to wage war against Russia. To the astonishment of the world the Japanese had defeated Russia by 1905. The Russian navy was convincingly beaten and its main fleet was sunk. Japan had arrived as a powerful nation.

Having defeated a great European country the Japanese government expected to be treated as an equal by other powerful states. In particular, the Japanese government wanted an empire in Asia. This empire could supply raw materials for the increasing numbers of Japanese factories. The Western nations were very unhappy at the idea of a Japanese empire. This was a threat to their own interests in Asia. The argument about a possible Japanese empire centred on China.

In the First World War Japan joined forces with Britain and France and declared war on Germany. Japanese forces occupied all the German territories in the Pacific. The Japanese government also used the war to start to build up an empire in the area of China known as Manchuria. The Japanese were disappointed by the 1919 peace settlement. They were on the winning side and they expected more rewards than they got. This led to a great sense of resentment towards Britain, France and America.

SOURCE A

A Japanese painting celebrating the defeat of the Russian navy at Tsushima in the war of 1904–5.

Japanese troops interrogating a Chinese prisoner in Manchuria. The League did little to stop the Japanese occupation.

Attack on Manchuria

The army was a very powerful force in Japan. In the 1920s the power of the army grew to a point where politicians could no longer tell soldiers what to do. Army officers wanted to increase Japanese control in Manchuria. The army took the initiative in September 1931 when they organised an armed clash with Chinese forces in Manchuria. War followed. Japan won the war in Manchuria and set up a puppet government.

The invasion of Manchuria was a clear test of the League and collective security. Both China and Japan were members of the League. Would the League use economic sanctions or war to stop the Japanese take-over? In fact, the League did virtually nothing. A group known as the Lytton Committee was sent to Manchuria to find out what was happening. It took months to carry out its work, by which time Japan was firmly in control. Eventually it criticised both Japan and the government of China.

The League Council accepted the Lytton Committee Report. It criticised Japan but did not recommend a trade ban or the use of force. Even though the League did little Japan was not prepared to accept any criticism and left the League in 1933.

SOURCE C

The failure to take firm action over Manchuria was a great blow to the image of the League of Nations. People who expected the League to keep the peace began to despair. The English newspaper, the Manchester Guardian, *expressed a widespread concern about the failure of the League in Manchuria in December 1931.*

The League Covenant [the charter of the League setting out its principles] can apparently be ignored with impunity. Japan has ignored it by invading Manchuria; the nations represented on the League Council have ignored it by refusing to insist on the withdrawal of Japanese troops. The Covenant has failed to save China from aggression as completely as a signed and ratified treaty failed to save Belgium from German aggression in 1914. The Great Powers, despite all their fine gestures, have to their great shame not even seriously protested against, let alone resisted, such a state of affairs.

The failure of the League

>> **Activity**

1 Read Source E. Explain in your own words what this interpretation says about why no other country was ready to stop Japan taking over Manchuria.

2 Does the information on page 55 on other countries' reactions to the invasion of Manchuria support the interpretation in Source E, or does it suggest additional reasons why Japan was not stopped?

SOURCE E

Gaetano Salvemini was an Italian historian. Writing in 1954 he described Western attitudes towards the crisis in Manchuria.

In the Far Eastern crisis of 1931 and the following years, Japan and China, owing to their great distance from Europe, might as well have been on the moon. If a man sees a cat crushed under a car, he loses his appetite; yet the same man can calmly eat his breakfast while reading in his morning paper that thousands of men, women and children have been engulfed in some terrible earthquake. The Japanese Government could count on the ignorance of people too busy with difficulties at home to be bothered about events in remote lands. People's minds in both America and Europe were with the economic depression that had started in 1929 and was at its worst in 1931–2.

SOURCE D

THE DOORMAT

Both of the cartoons on these two pages were produced by the British artist, David Low. In this picture the League is shown as a doormat and a Japanese officer walks over it.

The missing powers

Two powerful countries with an interest in this part of Asia were not members of the League. These were the USA and the USSR. The USSR was worried about the actions of the Japanese. The move in Manchuria was seen as a challenge to Soviet power in East Asia. However, the government of the USSR was busy at the time, dealing with chaos at home as peasants were forced to live on new collective farms. In addition, the USSR had no allies who might join forces against Japan, and Soviet leaders were not ready to act alone.

Some members of the American government were appalled by the Japanese aggression. However, President Hoover believed in isolationism and did not want to get involved in the conflict between China and Japan. As a result the USA refused to support the idea of economic sanctions against Japan. This greatly weakened the ability of the League to threaten trade sanctions. Members of the League knew that if they refused to trade with Japan the USA might simply carry out the trade instead.

The sympathetic powers

Italy and Germany were important members of the League. They were happy with Japanese aggression. Italy was not interested in the Far East but, like Japan, was keen to build up its own empire. Germany had investments in China, but its main concern was to see if the Japanese would get away with the use of force. As a result, Italy and Germany offered no opposition to Japan.

The worried powers

The French were completely preoccupied with the German threat in Europe. While they disapproved of Japanese actions the French had no wish to get involved in a war in Asia. The use of French and British forces against Japan would weaken defences against Germany in Europe. In public the French government condemned Japanese action; in private messages were sent to the Japanese to let them know that France sympathised with the difficulties faced by Japan in China.

Members of the British government were in a difficult position. They did not feel that the British navy was in a position to take on the Japanese. The advice from military leaders was that a war with Japan might be disastrous. Vital parts of the British Empire – India, Singapore and Hong Kong – could well be lost if fighting broke out between Britain and Japan. British businesses did considerable trade with Japan and the government was unwilling to lose the trade. Although the British government was worried about Japan it was not prepared to take firm action.

SOURCE F

Japan is shown here as a gangster defying the judges of the League.

> *How can you tell that the artist was not impressed by the way the League dealt with Japan?*

Mussolini and Italian

Italy before Mussolini

Italy had many political problems in the years after the First World War. Italians felt cheated. About half a million Italian soldiers had been killed in the war. Italians expected payment for this sacrifice from the peace settlement. However, the peace treaties were a great disappointment because the Italians failed to get all the land they expected. It became known as the 'mutilated peace'. At home there were deep divisions between those who supported the ideas of the Russian Revolution and those who hated socialism and communism. Few people respected the Italian parliament. Five governments were formed between 1919 and 1922 and none of them was able to take control of the situation.

Mussolini: the man

Benito Mussolini was born in 1883. Before the First World War he had been a socialist journalist. He left the socialist party because he supported the war and other socialists did not. In 1919 Mussolini began to organise gangs of angry ex-servicemen into a powerful political force. They were known as 'fascists', because they belonged to a 'fascio' or armed squad. The fascists soon got a reputation for attacking and beating up their enemies. Mussolini loved parades and uniforms. The fascist fighters wore distinctive black shirts. Throughout his early political career he kept changing his policies. He was ready to drop any belief that got in the way of his search for power. Once in power, Mussolini encouraged Italians to look up to him as a special leader with extraordinary powers. He was called 'duce', which is the Italian for 'leader'.

Mussolini in military uniform.

The fascist take-over

Mussolini came to power in 1922. His followers staged a dramatic march on Rome to get publicity and to show how strong they were. Italy was in chaos. The king of Italy turned to Mussolini because he thought the fascists would improve law and order and stop Italy turning towards communism. At first the fascists did not have complete control and had to share power with other parties. After rigged elections in 1924 Mussolini strengthened his grip on power. The leader of the rival Socialist Party was murdered. From 1925 Mussolini began to rule Italy as a dictator. In 1926 all other parties were banned. Leading communists and socialists were imprisoned.

Some were murdered. Widespread use was made of propaganda to convince Italian people that Mussolini was an almost super-human leader. Posters were put up throughout the country saying, 'Mussolini is always right'. The voting laws were changed in 1928 so that only fascist men could vote, and the only permitted candidates were fascists. Not surprisingly, Mussolini did well in the elections that followed. In 1929 Mussolini came to an agreement with the Pope about the place of the Catholic Church in Italy. In return for giving the Church special privileges Mussolini made sure that the Church would not challenge fascism.

fascism

The dead bodies of Mussolini and his lover, Clara Petacci, displayed hanging from a garage after they had been tried and executed by Italian partisans in Milan in 1945.

Discussion points

> Why do you think some Italian people turned to Mussolini in the early 1920s?

> How did Mussolini strengthen his power in the 1920s?

Mussolini goes to war

By 1930 the fascist revolution at home was largely over. In the 1930s Mussolini looked to foreign policy for further triumphs. In 1935–6 Italy invaded and conquered Abyssinia (modern Ethiopia). He made an agreement to work with Hitler in 1936; the link between Germany and Italy was called the Rome–Berlin Axis. In 1940, when it looked as if Germany was going to win the Second World War, Mussolini joined forces with Hitler and went to war against France and Britain. The war was a disaster for Mussolini. His forces were defeated in North Africa by Britain and the USA. By 1943 Italy itself had been invaded. Mussolini was overthrown by other fascists and imprisoned. Hitler sent German paratroopers to rescue him. For the last two years of the war Mussolini ruled part of northern Italy, but real power lay with the Germans. He was captured and killed by anti-fascist fighters in April 1945 and his dead body was put on public display in Milan.

THE KEY IDEAS OF ITALIAN FASCISM

> Italians should take a fierce pride in their country.

> War is good for a country. Young Italian men should be ready to fight.

> Italy should establish an empire in Africa.

> No other political parties are allowed.

> Communism and socialism are the enemies of fascism.

> Democracy is useless. Italy needs a strong powerful leader who can tell people what to do.

> The place of women is at home. Italian women should have as many children as possible.

> A great country should be self-sufficient. The government should tell firms what to produce to bring this about.

The conquest of Abyssinia

Italy conquered Abyssinia in 1935–6. Some historians see a direct link between the crisis over Abyssinia and the outbreak of world war in 1939. In 1977 a British historian called Anthony Adamthwaite wrote: 'If there was a turning-point on the road to war it was the Abyssinian crisis of 1935-6. The crisis was the major step towards war.'

What were the results of the invasion of Abyssinia?

The search for an empire

In the late nineteenth century Italy tried to conquer the African state of Abyssinia (known today as Ethiopia). The attempt ended in disaster. In 1896 the Abyssinians destroyed an Italian army at Adowa. The battle stopped Italy for a while but after Adowa many Italians wanted to take revenge.

Mussolini looks south

By the early 1930s Italy was suffering from the Depression. Mussolini wanted a successful war to strengthen his position at home. He was also disturbed by the rise of Hitler. Hitler was planning to dominate central Europe, so Mussolini decided to look south and make Italy a great Mediterranean power. This led him to think about an Italian return to Abyssinia.

SOURCE A

Extracts from statements by Mussolini in 1935:

Whatever it costs, I will avenge Adowa. We have been patient with Ethiopia for forty years. Now, we have had enough!

The Stresa Front

France and Britain were keen to stop Italy joining forces with Germany. In return, they seemed ready to give Italy a free hand in Africa. In April 1935 Mussolini met the French and British prime ministers in the Italian town of Stresa. They condemned German breaches of the Treaty of Versailles. People began to talk about the Stresa Front: an anti-German grouping of Italy, Britain and France. The Stresa agreement was vague: the declaration talked only about the need to 'keep the peace in Europe'. Mussolini understood this to mean that France and Britain would not object to the Italian use of force outside Europe. Mussolini thought that in return for supporting France and Britain in Europe he would be allowed to attack Abyssinia without any interference.

The Anglo–German Naval Agreement

The British government greatly weakened the Stresa Front in June 1935. Britain signed a treaty with Germany over the strength of their navies. This fixed the size of the German navy at 35 per cent of the British navy. The agreement allowed Germany to have submarines. The French and the Italians were annoyed by the Naval Agreement. They had not been consulted and the agreement was in breach of the Versailles Treaty.

Invasion

The Italian attack on Abyssinia began on 3 October 1935. Symbolically, one of the first Italian actions was the bombing of the town of Adowa, scene of the Italian defeat in 1896.

Britain and France were caught in a dilemma. They did not want to annoy Mussolini, but they also wanted to support the League of Nations and the idea of collective security. Abyssinia was a member of the League of Nations. The League condemned Italian action and imposed a trade ban. However, the ban did not include the trade in oil and petrol. This was crucial. As long as the Italians had petrol they could continue the war. Limited sanctions did not work.

Italian troops say farewell to their families at Rome railway station before departing for Abyssinia in 1935.

The Italian invasion of Abyssinia.

The Hoare–Laval Pact

The reaction of the French and British governments was half-hearted. In December 1935 the British Foreign Secretary, Hoare, had secret talks with Laval, the Prime Minister of France. They designed a compromise, known as the Hoare–Laval Pact, under which Abyssinia would have been divided in two, with Italy given the richer part. The war was going badly for Mussolini and he might have accepted the deal. However, the details of the Pact were leaked to the press. There was uproar in Britain. People saw it as a surrender to Italian aggression. The Pact was scrapped and Hoare was forced to resign.

After the failure of the Hoare–Laval Pact Britain and France took a tougher line against Italy. In March 1936 they finally decided to ban the sale of oil and petrol to Italy but by this time it was too late. In May 1936, before the oil and petrol ban had started properly, Italy won the war. The League had failed and on 15 July all the sanctions against Italy were ended.

>> Activity

1 What happened at the Battle of Adowa?

2 Why was Mussolini keen to conquer Abyssinia?

3 What was the Stresa Front? What was the Anglo-German Naval Agreement?

4 What was the Hoare–Laval Pact? Did it succeed?

5 Why do you think the sale of oil and petrol was important to the Italian army in Abyssinia?

SOURCE E

Hailie Selassie, addressing the League of Nations in June 1936. Despite his passionate pleas, the League was unable to stop the Italian conquest.

After Abyssinia

The League of Nations was broken by the Abyssinian crisis. Afterwards no one took it seriously. The failure of the League was highlighted by Hailie Selassie, the Abyssinian emperor, who made a passionate speech to the League Assembly after his country had been conquered.

SOURCE C

Extract from Hailie Selassie's speech to the League Assembly, 30 June 1936:

I was defending the cause of all small peoples who are threatened with aggression. Ethiopian warriors asked only for means to defend themselves. On many occasions I have asked for financial assistance for the purchase of arms. That assistance has been constantly refused me. The problem is a much wider one than that of Italy's aggression. It is the very existence of the League of Nations. God and history will remember your judgement. Are states going to set up a terrible precedent of bowing before force? What reply shall I have to take back to my people?

SOURCE D

The Italian government showed its contempt by sending a sneering message to the League. On 30 June 1936 the new Italian Foreign Minister, Count Ciano, responded defiantly to the speech of Hailie Selassie.

Italy views the work she has undertaken in Ethiopia as a sacred mission of civilisation, and proposes to carry it out according to the principles of the Covenant of the League of Nations. Italy will consider it an honour to inform the League of Nations of the progress achieved in her work of civilizing Ethiopia.

A discredited League

In the crises that followed Abyssinia, the League was completely helpless. When the Spanish Civil War broke out in 1936 Germany and Italy sent help to the anti-government side. The Spanish government appealed to the League: the League did nothing. In 1938–9, as the Second World War drew close, the League played no part in serious attempts to avoid conflict. When war broke out in September 1939 none of the countries involved bothered to tell the League that a war was taking place.

SOURCE F

Litvinov, the Soviet Foreign Minister, described the failure of the League in a speech to the League Assembly in September 1938.

The League was created as a reaction to the world war. Its object was to make that the last war, to safeguard all nations against aggression, and to replace the system of military alliances by the collective organisation of assistance to the victim of aggression. In this sphere the League has done nothing.

Germany and Abyssinia

Hitler was deeply interested in the crisis in Abyssinia. He wanted to know how far Britain and France would go to stop the Italians. He was not impressed at the confused and feeble response of the democracies.

SOURCE G

A German newspaper commented unfavourably on the way the British had behaved over Abyssinia.

The English like a comfortable life, compared to us Germans. They avoid sustained effort, if possible. After the war, the British masters of the world thought that they had earned a rest. Today the Italians have complete control over Abyssinia. The League and the London government know that only the use of great force can drive the Italians out of Abyssinia, but they are not prepared to use such force.

Münchener Zeitung, May 1936

SOURCE H

Britain's anxiety to avoid war led Hitler to despise the British.

The modern British Empire shows all the marks of decay and unstoppable breakdown. Britain will regret her softness. It will cost her the British Empire.

Adolf Hitler, 1936

The fall of the Stresa Front

After Abyssinia the British and French governments hoped to re-establish a good relationship with Italy. Mussolini had different ideas. He had been annoyed by what he saw as British and French double dealing. Instead he turned to Hitler. The German leader had not interfered over Abyssinia. In January 1936 Mussolini thanked Hitler and made it clear that he was happy for an increase in German control over Austria. This was a significant development. In 1934 Mussolini had opposed German expansionism towards Austria. The Stresa Front against Germany had collapsed.

The Axis and the Anti-Comintern Pact

By November Mussolini was talking of a new force in European politics – a linking together of the fascist states of Italy and Germany called the Rome–Berlin Axis. Later in the same month the leaders of Germany, Italy and Japan signed the Anti-Comintern Pact (Comintern was the Soviet organisation whose job was to spread communism world-wide). On one level the Anti-Comintern Pact was simply an agreement to work together against communism. As far as Hitler was concerned it was much more important than that; it was a step towards an alliance of those countries that wanted to take land off their neighbours.

THE BENEFITS OF THE ABYSSINIAN CRISIS FOR HITLER:

> The League was unlikely to stop German aggression any more than it had stopped Mussolini.

> The anti-German Stresa Front fell apart.

> The crisis provided Hitler with an opportunity for his first act of aggression – the sending of German troops into the Rhineland area.

> The Rome–Berlin Axis and the Anti-Comintern Pact strengthened the position of Hitler.

>> Activity

Explain in your own words the consequences of the Italian conquest of Abyssinia. In your answer you should mention:

a the reputation of the League;

b the advantages of the crisis for Hitler.

The rise and fall of the League of Nations

THE ESTABLISHMENT OF THE LEAGUE

> The idea of a League of Nations was discussed by American, British and French politicians during the First World War, as an organisation that would prevent future war.

> The American President, Woodrow Wilson, was very keen on the idea of the League. He was very idealistic but not very practical about how the League should work.

> The League was set up as part of the Treaty of Versailles, 1919. It began work in 1920. Its headquarters was in Geneva, Switzerland.

> The plan was that the League would bring peace to the world through a system called 'collective security'. Collective security meant that the members of the League would act together to punish and stop any country that attacked another state. This punishment could be either economic sanctions: a ban on trade with an aggressor country; or military action: the use of war.

THE ORGANISATION OF THE LEAGUE

> Decisions were taken by the Council. This small group was dominated by a few powerful countries who were permanent members. At first the permanent members were Britain, France, Italy and Japan. Other countries took it in turns to have temporary membership of the Council.

> At first it was expected that the USA would be a leading member of the League. President Wilson had a disagreement with the US Senate about the League. In 1920 the Senate refused to let the USA join the League.

> Any decisions taken by the Council had to be unanimous: every member of the Council had to agree before any action could be taken.

> All member states could send representatives to the Assembly. This was a place to discuss the problems of the world. It had little real power.

THE WORK OF THE LEAGUE

The League was responsible for several organisations that did good work in a number of fields. These organisations still exist today as part of the United Nations and included:

> The Refugee Organisation which helped the victims of war;

> The International Labour Organisation which tried to improve working conditions;

> The Health Organisation which encouraged schemes to improve healthcare.

Burying the war dead, 1918. The League was intended to prevent the repetition of scenes like this.

SUCCESSES IN PEACE-KEEPING

The League made some progress in solving arguments between states during the 1920s. Often the success stories involved arguments between smaller countries:

1920: an argument was settled between Finland and Sweden about the Åland Islands;

1922: the League rescued Austria from a financial crisis;

1925: action by the League stopped war from breaking out between Greece and Bulgaria;

1926: Germany joined the League as part of the Locarno settlement;

1934: the Soviet Union became a member of the League.

THE LEAGUE! PAH! FANCY SUGGESTING NATIONS COULD UNITE FOR *PEACE*.

A David Low cartoon criticising the League's failure to take effective action during the Spanish Civil War, 1936.

FAILURES IN PEACE-KEEPING

From the beginning, the League found it difficult to stop powerful countries from attacking other states. The weakness of the League became clear to the world in the 1930s:

1923: Italy seized the Greek island of Corfu. The League could not agree on any action;

1931: Japan attacked the Chinese province of Manchuria. The League did little and Japan remained in Manchuria. Japan did not like being criticised by the League and left the organisation in 1933;

1934: Hitler had despised the League since it was set up. A year after he took power, Germany left the League;

1935: Italy invaded Abyssinia. The League tried to stop Italy through the use of economic sanctions. These did not include a ban on the sale of oil and they failed. After this the League was not taken seriously.

WHY DID THE LEAGUE FAIL?

Some powerful countries were not members

The League was greatly weakened by the refusal of the USA to join. If America had joined, the League would have had more power and authority. Other powerful countries were either excluded or chose to leave. Germany did not join until 1926. The USSR was excluded until 1934, by which time Germany had left the League.

Britain and France could not always agree

In the absence of the USA the most powerful states in the League were Britain and France. They did not trust each other and often disagreed about how the League should work. The rule that Council decisions had to be unanimous made it even more difficult for the League to make decisions.

The League lacked teeth

Collective security did not work. France, Britain and other members were more concerned about their own interests than the authority of the League. As a result they were reluctant to get involved in collective security. The League could not make powerful countries obey its rulings.

The Depression undermined the League

The League was weakened by the Great Depression that swept the world after 1929. At a time of economic crisis governments were less interested in what happened in faraway places. Japan and Italy were able to invade other countries without being punished effectively by the League.

From the Rhineland to the 'Anschluss'

In 1936 Hitler defied the Treaty of Versailles. He ordered German troops to march into the Rhineland. Two years later he broke the Treaty again by uniting Germany with Austria.

What can we learn about Hitler from the crises over the Rhineland and Austria?

SOURCE A

German troops march into the Rhineland in 1936. This action was a clear breach of the Treaty of Versailles.

The risk of war

Hitler took considerable risks in moving into the Rhineland. There was a good chance that France would send troops to resist the German forces and this would mean war. The German army was not ready for war. No one in Germany knew how the French would react. Many German generals were unhappy at Hitler's plan. If the French had sent an army into the Rhineland they could easily have outnumbered the German forces. The first troops into the Rhineland were ordered to retreat if they met with French resistance. In the days immediately after the invasion the German generals called upon Hitler to retreat. He refused.

Hitler the peacemaker?

Instead of giving way, Hitler tried to show the world that the action in the Rhineland was reasonable. The ambassadors of Britain, Italy and France were told that Hitler had important new plans for long-term peace in Europe. He proposed a 25-year agreement between Germany and France and Belgium: Germany promised not to attack its western neighbours. Hitler also suggested that there should be a demilitarised zone on either side of the French–German borders. He talked about Germany returning to the League of Nations. These were not serious proposals, but they made Hitler seem reasonable. Many people were taken in by his proposals. In Britain, for example, the Labour politician Arthur Henderson said that Hitler's offer of the 'olive branch…ought to be taken at face value'.

SOURCE B

François Poncet was the French ambassador to Germany in 1936. In 1949 he looked back at Hitler's policy of military action and skilful politics.

Hitler smacked his enemy in the face, and as he did so he declared: 'I bring you proposals for peace!'

On the day of the reoccupation Hitler spoke to the Reichstag. Again, his intention was to convince the world that the action in the Rhineland was not worth fighting for. He suggested that he was actually trying to build a new peaceful Europe.

SOURCE C

I have never forgotten my duty to uphold European civilisation. It should be possible to end this useless conflict between France and Germany which has lasted for centuries. Why not replace it with the rule of reason? The German people have no interest in seeing the French people suffer.

Hitler speaking to the Reichstag, 7 March 1935

The reaction of the French and the British

French ministers and generals met in emergency session on the day of the occupation. They thought about sending the French army to fight. In the end the French decided to protest but not to fight.

In Britain hardly anyone wanted to go to war over the Rhineland. Many British people approved of what Hitler had done; this was German territory, and they thought the German army had a right to be there. One politician said that the British did not care 'two hoots' about the Rhineland. The British government sympathised with this view. They took no action.

The Rhineland crisis showed that Hitler could seize an opportunity on the spur of the moment. He had been planning to wait until 1937, by which time the German army would have been stronger due to rearmament. However, he recognised that the Abyssinian crisis provided an unusual opportunity. Britain, France and the League of Nations were overwhelmed by the crisis in Abyssinia and there was a reluctance to get involved in any more conflicts.

SOURCE D

Years later Hitler looked back with pride to the Rhineland crisis.

The forty-eight hours after the march into the Rhineland were the most nerve-racking in my life. If the French had then marched into the Rhineland we would have had to withdraw with our tails between our legs, for the military resources at our disposal would have been wholly inadequate for even a moderate resistance.

What would have happened in March 1936 if anyone other than myself had been in charge of Germany! Anyone else would have lost his nerve. I had to lie. We were saved by my unshakeable obstinacy and my remarkable daring. I threatened, unless the situation ceased in twenty-four hours, to send six extra divisions into the Rhineland. In fact, I only had four brigades.

The 'Anschluss': the German take-over of Austria

In early 1938 Austria was in a state of crisis. Local Nazis were making life difficult for the government of Chancellor Kurt Schuschnigg. Hitler did not have complete control over these Austrian Nazis, and they sometimes acted without waiting for orders from Berlin. In January 1938 it was discovered by the Austrian authorities that there was a plot by Austrian Nazis to create chaos in Austria by killing the German ambassador. Austrian Nazis hoped that in the turmoil the German government would take over Austria.

The Austrian leader, Schuschnigg, visited Hitler for crisis talks in Germany in February 1938. Schuschnigg was badly treated at this meeting. Hitler raved and shouted at him for two hours. He demanded that Nazis be allowed to join the Austrian government and be given control of law and order. Schuschnigg felt that he had no option and agreed to Hitler's terms.

When Schuschnigg got back to Austria he was in a difficult situation. He took very seriously Hitler's threat of force unless Nazis were given more power in Austria. There was no chance of help from abroad. The British had made it clear that they would not stop a German take-over.

SOURCE E

On 12 February 1938 Hitler ranted at Schuschnigg.

The whole history of Austria is just one uninterrupted act of treason. This must come to an end. I can tell you, here and now, Herr Schuschnigg, that I am absolutely determined to end this. Germany is one of the Great Powers and no other state will raise its voice if Germany settles its border problems. I have achieved everything I set out to do, and have become perhaps the greatest German in history. Listen. You don't really think that you can move a single stone in Austria without my hearing about it the very next day, do you? You don't seriously believe that you can stop me, or even delay me for half an hour, do you?

The plebiscite

On 9 March Schuschnigg made one last desperate attempt to keep Austria independent. He announced that there would be a plebiscite, or referendum, in Austria to decide whether Austrians wanted their country to remain independent. He fixed the lowest age of voting at twenty-four, so that young Nazis would not be able to vote. Hitler was enraged when he heard about the plebiscite plan. He feared that Schuschnigg would win the plebiscite and he ordered the army to invade before the plebiscite. On 11 March 1938 the German army invaded Austria. Arrests began immediately of enemies of the Nazis. In the city of Vienna alone 76,000 people were arrested in the aftermath of the invasion. On 12 March Hitler himself crossed into Austria. He went to his own home town of Linz where he was greeted by cheering crowds.

SOURCE F

Schuschnigg made a radio broadcast on 11 March.

Men and women of Austria. Today we have been faced with a difficult situation. The German government gave us an ultimatum: appoint as Chancellor a candidate nominated by Germany, otherwise German troops will march into Austria. There is no truth in the stories that there has been unrest, that streams of blood have flowed and that the government could not maintain order.

The Austrian government has decided to yield to force. Because we do not want to shed German blood, we have ordered our armed force to offer no resistance if the invasion is carried out.

SOURCE G

An extract from Hitler's speech to the people of Linz, 12 March 1938:

I left this town years ago with precisely the same beliefs as I have today. Imagine how deeply I feel now that I have brought my beliefs to fulfilment. Providence gave me a mission to restore my dear homeland to the German Reich. I believed in that mission, I have lived and fought for it, and I believe I have now fulfilled it.

SOURCE H

Austria, 12 March 1938: cheering crowds greet the arrival of the German army.

>> Activity

Look back at pages 64–67.

1 Using information from this unit explain how Hitler sent troops into the Rhineland and Austria.

2 What evidence can you find to support the following statements about Hitler:

    a He was prepared to gamble and take great risks.

    b He was skilled at propaganda.

    c Sometimes he acted like a madman.

    d He did not believe that France or Britain would take action to stop his aggression.

    e He had no respect for plebiscites or democratic votes.

3 What else can you learn about Hitler from his actions over the Rhineland and Austria?

Munich and the destruction of

The peace treaties at the end of the First World War had created a new country called Czechoslovakia. In 1938 Britain and France signed the Munich Agreement that broke up Czechoslovakia and gave much of it to Germany.

What happened at Munich?

The Sudeten Germans

There were about 3 million German speakers in Czechoslovakia. They were a large minority in a country dominated by Czechs and Slovaks. They were known as Sudeten Germans and were concentrated in the border areas. Nazis were active among the Sudeten Germans. The local Nazi leader, Konrad Henlein, led a political party called the Sudeten German Party that received money from Hitler. Henlein claimed that the Sudeten Germans were not treated fairly. He took part in negotiations with the Czechoslovak government but these got nowhere.

Hitler met Henlein on 28 March 1938 to give him instructions. He told the Sudeten leader to keep making demands that the Czechoslovak government could not possibly accept. By dragging out the negotiations, Hitler hoped to create a crisis over Czechoslovakia.

SOURCE A

A tearful woman gives the Nazi salute to the German forces as they cross into Czechoslovakia during the German takeover of the Sudetenland.

Support from Britain and France?

The government of Czechoslovakia looked to Britain and France for help. British leaders had no treaty with Czechoslovakia. The leaders of the British armed services could not see any way that Britain could help. By March 1938 Chamberlain was saying in private that Czechoslovakia could not be saved.

France had signed a treaty with Czechoslovakia in 1925. This said that France would give Czechoslovakia military help if it was attacked by Germany. In April 1938 there was a change of government in France. The new Prime Minister, Daladier, was not keen on the idea of going to war with Germany over Czechoslovakia. His Foreign Minister, Bonnet, tried to find a way of avoiding war without clearly going back on the promise to Czechoslovakia.

Hitler prepares to act

Hitler was sure that neither Britain nor France would intervene if he attacked Czechoslovakia. In April he visited Rome and was told by Mussolini that Italy would support Germany. On 30 May Hitler let his generals know that he had decided to 'smash Czechoslovakia by military action in the near future'.

The British and the French governments reacted to the crisis by putting pressure on the Czechoslovaks to make concessions. The British government sent a politician called Lord Runciman to Czechoslovakia in July to try to work out a settlement between the two sides. Runciman was biased in favour of the Sudeten Germans. He recommended to the British government that the Sudetenland should be separated from Czechoslovakia.

Czechoslovakia

SOURCE B

The mood of some French people was described by the novelist Jean-Paul Sartre. Sartre was a left-wing intellectual who lived in this period. A character in one of his novels, set in 1938, explained why it was wrong for France to think about going to war over Czechoslovakia.

I know what the Czech government is like. I know what tyrants they can be. Is it right that France – the land of liberty – should allow Frenchmen to be killed so that the Czech government should continue to torment the Sudeten Germans? Is that a good enough reason why an educated young Frenchman should end up ten feet underground? We ought to say to our Government, 'If the Sudeten Germans want to join Germany, that's fine, its none of our business.'

J-P. Sartre, The Reprieve

>> Activity

Look at the sources on this page. They shed light on Western attitudes to Czechoslovakia. What can we learn from these sources about why some people in France and Britain were not ready to stand by Czechoslovakia?

SOURCE D

An extract from the Runciman Report on the Sudetenland:

I have much sympathy with the Sudeten case. It is a hard thing to be ruled by an alien race. Czechoslovak rule in the Sudeten areas for the last twenty years has been marked by discrimination, to a point where the German population was inevitably moving in the direction of revolt. The Sudeten Germans felt that in the past they had been given many promises by the Czechoslovak Government, but that little or no action had followed. Czech officials and Czech police, speaking little or no German, were appointed to purely German districts; Czechs were encouraged to settle on land in the middle of German populations. Czech firms were favoured against German firms. The State provided work and relief for Czechs more readily than for Germans.

The feeling of the Sudeten Germans until about three or four years ago was one of hopelessness. But the rise of Nazi Germany gave them new hope. I regard their turning for help to their kinsmen and their desire to join the Reich as a natural development.

SOURCE C

" Why should we take a stand about someone pushing someone else when its all so far away .. "

INCREASING PRESSURE.

A British cartoon of the time criticising British and French attitudes to German aggression.

The Munich crisis

Hitler was ready to go to war against Czechoslovakia in the summer of 1938. Many of his leading generals disagreed. They were afraid that Britain and France would fight and they did not feel that Germany was ready for a large-scale war. Hitler refused to listen to the generals. He was sure that Britain and France would do nothing.

Tension rose in early September. Henlein ordered local Nazis to attack Czech and Jewish targets. As a result of this violence, negotiations between the Sudeten Germans and Prague were broken off. Henlein left Czechoslovakia on 15 September. In Germany much publicity was given to his stories of the mistreatment of Sudeten Germans.

SOURCE E

Mussolini, Hitler and Chamberlain meet at Munich. (Hitler's interpreter, Schmidt, is sitting on his left.)

Chamberlain flies to Germany

Chamberlain met Hitler in Germany at Berchtesgaden on 15 September. Hitler complained to Chamberlain about the treatment of the Sudeten Germans. Chamberlain gave in to Hitler. He agreed with him that the Sudetenland should be annexed by Germany. In return he asked Hitler not to use force to take control. Chamberlain returned to London and got Cabinet support for a peaceful German take-over. The French leaders Daladier and Bonnet came to London on 18 September and agreed to support the partition of Czechoslovakia in return for a British promise to defend what was left of the Czechoslovak state. A day later the Czech President, Beneš, was told that he must hand over the Sudetenland. Beneš was extremely unhappy about this, and at first he refused to co-operate. By 21 September he realised that he was powerless to resist without Allied support so he reluctantly agreed to the take-over.

Hitler did not want a peaceful settlement. He wanted to destroy Czechoslovakia by force. He was annoyed when Chamberlain came to see him for a second time on 22 September at Bad Godesberg with news that Britain, France and Czechoslovakia had agreed to his proposals. To Chamberlain's horror, Hitler then refused to accept the deal he had suggested a week earlier. Hitler made new demands: that the German take-over should be immediate, that there should be votes on whether to stay in Czechoslovakia in additional areas, that the claims of Hungary and Poland to other parts of Czechoslovakia needed consideration. Chamberlain tried to get him to compromise, but he refused. Chamberlain returned to London disappointed.

War?

At this point a war between Britain and Germany seemed a real possibility. The British government prepared to issue 38 million gas masks and anti-aircraft guns were put in place. Chamberlain tried once again to get Hitler to find a peaceful solution. He sent Sir Horace Wilson to talk to Hitler on 26 and 27 September. Hitler was not in a mood for negotiation. He told Wilson several times that he was going to 'smash the Czechs'.

SOURCE G

Sudeten Germans greet the German invasion in October 1938. The banner offers thanks to Hitler.

SOURCE F

When Horace Wilson suggested that an attack on Czechoslovakia could lead to war with France and Britain Hitler replied:

If France and England strike, let them do so. It is a matter of complete indifference to me. I am prepared for every eventuality. It is Tuesday today, and by next Monday we shall be at war.

An invitation to Munich

On 28 September Chamberlain was in the middle of a speech to parliament describing the negotiations when he was passed an important note. The note told him that Hitler had agreed to a conference at Munich with representatives of Britain, France and Italy. The conference would try to explore a peaceful solution to the crisis over Czechoslovakia. There was wild cheering among MPs, who were relieved to hear that war might be avoided.

The Munich Conference began on 29 September. A day later the British and French Prime Ministers agreed with Hitler on the terms of the annexation of the Sudetenland. Czechoslovakia was not represented at the conference. The conference did not involve any real negotiations. Britain and France simply agreed to give Hitler what he wanted. On 1 October German troops marched unopposed into the Sudetenland. The Czech President, Beneš, was forced to go into exile.

SOURCE H

On 30 September the German general, Jodl, wrote about the Munich Agreement in his diary.

The Pact of Munich is signed. Czechoslovakia as a power is out. The genius of the Führer and his determination not to avoid the risk of world war have again won us victory without the use of force.

>> Activity

1 Who was Konrad Henlein? What part did he play in the Czechoslovak crisis?

2 What happened when Chamberlain met Hitler on 15 and 22 September 1938?

3 What was agreed at the Munich Conference?

4 What clues can you find as to why Chamberlain and Daladier decided to give way to Hitler over Czechoslovakia?

5 What can we learn from the Munich crisis about the personality of Hitler?

Different views of appeasement

Since 1945 historians have disagreed passionately about Chamberlain's policy of trying to satisfy Hitler's demands, known as 'appeasement'. There have been two conflicting views: some historians say appeasement was cowardly and stupid because it encouraged Hitler to demand more and more; other historians are much more sympathetic and say that Chamberlain's decisions made a lot of sense at the time.

Was the British policy of appeasement justified?

TWO INTERPRETATIONS OF CHAMBERLAIN'S RESPONSE TO HITLER

Interpretation A

Chamberlain was foolish. He misunderstood Hitler. Chamberlain thought that Hitler was a reasonable man. He was wrong.

Interpretation B

Chamberlain was no fool! It's easy to look back and criticise Chamberlain but he was in a difficult position. Appeasement seemed sensible at the time.

>> Activity

1 Look back to the story of how Hitler took over Austria and the Sudetenland (pages 68-71). Do you think that Chamberlain took the right approach to Hitler?

2 Consider the following four factors that led Chamberlain to believe in appeasement. For each factor work out whether it fits in with Interpretation A or Interpretaton B.

SOURCE A

Neville Chamberlain.

FACTOR 1
THE PERSONALITY OF CHAMBERLAIN

Like many people who had lived through the First World War, Chamberlain was horrified at the idea of another war. He believed passionately in the importance of peace.

SOURCE B

Writing before he became Prime Minister Chamberlain said:

War wins nothing, cures nothing, ends nothing. When I think of the 7 million young men who were cut off in their prime, the 13 million who were maimed or mutilated, the misery and suffering of the mothers and the fathers...in war there are no winners, but all are losers.

Chamberlain was not used to dealing with fanatics like Hitler. He was a great believer in the power of talk and negotiations. In 1937 he said to the Soviet ambassador to London: 'If only we could sit down at a table with the Germans and run through all their complaints and claims. That would greatly reduce the tension.' Chamberlain was an honest man and assumed that other leaders were also honest. He believed Hitler when the German leader said that after Czechoslovakia there would be no more threats to peace in Europe. Hitler was, in fact, lying. On his return from Munich Chamberlain told his colleagues that Hitler now respected him. This was not true. In private Hitler described Chamberlain as a worm and said that he would like to kick him down a flight of stairs.

SOURCE C

Chamberlain's comments to the Cabinet at the time of the Munich crisis were summarised in the Cabinet records:

He [Chamberlain] also had in mind that you could say more to a man face to face than you could put in a letter. He thought that doubts as to the British attitude would be better removed by discussion than by any other means.

In his view, Herr Hitler had certain standards. He had a narrow mind and was violently prejudiced on certain subjects; but he would not deliberately deceive a man whom he respected. He was sure that Herr Hitler now felt some respect for him. When Herr Hitler announced that he meant to do something, it was certain that he would do it. Hitler had said that once the present situation had been settled he had no more territorial ambitions in Europe. To miss all this would be a great tragedy. A peaceful settlement of Europe depended upon an Anglo–German understanding.

FACTOR 2
CONCERN FOR THE EMPIRE

The British Empire mattered a great deal to British politicians in the 1930s. The most powerful voices in the Empire were those of the self-governing countries, known as the dominions – Canada, Australia, New Zealand and South Africa. The dominions were great supporters of appeasement and made it very clear at the time of Munich that they would not back Britain if it came to a war over Czechoslovakia.

On 1 September 1938 Chamberlain was told that the South African and Australian governments would not give military support if war broke out. On 24 September the South African parliament voted in favour of neutrality if war broke out between Germany and Britain. It was clear to Chamberlain that an aggressive policy towards Germany would split the British Empire.

The Empire influenced Chamberlain in another way. Much of the Empire was in Asia where Britain faced another threat in the form of the rise of Japan. British military leaders were terrified at the idea of a war with both Germany and Japan. The generals and admirals did not believe that Britain was strong enough to fight both countries at the same time. The military leaders supported the idea of appeasement of Germany.

SOURCE D

The Defence Requirements Committee 1936 stated:

It is a cardinal requirement of our national and Imperial security that our foreign policy should be so conducted as to avoid a possible development of a situation in which we might be confronted simultaneously with the hostility of Japan in the Far East, Germany in the West and any power on the main line of communication between the two.

SOURCE E

A criticism of appeasement. This David Low cartoon of the time suggests that Hitler was effortlessly destroying small countries who had put their trust in Britain and France.

FACTOR 3
THE SLEEPING SUPERPOWERS

If Britain had been given effective support by the USA or the USSR its leaders could have taken a harder line towards Germany. This was not possible because the USA maintained its 'isolationist' policy and the British leaders did not trust the communist USSR.

Until the late 1930s American spending on defence was very limited. As a result, the Americans did not have the military strength to match their economic strength. Although the USA was a very rich country, in 1937 it spent only 1.5 per cent of its national income on defence. By contrast, Germany was spending 23.5 per cent of its total income on defence in the same year. The USA was rightly described as a 'sleeping giant'. As a result of the long-standing policy of isolation, the American armed forces were in no position to fight. In 1937 the USA had a small standing army, largely equipped with inefficient, old-fashioned weapons. The American air force was considerably outnumbered by the German and Japanese air forces.

The American President, F. D. Roosevelt, hated war. He was also a realistic politician who tried to respond to the mood of the American people. America had been devastated by the Depression and the American people were concerned with the need to rebuild their own country. Many Americans were not interested in what happened in Europe. Other Americans did care about the wider world but felt that the USA should try to stamp out war and the arms trade. A temporary Neutrality Act was passed in 1935 and this was made permanent in 1937. As result, Chamberlain could expect no help from America in any struggle with Germany.

SOURCE F

Roosevelt in 1936:

We shun political commitments which might entangle us in foreign wars. We are not isolationists except insofar as we seek to isolate ourselves from war.

SOURCE G

The Soviet Union was another source of potential support against Hitler. The Soviet Red Army was large but the British authorities did not have a very high opinion of its ability. The British leaders hated communism. The unreliability of the USSR was heightened by the purges that Stalin carried out in the late 1930s. The Soviet leader accused many leading communists of treachery and many of them were killed. In 1937 the purges reached the Red Army. Stalin destroyed almost his entire military leadership: 35,000 leading officers were executed, including nearly all his top military experts. Of the 80 members of the Supreme Military Council, 75 were executed. This greatly weakened the fighting capacity of the Soviets. It also convinced British leaders that Soviet military help against Germany was of little use.

Chamberlain knew that without support from other powerful countries, war with Germany was risky. In the First World War, Britain and France fought Germany with allies in Russia, Italy and Japan. Even with these allies Britain and France were only able to defeat Germany when the USA entered the war. In the late 1930s Britain and France had no powerful allies. If it came to war they could not be sure of winning.

A German cartoon of 1937 shows Russia at war with itself. A two-headed creature (with the face of Stalin) attacks itself. At this time Stalin's purges were greatly weakening the strength of the Soviet army.

FACTOR 4
PLAYING FOR TIME

Appeasement was a complex policy. It was not just a question of giving in to Hitler. The negotiations were accompanied by a policy of rearmament so that, if necessary, aggression could be resisted by force.

Between 1934 and 1938 Britain increased four-fold the amount of money spent on defence. One view of appeasement is that it gave Britain time to rearm so that when the crisis with Germany finally came to a head in 1939 Britain was better prepared. At the time of Munich in 1938 Chamberlain felt that rearmament had not gone quite far enough for Britain to risk a war. His military advisers urged him to play for time.

SOURCE H

Advice from the British military leader, General Ismay, to Chamberlain at the time of Munich:

From the military point of view time is in our favour. If war has to come, it would be better to fight her in say 6–12 months than to accept the present challenge.

At the end of the war Hitler himself looked back to Munich and wondered if he had not made a mistake. He felt cheated by the Munich deal. He told his assistant, Bormann, that Germany should have gone to war in 1938 over Czechoslovakia.

SOURCE I

We ought to have gone to war in 1938. Although we were ourselves not fully prepared, we were better prepared than the enemy. September 1938 would have been the favourable date.

Adolf Hitler, February 1945

>> Activity

Why did a policy of appeasement make sense to Chamberlain?

In your answer you could mention the following factors:

> Chamberlain's own character
> The needs of the British Empire
> A lack of support from the USA and the USSR
> Plans for rearmament

SOURCE J

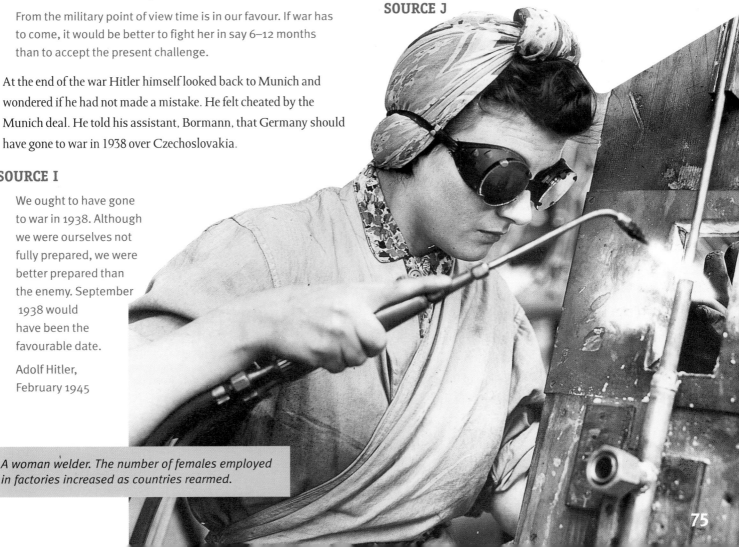

A woman welder. The number of females employed in factories increased as countries rearmed.

The Nazi–Soviet Pact

In 1939 Stalin amazed the world by doing a deal with his deadly enemy, Hitler.
Within a few days of the signing of the Nazi–Soviet Pact the Second World War broke out.

Why did Stalin agree to the Nazi–Soviet Pact?

Communist beliefs

As a communist Stalin believed that there was little difference between the fascist dictatorships and the Western democracies. Germany, Italy, Britain and France were all, to him, capitalist states and potential enemies of the Soviet Union. The most important task for him was to ensure that they did not unite to fight against the USSR. He was perfectly happy to do a deal with either.

Communist writers taught that capitalist powers were naturally aggressive. Countries attacked each other to get more markets or raw materials. Stalin believed this and expected that sooner or later there would be another war like the First World War. His concern was that capitalist countries did not gang up together against the Soviet Union. He tried to make sure that the USSR was on the winning side in any war among capitalist countries.

SOURCE A

In 1925 Stalin stated that sooner or later there would be another world war.

Should such a war begin we will not be able to stand idly by. We will have to take part, but we will be the last to take part so that we may throw the decisive weight onto the scales, a weight that should prove the determining factor.

Reacting to Hitler

The rise of Hitler posed a problem for Stalin. As early as January 1934 Stalin made it clear that he was prepared to do business with Hitler. In that month he made a speech stating that the USSR could work with any country that did not threaten it. At this stage Hitler had no interest in good relations with Stalin and this early attempt by Stalin to do a deal with Nazi Germany was not successful.

SOURCE B

Hitler had always hated Soviet communism. This Nazi election poster of 1932 shows Bolshevism as an armed monster.

Support for the League and collective security

Having failed to establish a relationship with Hitler, Stalin turned instead to the Western powers. In September 1934 the Soviet Union suddenly joined the League of Nations. Before that the Soviet government had referred to the League as 'a gang of robbers'. In 1935 communist parties across the world were ordered to stop trying to organise revolution. Instead they co-operated with any anti-fascist forces.

The Soviet Foreign Minister was Maxim Litvinov. Between 1934 and 1938 he tried to build links with Britain and France, in order to counter the threat from Germany. He was a great believer in the idea of collective security: by standing together, the countries of Europe could stop German aggression.

Appeasement and the Soviets

The policy of appeasement disappointed Litvinov and Stalin and forced them to think again about the value of a link with Britain and France. With regards to the Rhineland, Austria and at Munich the Western Allies seemed too ready to ignore Hitler or do a deal with him. Stalin had never really trusted the British and the French. He suspected that their secret aim was to encourage a war between Nazi Germany and the Soviet Union in the hope that the two sides would destroy each other.

SOURCE C

Maxim Litvinov, Soviet Foreign Minister 1934–9. He tried to link up with Britain and France to build an anti-German alliance. The Western powers did not trust the Soviets and the alliance came to nothing.

SOURCE D

In June 1938 the Soviet Foreign Minister, Litvinov, reflected on the crisis over Czechoslovakia.

The entire diplomacy of the Western powers over the last five years has been an attempt to avoid any resistance to German aggression and to agree to every demand for fear of arousing German disapproval. The Soviet Government takes no responsibility for future developments.

SOURCE E

At the height of appeasement the government of the USSR began to show its annoyance with both Germany and the Western powers of Britain and France. This view is seen in an extract from the official party newspaper, Pravda, in September 1938.

The Soviet Union is indifferent to the question which imperialist brigand falls upon this or that country, this or that independent state.

SOURCE F

Stalin made this speech on 10 March 1939:

Britain and France have rejected the policy of collective security and have taken up a policy of non-intervention and neutrality. The policy of non-aggression is a way of encouraging aggression. Britain and France are encouraging the Germans to march east. They are saying to Germany, 'Just start war on the Bolsheviks and everything will be all right.'

>> Activity

What can we learn from these sources about how appeasement affected the way the Soviet Union viewed Britain and France?

A Soviet offer to the West

By the spring of 1939 there was a real possibility of Britain and France going to war with Germany. What was not clear was the position of the Soviet Union. Both sides wanted a deal with the Soviet Union. For a while it still seemed that the Western powers would succeed in winning Soviet support. On 17 April 1939 the Soviet Foreign Minister, Litvinov, outlined the basis for a treaty to France and Britain. This would have involved all three promising to defend the existing borders of the states of Eastern Europe from German attack, and each country promising to help the others in case of German attack.

A change of foreign minister

It took Britain six weeks to reply to this offer. Stalin was not impressed that it took so long. He thought it indicated that the Western allies were not serious about an alliance. He began to look towards Germany for a deal. Stalin indicated a change of approach in May. He dismissed Litvinov and appointed Molotov to be the Soviet Foreign Minister. Litvinov had been on friendly terms with some Western politicians. His dismissal was a sign that Stalin was open to offers from Nazi Germany. Exploratory talks began between the Soviets and the Germans in May. These were secret talks and the British and the French knew nothing of them. Contacts between the Germans and the Soviets continued through the summer. Germany made it clear that, if the Soviet Union stayed neutral, the Soviet government could increase its territory in Eastern Europe.

SOURCE G

Hitler explained the consistency of his foreign policy on 11 August 1939 in conversation with Carl Burckhardt, the High Commissioner of the League of Nations in Danzig.

Everything that I undertake is directed against Russia; if the West is too stupid and too blind to understand this, then I will be forced to reach an understanding with the Russians, smash the West, and then turn all my concentrated strength against the Soviet Union. I need the Ukraine so that no one can starve us out again as in the last war.

Failure in Leningrad

Public talks between the Western powers and the Soviets carried on in the early summer of 1939 but they got nowhere. On 12 August British, French and Soviet military leaders met for talks in Leningrad. The Soviet delegates asked the British and the French if they could ensure a right of passage for Soviet troops through Polish and Romanian territory. The British and the French said 'no'. The Polish and Romanian governments did not want Soviet troops entering their territory on the way to fight the Germans. The Soviet generals were exasperated by this. Voroshilov, the leader of the Soviet delegates, said, 'Are we supposed to beg for the right to fight our common enemy?' The talks ended in failure on 21 August.

SOURCE H

Soviet troops in 1938. At this time, Stalin was unsure whether to use these forces against Germany.

Hitler sends a letter

The Soviets were further annoyed that the British and French delegates did not include senior ministers or top generals. As a result they did not have the power to sign a treaty. The Germans did things differently. On 20 August Hitler took the unusual step of writing a personal letter to Stalin offering high level talks in Moscow. Stalin was impressed by this.

SOURCE I

Hitler sent this personal letter to Stalin on 20 August:

The tension between Germany and Poland has become intolerable. A crisis may develop any day. In my opinion it is desirable for our two states to enter into a new relationship, without losing any time. I propose that you receive my foreign minister in Moscow. He will have the fullest power to sign the pact. I should be glad to receive your early answer.

SOURCE J

Stalin replied to Hitler the next day.

I thank you for your letter. I hope that the German–Soviet Non-Aggression Pact will mark a decided turn for the better in the political relations between our two countries.

Ribbentrop calls on Stalin

On 23 August, two days after the talks with Britain and France had broken down, Hitler sent Ribbentrop, his Foreign Minister, to Moscow. Ribbentrop, unlike the British and the French delegates, was a senior figure and he had full power to negotiate and sign a non-aggression treaty.

In Moscow, Ribbentrop met Stalin and began bargaining. Stalin was particularly interested in a secret section of the proposed treaty. In the so-called 'secret protocol', Germany and the Soviet Union agreed to carve up most of the territory that lay between their two countries. The Soviet Union was offered control of vast areas of territory, including Finland, Latvia, Estonia, Lithuania, and parts of Belarus and the Ukraine that were ruled by Poland. The pact was soon signed. Stalin celebrated by drinking champagne with Ribbentrop and proposing a toast to Hitler: 'I know how much the German people loves its Führer; I should therefore like to drink his health'.

SOURCE K

Molotov signs the Non-Aggression Pact with Germany. Ribbentrop, Stalin and others look on.

The two choices

Focus

By the middle of August 1939 Stalin was faced with two clear choices. He opted for the German offer. Look at the following details of the two offers. Can you work out why Stalin found the German offer more attractive?

The British and French offer

The British and French offered a military agreement with the Soviet Union. If Germany attacked Poland, the Soviet Union would join Britain and France and go to war against Germany. The theory was that the threat of war from Britain, France and the Soviet Union would be enough to stop Hitler from sending his troops into Poland. It was not at all clear how this military agreement would work in practice. The Polish government disliked the Soviet leaders and refused to accept that Soviet troops could enter Poland. By signing, the Soviet Union risked getting involved in a war. In return, the Soviet Union would receive support from Britain and France if German troops attacked Soviet territory. The Soviet Union would not gain any additional land by signing.

The German offer

The Germans offered a non-aggression pact with the USSR. This meant that each side promised not to attack the other. In addition there was a secret offer to divide up much of Eastern Europe between Germany and the USSR. In return for allowing the Germans to conquer most of Poland, the USSR would be given control of the Baltic states and parts of Belarus, the Ukraine and the remainder of Poland. These were territories that Russia had controlled before the 1917 Revolution. By signing the Soviet Union avoided, at least for a while, involvement in a war. In return the Soviet Union would be given control of huge areas in Eastern Europe.

>> Activity

Look at these interpretations of the negotiations in 1939. Do they help us to understand why Stalin agreed to a deal with Germany?

SOURCE L

A modern British historian has tried to explain Stalin's decision.

Stalin was presented with a choice, an agreement with France and Great Britain or one with Germany. On 23 August 1939 von Ribbentrop and Molotov signed the German–Soviet non-aggression pact in Moscow. This pact made war in Europe inevitable. Why did Stalin not opt for an agreement with France and Great Britain? Stalin decided that war was inevitable, with Germany the aggressor, so he set out to make sure that the Soviet Union came out on top.

M. McAuley, *The Soviet Union since 1917*, 1981

SOURCE M

In November 1958 Khrushchev, the Soviet leader, explained his view of how the Second World War could have been avoided.

Given a more far-sighted policy on the part of the Western Powers, co-operation between the Soviet Union, the United States and France could have been established much earlier, in the first years after Hitler seized power in Germany. Then there would have been no occupation of France, no Dunkirk and no Pearl Harbor. It would have been possible to save millions of human lives.

SOURCE N

In his memoirs Churchill, the former British Prime Minister, said that the Western powers had missed a big opportunity in 1939.

There can be no doubt that Britain and France should have accepted the Russian offer. The alliance of Britain, France and Russia would have struck deep alarm into the heart of Germany in 1939 and war might have been averted. If Mr Chamberlain on receipt of the Russian offer had replied: 'Yes. Let us three band together and break Hitler's neck', history might have taken a different course.

W. Churchill, 1948

SOURCE O

The official Soviet view of the pact was expressed in 1985 by a communist historian called Vasili Ryabov.

The Soviet government knew that it would be a short-lived agreement. Yet it was the right step to take in the situation. History proved the Soviet Union right. Almost two years of peace followed and this showed that the right step had been taken. From 1939 to June 1941 the total strength of the Soviet armed forces rose 2.8 times to well over five million. The strengthening of Soviet air defences also received considerable attention.

SOURCE P

A cartoon of the time from a Turkish newspaper ridiculing the unlikely alliance of Hitler and Stalin.

>> Activity

Explain in your own words why you think Stalin agreed to do a deal with Hitler. In your answer you could mention:

> Stalin's beliefs as a communist;

> the failure of appeasement;

> the weakness of the British and French offer in 1939;

> the strength of the German offer in 1939.

Hitler's war

German forces entered Polish territory on 1 September.
Two days later, on 3 September 1939, the British and the
French governments declared war on Germany.
The Second World War had begun.

Why did the Second World War break out?

SOURCE A

In March 1939 Germany invaded what
was left of Czechoslovakia. Britain and
France took no action. Hitler then turned
to Poland. Having taken Czechoslovakia
without any resistance, he thought that
Britain and France would not try to stop
him over Poland. Hitler said that the city
of Danzig must be returned to Germany
and Germany must have access to
Danzig through Polish territory. The
Treaty of Versailles had taken Danzig
from Germany and put it under League
of Nations control.
The fall of Czechoslovakia, however, had
convinced the British and the French that
appeasement had failed. Chamberlain's

*An angry and bewildered crowd of people look on as German
forces take control of the remnants of Czechoslovakia, March 1939.*

reaction when he heard the news from Czechoslovakia was to say,
'After this I cannot trust the Nazi leaders again.' On 31 March the
British government stated that Britain would stand by Poland in
case of war. British politicians had concluded that Hitler had to be
stopped otherwise he would eventually challenge the existence of
the British Empire. Similarly, the French Prime Minister, Daladier
decided that only war would stop Hitler from dominating Europe
and controlling France. Hitler thought that Chamberlain and
Daladier were bluffing.
On 23 August 1939 the Nazi–Soviet Non-Aggression Pact was
signed. This was part of Hitler's plan for the conquest of Poland.
He thought that without Soviet support Britain and France would
not feel strong enough to risk a war with Germany. The pact led

Hitler to make an enormous mistake. He did not realise that by
this stage Britain and France were prepared for war.

The governments of Britain and France were not as frightened by
the German–Soviet Pact as Hitler had hoped. They did not think
much of the Soviet army so they were not too worried by Soviet
neutrality. Italy and Japan were annoyed by the news of the pact
and they refused to help Hitler. The loss of Italy and Japan was
good news for leaders in Britain and France. The British
government was also heartened to know that the dominions of
Canada, Australia and New Zealand supported a new tough line
and had abandoned appeasement. To Hitler's surprise, Britain
and France responded to his attack on Poland by declaring war.

Hitler's mistake

>> Activity

A number of factors encouraged Hitler to believe that an attack on Poland would not lead to war with Britain and France:

> His experience of appeasement led him to think that British and French politicians were not prepared to fight.

> His key advisers told him that the British and the French would not go to war.

> He overestimated the impact of the Nazi–Soviet Pact on Britain and France.

> Hitler did not understand the motives of the Western leaders.

Look at the sources opposite. Can you see any links between them and the factors which led Hitler to misjudge the attitude of Britain and France?

SOURCE B

A London newspaper vendor with the headline that war is declared, 3 September 1939.

SOURCE C

This was the view of Ribbentrop, the German Foreign Minister, in May 1939.

It is certain that within a few months not one Frenchman nor a single Englishman will go to war for Poland.

SOURCE D

Hitler in August 1939:

Our enemies have men who are below average. No personalities. No masters. No men of action. Our enemies are little worms. I saw them at Munich. They will be too cowardly to attack. They won't go beyond a blockade. My only worry is that Chamberlain or some other such pig of a fellow will come at the last moment with proposals.

SOURCE E

Albert Speer was Hitler's Minister of Armaments. He later recalled Hitler's reaction when he heard the news that the German–Soviet Pact had been signed:

He stared into space for a moment, flushed deeply then banged on the table so that the glasses rattled and exclaimed in a voice breaking with excitement. 'I have them! I have them!'

SOURCE F

Hitler's reaction to the news that Britain intended to declare war:

When I finished [reading out the British ultimatum] there was complete silence. Hitler sat immobile, gazing before him. After an interval, which seemed like an age he turned to Ribbentrop. 'What now?' asked Hitler with a savage look, as though implying that his foreign minister had misled him about England's probable reaction.

P. Schmidt, *Hitler's Interpreter*, 1951

SOURCE G

In October 1939, after the war had started, Hitler was puzzled by the British attitude.

Why do they fight, they have nothing to gain? They have no definite objectives. We want nothing from Great Britain or France. I have not a single aspiration in the West. I want England to retain her Empire and her command of the seas unimpaired.

Complex causes?

During and immediately after the Second World War the cause of the conflict seemed very simple: the war was caused by the aggression of Hitler. More recently, historians have argued about the part played by Hitler. Some of them have put more emphasis on other causes. Several of these causes have been explored in earlier sections of this book.

ONE WAR: MANY CAUSES

The Treaty of Versailles, 1919

Most Germans disliked the terms of the Treaty of Versailles. They were unhappy at the way land was taken from Germany.

The failure of the League of Nations

After the First World War people hoped that the League of Nations would sort out arguments between states. The League and its policy of collective security did not work well. It was unable to stop aggression in Manchuria and Abyssinia.

The Depression of the early 1930s

The political results of the Depression made the world a more dangerous place – there was an increase in:

> isolationism in the USA;

> support for the Nazi Party in Germany;

> disarmament and a sense of weakness in France and Britain.

The Policy of Appeasement

Britain and France were reluctant to take a firm line against Germany 1936–1938.

Stalin's decision in August 1939

The Soviet leader rejected an alliance with Britain and France. Instead he signed an agreement with Nazi Germany.

An argument among historians

Debate about the start of the war has centred on a number of questions:

> How far was Hitler to blame for the war?

> Did Hitler have a plan to get Germany involved in a world war?

> Were Hitler's policies before 1939 any different from those of earlier German leaders, such as Wilhelm II and Stresemann?

SOURCE H

Great controversy was caused in 1961 when A. J. P. Taylor wrote a book called The Origins of the Second World War. *He argued that:*

The British government, not Hitler, took the lead in dismembering Czechoslovakia. The British government in 1939 gave Hitler to believe that they were more concerned to impose concessions on the Poles than to resist Hitler.

Taylor asserted that:

> Hitler did not stick to a grand plan. He made his policies up as he went along.

> He hoped to make gains through threatening war but wanted to avoid war.

> Hitler's views were similar to those of many other Germans.

> Other factors, besides the personality of Hitler, played a crucial role in the outbreak of war. These factors include the appeasement policy of Britain and France.

>> Activity

Look at the table 'One war: many causes'. Can you explain any links between the causes and the outbreak of war between Britain and France on one side and Germany on the other side?

SOURCE I

Followers of Hitler marching at a Nazi rally at Nuremberg.

> *How far was there a long-term plan behind Nazi acts of aggression?*

SOURCE J

Alan Bullock is a leading modern British biographer of Hitler. He wrote an important book about Hitler in 1991. Bullock disagrees with Taylor, arguing that:

> there was a consistency in Hitler's thinking from 1924 when he wrote *Mein Kampf* until his death in 1945 – he wanted to set up a German empire in Eastern Europe;

> Hitler knew that sooner or later a great war would be necessary to achieve a German empire in Eastern Europe.

> no other German leader would have dared to carry out foreign policy in the way that Hitler did;

> a major responsibility for causing the Second World War lies with Hitler.

>> Activity

Look at these quotations. Which do you think come from Bullock and which from Taylor?

a I find it difficult to imagine under any other German leader the extraordinary successes of the Nazis between 1930 and 1933 and the foreign policy and military successes of 1936–1941.

b In one sphere Hitler changed nothing. His foreign policy was the same as that of his predecessors and indeed of virtually all Germans. Like them Hitler, too, wanted to free Germany from the restrictions of the peace treaty; to restore a great German army; and then to make Germany the greatest power in Europe.

c Hitler never doubted that the racist empire in the east would have to be won by force.

d The vital question concerns Great Britain and France. They were the victors of the First World War. They had the decision in their hands. It was perfectly obvious that Germany would seek to become a great power again. Why did the victors not resist her?

The 1930s: the road to war

THE IMPACT OF THE DEPRESSION

After Locarno in 1925 it seemed that the world was entering a new period of peace. The years of optimism ended with the Wall Street Crash in October 1929. Many American investors were ruined when millions of dollars were wiped off the value of shares. This led to a great economic crisis that swept the whole world. Most governments made matters worse by 'protectionism': putting up taxes on imports.

The Depression had serious political consequences that made war more likely:

> The USA became more isolationist. Roosevelt was elected as US President in 1932. He was more concerned with rebuilding the American economy than foreign affairs.

> The Depression encouraged extreme politics in Germany. The fanatical nationalist, Hitler, became Chancellor in 1933.

> In Italy and Japan, leaders were keen to win new territory to offset the effect of the economic crisis.

> Both Britain and France went through political turmoil and felt less able to take a firm line against aggressive nationalism.

A CATALOGUE OF AGGRESSION

Japan, Italy and Germany went on the offensive in the 1930s. In each country the leaders believed in aggressive nationalism. They challenged the peace by seizing land from other countries. At first, other powerful countries did virtually nothing to stop them.

1931: Japan seized the Chinese province of Manchuria. Japan was criticised by the League of Nations but no action was taken to stop Japanese aggression.

1932–3: A major disarmament conference ended in failure. The new leader of Germany, Adolf Hitler, took Germany out of the conference. Germany also left the League of Nations.

1935–6: Italy conquered the African state of Abyssinia (modern Ethiopia). The League of Nations imposed a ban on trade with Italy but this did not include restrictions on the sale of petrol. The trade ban did not stop Italy from conquering Abyssinia.

1936: Hitler marched German troops into the Rhineland. The positioning of German forces in this border area was forbidden by the Treaty of Versailles. The government of France considered sending troops to stop the Germans but they decided to take no action.

1938: In March Germany annexed Austria. The unification of Germany and Austria was called the 'Anschluss'. In September Germany annexed the Sudetenland area of Czechoslovakia. Britain and France agreed to the takeover of the Sudetenland.

1939: Germany invaded the remaining part of Czechoslovakia in March. Hitler then threatened Poland and demanded control of the city of Danzig.

A crowd of unemployed men in the USA – the economic crisis soon spread to much of the rest of the world.

THE COLLAPSE OF THE LOCARNO SETTLEMENT

> In 1925 Britain, France, Italy and Germany accepted the borders in Western Europe established in the Treaty of Versailles. Agreement between these powerful countries ended in the 1930s.

> Germany left the League of Nations in 1933.

> In 1935 an anti-German grouping of Britain, France and Italy was established called the Stresa Front.

> In 1936, after Abyssinia, the Stresa Front fell apart.

> Italy, Germany and Japan signed the Anti-Comintern Pact in 1936; they pledged to fight against communism.

APPEASEMENT

In every international crisis between 1931 and 1938 Britain and France refused to use force to stop aggression. Often they tried to negotiate a deal and to give way to the aggressor states. This was called 'appeasement'. It was the policy of the British Prime Minister, Neville Chamberlain. The climax of appeasement came at the Munich Conference in September 1938. Here Britain and France agreed to the carving-up of Czechoslovakia: the Sudetenland area was handed over to Hitler.

Appeasement has been widely criticised as a weak response to aggression. Some critics say that appeasement encouraged more aggression. Recently historians have been more sympathetic and have tried to understand why Chamberlain believed in appeasement.

> Appeasement was based on the idea that Mussolini and Hitler were reasonable men who had just grievances.

> The richest country in the world was the USA. Its policy was 'isolationist' – Americans wanted nothing to do with foreign problems. Without American support it was hard for Britain and France to take action against aggression.

> British leaders were very worried about the defence of the British Empire. They avoided conflict in Europe in order to protect the Empire.

> Under Chamberlain, appeasement went hand in hand with rearmament. He wanted to make sure that Britain was properly armed before risking war in Europe.

THE END OF APPEASEMENT

Having been successful in the Rhineland, Austria and the Sudetenland, Hitler continued his aggressive foreign policy. In March 1939 he seized the remaining parts of Czechoslovakia.

In the early summer of 1939 Hitler prepared for a war against Poland. He created a crisis over the city of Danzig. He did not believe that Britain or France would help Poland.

The complete take-over of Czechoslovakia led to an abandonment of appeasement in Britain and France. They got ready for war with Germany. Hitler thought they were bluffing.

Both sides tried to win the support of Stalin, the Soviet leader. Hitler was successful. A German–Soviet Pact was signed in August 1939. Hitler felt that without Soviet support Britain and France would not risk war.

On 1 September 1939 Hitler invaded Poland. To his surprise Britain and France responded by declaring war on 3 September 1939. The Second World War had begun.

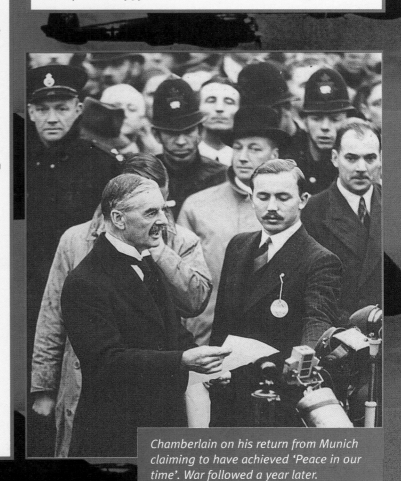

Chamberlain on his return from Munich claiming to have achieved 'Peace in our time'. War followed a year later.

87

The Second World War

Blitzkrieg in Poland

The Second World War began when Germany invaded Poland on 1 September 1939. Britain and France had pledged to defend Poland. On 3 September the French and the British governments declared war on Germany. The French and the British could do very little to stop a German victory in Poland. By the end of the month, Polish resistance had collapsed. On 17 September Soviet forces crossed the Polish frontier and took control of part of eastern Poland. This was part of the deal Hitler had struck with Stalin before the war in the Nazi–Soviet Pact. Stalin also moved his troops into the Baltic states of Latvia, Lithuania and Estonia.

In Poland and each of the following campaigns Hitler's methods became known as a 'Blitzkrieg' or lightning war. Blitzkrieg involved the use of overwhelming force, in as short a time as possible, in order to crush the enemy. Extensive use was made of tanks and other armoured vehicles. The Germans had much success with this technique.

The phoney war

Having succeeded in the east, Hitler's thoughts turned west. He began to make plans for an attack on France. Meanwhile the British and the French tried to weaken Germany by stopping German trade by sea. In particular they tried to cut off the supply of iron ore from Scandinavia. From October 1939 to April 1940 there was little fighting between Britain, France and Germany. This period became known as the 'phoney war'.

Fighting did take place in the winter of 1939–40 between the USSR and the small Baltic state of Finland. The Finnish army fought with great skill and ferocity and it took from October 1939 to March 1940 for the USSR to defeat her small neighbour. Eventually Finland was defeated and forced to give territory and a naval base to the USSR. The Soviet struggle to defeat Finland convinced Hitler that the

Hitler visiting Paris in 1940 after the defeat of France.

Red Army could easily be beaten by Germany. His secret long-term plan was to turn against the Soviet Union and set up a new German empire in the east.

In April 1940 the French and the British started mining Norwegian waters to stop the trade in iron ore. Germany responded by invading Norway and Denmark. The fall of Finland, Norway and Denmark led to a political crisis in Britain and France. Both prime ministers were forced to resign. In Britain Winston Churchill came to power in May 1940.

The fall of France

After months of waiting Hitler struck west in May 1940. The Netherlands, Belgium and France were invaded and rapidly defeated by German forces. A British army was forced to flee from the continent back to Britain from the port of Dunkirk. Germany took direct control of much of France, leaving part of the south and and south-east of the country under a puppet French government, with its capital in the town of Vichy. At this point it seemed that Hitler had virtually won the war. France was beaten and much of Europe was occupied. Only Britain remained to fight Germany. Sensing that the war was nearly over Mussolini joined forces with Germany in June 1940. He wanted Italy to get some of the rewards of victory.

Having defeated France, Hitler prepared for a German invasion of Britain. The German airforce, the Luftwaffe, set out to win control of the air over Britain. This was the first stage of the invasion plan. German planes bombed military sites, factories and the capital city, London, in August and September 1940. The British airforce, the RAF, fought back and the clash of the two airforces became known as the Battle of Britain. Although there were heavy losses on both sides, the RAF got the upper hand in the Battle of Britain and as a result Hitler was forced to put off his plans for an invasion of Britain.

The Italian attempt to share in Hitler's victory went disastrously wrong. An Italian army was defeated by Britain in North Africa, and Greece successfully stopped an Italian attempt to invade. Hitler was obliged to send German forces to north Africa and to Greece in order to help his ally.

German forces in the Soviet Ukraine, July 1941. Hitler's decision to attack the Soviet Union was one of the key turning-points in the war.

Hitler turns east

One of the great turning points of the war took place on 22 June 1941 when Germany invaded the Soviet Union in an operation known to the German leaders as Barbarossa. At first the blitzkrieg approach was successful for Germany. An army of over 3 million men stormed into the USSR, armed with over 3,000 tanks and 5,000 aircraft. Stalin was taken completely by surprise. German forces penetrated deep inside the Soviet Union capturing key cities such as Smolensk and Kiev. By mid-October over 3 million Soviet troops had been captured and the Germans were moving in on Moscow. At this point the campaign began to go wrong for Hitler. The German army reached the suburbs of the Soviet capital but met with fierce resistance and failed to capture the city. German troops were not equipped for the freezing Russian winter because Hitler thought that the war would be over in three months.

America joins the war: the attack on Pearl Harbor

While the battle for Moscow raged, the most powerful country in the world, the USA, became involved in the war. On 7 December 1941 the Japanese went to war against the USA with a surprise attack on the US naval base of Pearl Harbor. The result of this was that the USA joined forces with Britain and the USSR to fight Germany, Japan and Italy. In the end this was to swing the balance of the war decisively against Germany. At first Japan was all-conquering and in the early months of 1942 Japanese forces seized control of much of Eastern Asia and the islands of the Pacific.

The Japanese attack on the American fleet at Pearl Harbor. This led to American involvement in the war.

The tide turns

In the summer of 1942 the Germans renewed their attack on the USSR. They concentrated their forces in the south and tried to capture the southern city of Stalingrad. A fierce battle for the control of the city was fought in the autumn of 1942. The Soviet forces launched a counter-attack in November and the German army was eventually surrounded. At the end of January 1943 the German army at Stalingrad surrendered. The battle for Stalingrad was a crucial event. It proved that the Red Army could beat the German army. After Stalingrad Germany was on the defensive and the war began to go against Hitler.

There were further decisive battles in 1942. In June the USA stopped the tide of Japanese conquest at the Battle of Midway Island. After Midway, American forces began a slow process of capturing the islands of the Pacific from the Japanese. In October 1942 the German army in north Africa was defeated by British forces at the Battle of El Alamein. By May 1943 the Germans and Italians had been completely driven out of north Africa.

The Holocaust

Both the Germans and the Japanese treated many of their prisoners with extreme brutality. The most horrific atrocity of the war was the way millions of Jewish civilians were systematically murdered in Europe. This act is now known as the Holocaust. As German forces captured territory in Eastern Europe special army units massacred local Jews and other groups disliked by the Nazi Germans. In July 1941 the German leadership decided on a 'Final Solution' to the question of how Jewish people should be treated by the Nazi authorities. Death camps were set up to exterminate the Jewish population. Many were gassed to death; others were used as slave labour until they died. There can be no doubt that Hitler personally approved the decision.

The end game

After the decisive battles of 1942 the war went against Hitler and his allies. However, progress was slow:

> British and American forces landed in Italy in 1943. The Germans put up stiff resistance to the liberation of Italy. Rome was taken in June 1944 but it was not until 1945 that the whole of Italy was under British and American control.

> In January 1944 the Germans abandoned the siege of Leningrad, which had been going on for over two years. By the summer of 1944 the Germans were in retreat across the Soviet Union.

> France was invaded on 6 June 1944. This was known as 'D Day'. By 25 August the British and American forces had reached Paris. The Germans launched a counter-attack in December 1944 in the Ardennes area of Belgium. After some early success the German attack was turned back.

> The USA liberated territories in the Pacific taken by Japan. The Japanese forces put up ferocious resistance at every stage. In October 1944 the Americans invaded the Philippines. Over 170,000 Japanese soldiers were killed before the capital, Manila, was taken.

German power in Europe finally collapsed in April 1945. Soviet forces captured Berlin and Hitler committed suicide. The German forces finally surrendered on 8 May 1945 but the war continued against Japan. The American government was very worried at the level of Japanese resistance. The Americans expected a huge loss of life if they invaded and tried to conquer the islands of Japan. American scientists had been working for some years on the development of a new kind of weapon – the immensely powerful atomic bomb. In August 1945 two atomic bombs were dropped on the Japanese cities of Hiroshima and Nagasaki. The devastation caused by these bombs forced the Japanese government to surrender on 14 August 1945. The Second World War was over.

Discussion points

> In what ways was Germany successful between 1939 and 1941?

> Why was the attack on Pearl Harbor important?

> What happened in the Holocaust?

> How did the Second World War end?

The Holocaust. The greatest atrocity of the war was the systematic murder of millions of Jewish people.

The fall of the European empires

In the early twentieth century much of Africa, Asia and the Caribbean was controlled by European countries. These European empires all collapsed in the years after 1945.

THE CAUSES OF THE COLLAPSE OF EMPIRE

> The colonies suffered badly during the Depression of the 1930s. The imperialist European countries had encouraged their colonies to produce raw materials for European factories. The price of raw materials fell catastrophically during the Depression. The result was poverty and great unrest in the colonies.

> During the war much of the Asian territory held by the Europeans was conquered by the Japanese forces. Eventually the Japanese were defeated but the war had

fatally weakened the control of the Europeans. It was now clear to the local people that the Europeans could be beaten.

> After the war Britain, France and other European states faced many economic problems. They could no longer afford the cost of keeping their empires.

> After the war there was a rising tide of nationalism in the colonies. At the same time there was a decline in imperialist feeling in the European countries.

THE MAJOR EUROPEAN EMPIRES IN AFRICA AND ASIA

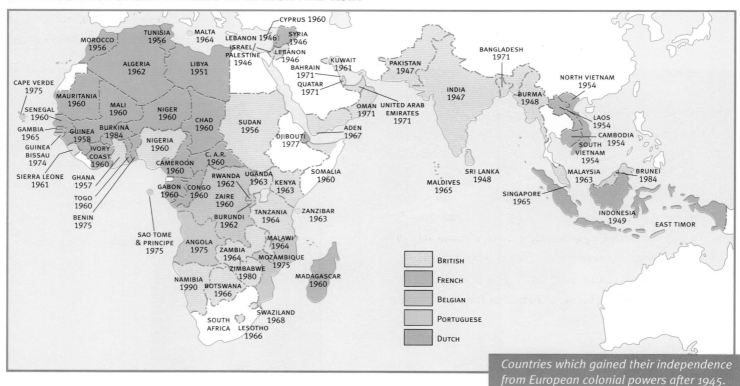

Countries which gained their independence from European colonial powers after 1945.

Handing over power

In the late 1940s there was a wave of de-colonisation in Asia and the Middle East. French forces left Syria and the Lebanon in 1946. The Philippines was given independence from the USA in 1946. At first the Dutch tried to fight nationalists in the Dutch East Indies but by 1948 the Dutch admitted defeat and granted independence to a new state known as Indonesia. Britain gave up control of the Indian sub-continent in 1947: two new states were created called India and Pakistan. A year later the British colonies of Burma and Ceylon (Sri Lanka) became free.

Independence came a little later for African and Caribbean countries. Most French and British colonies were given independence in the early 1960s. The sudden decision of the Belgian government to pull out of the Congo (modern Zaire) in 1960 led to a civil war. The end of European colonialism was complicated in those countries where a large number of European people had settled permanently. A bitter war was fought in Algeria from 1954 to 1962 between French forces and Algerian nationalists. The white minority in Rhodesia (modern Zimbabwe) refused to share power with the black majority until 1980. In South Africa there was a large minority of white people, largely descended from Dutch and British settlers. Britain had given independence to South Africa in 1910 but this white minority held on to power. It was not until 1994 that the black majority of South Africans were allowed to vote, and the black nationalist, Nelson Mandela, came to power.

The French tried to keep their old colonies in Indo-China, which included the modern countries of Vietnam, Laos and Cambodia. Local communists fought a war against the French. The Vietnamese communists defeated French forces in 1954 and won control of northern Vietnam. At this point the USA intervened and propped up a pro-western government in South Vietnam until 1975. The government of Portugal was extremely reluctant to grant independence to its African colonies of Angola and Mozambique. There was fierce fighting between nationalists and the Portuguese before independence was granted in 1975.

AFTER EMPIRE

> The history of the newly independent states was often troubled. The European states had imposed artificial boundaries, which sometimes led to ethnic unrest. The economies of most former colonies were undeveloped and relied too heavily on the sale of raw materials to the former colonial powers.

> The passing of their empires caused a sense of crisis in many European countries. There was a marked decline in power and status for those countries like Britain and France that had lost large world empires. Arguments over empire led to political turmoil and the fall of governments in France in 1958 and Portugal in 1975. Eventually most of the former colonial powers found a new identity as part of the European Community.

> The end of empire led to a large number of newly independent countries. Some of the leaders in these countries were unhappy that world politics was dominated by the conflict between the USA and the Soviet Union. A new 'non-aligned' movement began in 1955, when representatives from 29 countries met in Indonesia for the Bandung Conference setting up a loose organisation of states that were not allied to the superpowers.

Discussion points

> Why did the age of European empire come to an end?

> How did the transfer of power sometimes lead to violence?

> What have been the consequences of the end of empire?

The roots of the Cold War

Almost as soon as the Second World War ended, the winners started to argue with each other. In particular, a bitter conflict developed between the USA and the USSR. This struggle continued until the late 1980s. Walter Lippmann, an American journalist writing in the 1940s, called it a 'cold war' and the phrase has been widely used since.

Historians have produced three conflicting explanations for the start of the Cold War:

1 The USSR was to blame. Stalin planned for a communist take-over of the world. The take-over of Eastern Europe was the first step towards world control.

2 The USA was to blame. Soviet actions were defensive. The USA wanted to control its area of influence but refused to allow the USSR to do the same.

3 Neither side was to blame. The Cold War was based on misunderstanding and forces beyond the control of both sides.

Focus

As you find out more about the Cold War, try to work out which of these three explanations you find most convincing.

The long-term causes of the Cold War

The roots of the Cold War are to be found in earlier history. One historian said that the Cold War started, not in the 1940s, but in 1917, when the Russian Revolution took place and Soviet communism was born. By 1917 the USA was the richest country in the world. The two countries were both enormous and both had great natural resources. However, there was no chance of real friendship between them because the leaders of the new Soviet Union had extremely different beliefs from those of American politicians.

AMERICAN CAPITALISM

1 People should be free to make as much money as they can.

2 Factories and other property should be owned by individuals and companies.

3 The government should interfere as little as possible in the lives of ordinary people.

4 At elections people should be allowed to choose anyone they want for the government.

5 The Press should be able to criticise the government.

6 The government should not interfere in religion.

SOVIET COMMUNISM

1 Rich people are wicked and selfish. They should be forced to share their wealth.

2 Factories and other property should be owned by the state on behalf of all the people.

3 A communist government should get involved in every aspect of life.

4 At elections people should only be allowed to choose communists for the government.

5 The Press should never criticise a communist government.

6 Religious belief is nonsense and should be wiped out by the government.

Not only did American and Soviet leaders disagree totally. Each side was completely convinced that it was right and that other countries around the world should follow their lead. Americans believed that the answer to world problems was for other people to learn to live in an American way. The Soviet leaders were sure that their communist ideas would eventually spread to every country in the world. As a result the USA and the Soviet Union were very hostile towards each other after 1917. In 1919 the USA joined Britain, France and other countries in an attempt to destroy Soviet communism by force. They invaded the Soviet Union in support of the White Russians who were engaged in a civil war with the Bolshevik revolutionaries. This use of force failed but the hostility remained.

A female Soviet soldier meets American troops near the River Elbe, 1945. The smiles soon disappeared as the wartime allies became Cold War enemies.

The common enemy

The hostility between the the USA and the Soviet Union was suspended in 1941. They were linked by their common wish to destroy Hitler. As soon as it looked as though Hitler was going to be defeated the old tension began to re-emerge. Hitler predicted that once the war was over the two wartime allies would no longer have anything in common and would become hostile towards each other once again. The end of the war produced a difficult situation. Nazi power over Europe had been destroyed but what should replace it? In many countries there was no proper government. Decisions had to be made about the future of these countries. Inevitably, American and Soviet leaders had very different views on the best type of government for the countries of the new Europe. Shortly before his death, Hitler predicted the start of the Cold War.

'After the collapse of the German Reich, and until there is a rise in nationalism in Asia, Africa or Latin America, there will only be two powers in the world: The United States and Soviet Russia. Through the laws of history and geographical position these giants are destined to struggle with each other either through war, or through rivalry in economics and political ideas.'
Hitler's Political Testament, April 1945

Discussion points

> Explain in your own words the difference between American and Soviet ideas.

> Why did the destruction of Germany make a conflict likely between the USA and the USSR?

1945: the breakdown of the wartime alliance

The victory over Hitler created new worries for the winners. They had different views as to the future of Europe after the war. Before the end of 1945 deep divisions were emerging between the leaders of the USA and the Soviet Union.

Why did the wartime alliance fall apart in 1945?

Yalta and the argument over Poland

In February 1945 the leaders of Britain, the USA and the Soviet Union met at a place called Yalta. The three leaders were Churchill, Roosevelt and Stalin. The end of the war was in sight and they met to decide on the shape of the post-war world. Much of their time was spent discussing the future of Poland. They disagreed about how Poland should be governed.

YALTA: THE ATTITUDES OF THE LEADERS

> Roosevelt was already very ill – two months later he would be dead. Roosevelt was keen that democracy should be introduced into Eastern Europe. However, he trusted Stalin and wanted to make sure that the USA and the USSR remained on good terms after the war.

> Churchill was very concerned about the future of Poland and Eastern Europe. He did not trust Stalin. He wanted to stop Stalin from imposing communism on the territory taken by the Red Army. Britain had gone to war in 1939 to help Poland and Churchill did not want to abandon Poland to Soviet control.

> Stalin was obsessed with the security of the USSR. He wanted the Soviet Union to retain the Polish territory he had taken in 1939 as part of the Nazi–Soviet Pact. He also wanted to make sure that the new government of Poland would be friendly towards the Soviet Union.

Why was Poland the centre of attention at Yalta?

Poland was the largest country in Eastern Europe. Its post-war settlement was likely to set a pattern for the rest of Eastern Europe but the wartime allies had disagreed strongly about that settlement before Yalta.

Two different groups wanted to form the new government for Poland. Each group had a very different relationship with Stalin:

The London Poles

When the war broke out, some members of the Polish government fled to London and set up a 'government-in-exile'. They were strongly anti-Soviet. Much of Poland had been in the Russian Empire before 1917. The London Poles were Catholics and many were landowners: they hated both the idea of communism and Stalin because he had carved up their country through the German–Soviet Pact in 1939. In 1943 they were horrified to learn that the Soviet army had executed about 15,000 Polish officers and buried their bodies at a place called Katyn. Stalin knew that if the London Poles formed a Polish government, it would be hostile to the USSR.

The Lublin Poles

In July 1944 the USSR set up its own future government for Poland. This first met at the town of Lublin, and they became known as the Lublin Poles. They were mostly communists and Stalin felt that they could be trusted.

The Warsaw Uprising

The London Poles decided that their only chance of frustrating Stalin was to seize control of part of Poland before the Red Army did. In August 1944 Polish resistance fighters, loyal to the London Poles, attacked the German forces occupying Warsaw, the capital of Poland. The Soviet army was nearby but did nothing to help the Poles. Stalin did not want them to defeat the Germans. He wanted the Lublin Poles to take over after the war. The British and the Americans were appalled by the Soviet attitude. Without Soviet help, the Rising was ruthlessly smashed by the Germans and nearly 300,000 Poles were killed. The Germans sent the surviving people of Warsaw to concentration camps and when the Red Army finally took the city it was completely deserted. The Red Army went on to take control of the whole of Poland. By January 1945 the USSR announced that Poland had been liberated and the Lublin group was now in charge of Poland.

>> **Activity**

1 Explain in your own words the different attitudes of the leaders who met at Yalta towards Poland.

2 Who were the Lublin Poles and the London Poles?

3 What was the Warsaw Uprising?

4 Why do you think that Stalin refused to help the Warsaw rebels?

SOURCE A

German troops patrol the devastated streets of Warsaw after the abortive uprising.
> Why did Stalin fail to help the Warsaw Rising?

The meeting at Yalta

The three leaders had met before — at the Tehran summit in late 1943. The meeting at Yalta, in the Soviet Union, took place between 4 and 11 February 1945. Stalin had refused to leave the USSR so the two Western leaders had to go to him. The three men were pleased at the way the war was going. President Roosevelt talked about the friendly, 'family' atmosphere of the meeting but beneath the surface, serious disagreements existed.

The discussions at Yalta were very wide-ranging but the future of Poland dominated. The three leaders had previously agreed that the Soviet Union would take land from Poland and Poland would, in turn, be given German land. At Yalta they argued about the details and Churchill tried to limit the changes. He was worried about taking too much land from Germany and said: 'I do not want to stuff the Polish goose until it dies of German indigestion'. There was even greater disagreement about who should govern Poland.

Eventually, Truman and Churchill thought that they had won a major concession from Stalin: the Soviet leader agreed that the Lublin government should be expanded to include some of the London Poles and he accepted that free elections should be held as soon as possible in Poland. When asked how soon these elections could be held, Stalin replied: 'It should be possible within a month.'

>> Activity

Look at the Sources B and D. Summarise in your own words the details of the Yalta Agreement on Poland and Eastern Europe.

SOURCE B

The Yalta Agreement made the following statement about the future of Eastern Europe. This became known as the Declaration on Liberated Europe:

The three governments [USA, USSR, Britain] will assist the people in any European liberated state to form interim governments broadly representative of all democratic elements in the population and pledged to the earliest possible establishment through free elections of governments responsive to the will of the people.

SOURCE C

Churchill, Roosevelt and Stalin at Yalta, February 1945. Their discussions centred on the future of Poland.

SOURCE D

The Yalta Agreement included specific plans for the future of Poland.

A new situation has been created in Poland as a result of her complete liberation by the Red Army. This calls for the establishment of a Polish government which can be more broadly based than was possible before the recent liberation of the Western part of Poland. The Provisional Government should therefore be re-organised on a more democratic basis with the inclusion of democratic leaders from Poland itself and from Poles abroad. This Polish government shall be pledged to the holding of free elections as soon as possible. In these elections all democratic and anti-Nazi parties shall have the right to take part and to put forward candidates.

THE TERMS OF THE YALTA AGREEMENT

The final Agreement included a Declaration on Liberated Europe. This stated that each liberated country would be given an emergency government with representatives from any important non-fascist groups and that free elections would be held as soon as possible to set up a democratic government.

The borders of Poland were to be altered so that the USSR gained a huge amount of territory from eastern Poland. In return Poland was promised land taken from the eastern part of Germany.

The Lublin government in Poland was to be expanded so that it also included some of the London Poles. Free elections would be held in Poland as soon as possible.

The British and the Americans held many prisoners of war from Soviet territory. These were men from German-occupied lands who had chosen or been forced to join the German army. At Yalta it was agreed that they would be sent back to the USSR. About 10,000 of these men were executed on their return and many more were imprisoned.

The leaders agreed that Germany should be divided into occupied zones. Churchill argued that there should be a French zone, as well as a British, American and Soviet zone. This was because Churchill was keen to restore the power of France. Stalin and Roosevelt accepted this suggestion.

The USSR agreed to help in the war against Japan. In return the USSR gained control of island territories north of Japan. This turned out to be a very good deal for the USSR because Soviet troops did not have to do very much fighting before the Japanese surrender.

The leaders agreed to the setting up of the United Nations. Stalin successfully argued that each country should have a veto on the decisions of the powerful Security Council.

SOURCE E

One of the achievements of the Yalta conference was the decision to establish the United Nations.

>> Activity

The Yalta Conference covered many important topics and the table on this page gives a summary of the areas of agreement. Using the table and your knowledge of the background make a list of what Stalin gained from the Yalta Conference.

The weakness of the Yalta Agreement

Yalta was the high-point of the wartime alliance. To Roosevelt and many Americans it seemed like the beginning of a post-war period of co-operation. There was enthusiastic cheering in the American Senate when the Agreement was read out. In fact, the Yalta Agreement was flawed in a number of important ways:

YALTA: THE PROBLEMS

> The Soviets and the Americans interpreted it differently. The Agreement talked about the need for 'democracy' and 'free elections'. For Roosevelt democracy was the American system of free speech. Stalin's idea of democracy was a communist one, in which the communist party represented the people and no opposition was allowed.

> Yalta raised false expectations in the USA. People expected that Stalin would now allow western-style governments to be set up in Eastern Europe. They were bitterly disappointed when this did not happen.

> The Agreement tried to achieve compromise over the future of Poland. In fact, compromise was not possible. Either Poland was democratic or it was friendly towards the USSR. Leading figures in Polish society were anti-Russian. Stalin knew that he could only make sure that Poland was friendly by destroying free speech.

Yalta in practice

Roosevelt was proud of the Yalta Agreement. He was disappointed to see how Stalin put it into practice. Stalin paid only lip service to the idea of bringing non-communists into the government of Poland. At Yalta it was agreed that the Soviet Foreign Minister, Molotov, would negotiate the details of the new Polish government with the British and American ambassadors to Moscow. These talks were not successful. Molotov refused to let the London Poles play a significant part in the government. Harriman, the American ambassador, later said: 'We began to realise that Stalin's language was somewhat different from ours.' By the beginning of April Harriman was reporting to Truman that the talks had achieved nothing. At the same time Polish opponents of communism were dealt with ruthlessly. In March, 16 leaders of the Polish Resistance went, at the invitation of Stalin, to have talks with the Soviet authorities near Warsaw. They were promised their own personal safety. They were arrested and were never seen again.

SOURCE F

Roosevelt was now dying, but he managed to write a letter of criticism to Stalin:

I cannot conceal from you the concern with which I view the development of events since our fruitful meeting at Yalta. So far there has been a discouraging lack of progress made in the carrying out of the decisions we made at the Conference, particularly those relating to the Polish question. I am frankly puzzled as to why this should be and must tell you that I do not fully understand the attitude of your government.
F. D. Roosevelt, 1 April 1945

SOURCE G

Churchill was not pleased by the news from Poland. He wrote to Stalin on 29 April 1945.

The British went to war on account of Poland. They can never feel this war will have ended rightly unless Poland has a fair deal in the sense of independence and freedom, on the basis of friendship with Russia. It was on this that I thought we agreed at Yalta.

SOURCE H

Stalin refused to give any ground. In May, Stalin said the Americans were to blame for any bad feeling.

At Yalta it had been agreed that the existing government of Poland was to be reconstructed. Anyone with common sense could see that this means that the present [Lublin] government was to form the basis of the new government. No other understanding of the Yalta Agreement is possible. The Russians should not be treated as fools.

A new face at the White House

A key figure in the early stages of the Cold War was the American President, Harry Truman. It was only through chance that he became President. As Vice President he took over when Roosevelt died in April 1945. Truman was a Democrat politician from Missouri. He had made his reputation in domestic politics. He had only been Vice President for a few weeks and he had almost no experience of international politics. He was very different from Roosevelt and his personality played a part in the development of a tougher American policy. Roosevelt was much more diplomatic than Truman. Roosevelt was sure that the USA and the Soviet Union could remain friendly after the war. Just a few hours before he died Roosevelt sent a message to Churchill. The British leader had been trying to get Roosevelt to take a tough line on communist control in Poland. Roosevelt replied: 'I would minimize the general Soviet problem as much as possible.' To the last, Roosevelt remained convinced that the USA would stay on good terms with the Soviet Union. Truman was less certain about Soviet intentions.

SOURCE I

Harry Truman, the new American President, took a tougher line towards the Soviet Union than his predecessor, F. D. Roosevelt.

>> Activity

1 Explain in your own words why Roosevelt and Churchill were disappointed at the way Stalin put the Yalta Agreement into practice.

2 What evidence is there from Sources F–H, that the leaders had different interpretations of the Yalta Agreement?

Truman takes a tough line

Truman showed his different style as soon as he came to power. In April 1945 Truman spoke angrily to the Soviet Foreign Minister, Molotov. He insisted that the Soviets must carry out the Yalta Agreement and allow free elections in Poland. He would not listen to Molotov's explanations. As Molotov left he said: 'I have never been talked to like that before in my life.' To which Truman said: 'Carry out your agreements and you won't get talked to like that.'

SOURCE J

An American historian saw Truman's angry meeting with Molotov as a major step towards the start of the Cold War.

After only eleven days in power Harry Truman made his decision to lay down the law to an ally which had contributed more in blood and agony than we had – and about Poland, an area through which Russia had been invaded three times since 1914. The basis for the Cold War was laid on 23 April in the scourging which Truman administered to Molotov, giving notice that in areas of the most crucial concern to Russia our wishes must be obeyed.

D. F. Fleming, The Cold War and its Origins 1917–1960, 1961

SOURCE L

Truman described his new approach to the Soviet Union in May 1945.

We have to get tough with the Russians. They don't know how to behave. They are like bulls in a china shop. They are only twenty-five years old. We are over a hundred and the British are centuries older. We have got to teach the Russians how to behave.

The Potsdam Conference

The leaders of the USA, USSR and Britain met at Potsdam, near Berlin, between 17 July and 2 August 1945. This was the last of the great wartime summit meetings. The membership of the Conference showed that the wartime alliance was changing. At previous conferences the American leader had been Roosevelt; now it was Truman. Churchill was replaced halfway through by the Labour leader, Clement Attlee.

At Potsdam, Truman told Stalin that America had the atomic bomb. Churchill noticed the sense of power that Truman seemed to feel now that he had this powerful weapon. Later Churchill wrote: 'Truman was a changed man. He told the Russians where they got on and off and generally bossed this whole meeting.' The US government thought that it might take 20 years for the Soviet Union to develop an atom bomb. Truman believed that the bomb put the USA in a strong position in any arguments with the Soviet Union.

SOURCE K

The Allied leaders at Potsdam: Attlee, Truman and Stalin. The British and American leaders were new to their posts. Truman was determined to treat Stalin with firmness.

Focus

What was agreed at Potsdam? What were the areas of disagreement from the Potsdam discussions?

POTSDAM: AREAS OF AGREEMENT AND DISAGREEMENT

> German reparations were agreed. Each country was to take reparations from its own area of occupation. The Soviet Union was to receive some additional industrial equipment from the western zones of occupation: little of this was ever handed over.

> The details of the German–Polish borders on the rivers Oder and Neisse were finally agreed. The British and Americans disliked the position of the new border but could do little about it.

> It was agreed that the Nazi Party should be stamped out in all sectors of Germany.

> The Soviet Union wanted to play a part in the running of the rich German industrial area of the Ruhr. The USA rejected this idea.

> The Soviet Union wanted to share in the occupation of Japan. Truman firmly blocked this idea.

> The USA and Britain asked for a greater say in what went on in Eastern Europe. Stalin rejected this suggestion.

SOURCE M

Winston Churchill was the former British Prime Minister. He lost power in the 1945 general election. He made the famous 'iron curtain' speech in March 1946.

From Stettin in the Baltic, to Trieste in the Adriatic, an iron curtain has descended across the continent. Behind that line lie all the capitals of the ancient states of Central and Eastern Europe: Warsaw, Berlin, Prague, Vienna, Budapest, Bucharest and Sofia. All these famous cities lie in the Soviet sphere, and all are subject to a high and increasing control from Moscow. The Russian-dominated Polish government has been encouraged to make enormous and wrongful inroads upon Germany, and mass expulsions of millions of Germans are now taking place. The Communist Parties, which were very small in all of these Eastern states, are seeking everywhere to obtain totalitarian control.

The Iron Curtain

The new hostility towards the Soviet Union was encouraged by Winston Churchill in a famous speech on 5 March 1946. The speech was made at Fulton, Missouri. President Truman was in the audience and had seen the speech before it was given. Churchill called for an American–British alliance to meet the communist menace. At first some Americans felt that he was exaggerating. Gradually most Americans came to agree with him.

>> Activity

Look back at this unit. Explain in your own words how each of the following factors made the Cold War more likely:

a long-term hostility between the USA and the Soviet Union;

b arguments over the Yalta Agreements;

c the personality of Truman.

The Soviet take-over of Eastern Europe

After 1945 the Soviet Union took control of much of Eastern Europe. Historians are still debating the motives behind this take-over. Was this a defensive move or was this a step towards a take-over of the whole of Europe?

Why did Stalin take control of Eastern Europe?

Liberation?

The Soviet take-over was not complete until 1948 but it began before the end of the Second World War. As the Red Army drove the Germans westwards the Soviet leadership made sure that territory came under the control of people friendly to the Soviets. In most countries the Soviet government set up anti-fascist coalition governments, but gave local communists a leading position. These communist-dominated governments introduced nationalisation and took land away from the landlords. Opposition parties were gradually undermined. Elections were rigged. Eventually all opposition was destroyed and Soviet control was complete. The process was more rapid in some countries than in others.

THE SOVIET TAKE-OVER OF EASTERN EUROPE

Look at the following information about the stages of the Soviet take-over. How did the Soviet Union take control of Eastern Europe?

STAGE 1: THE TAKE-OVER OF POLAND

As we have seen, Stalin's first priority was control of Poland. At the end of June 1945 a few London Poles were included in the Polish government. However, it remained completely dominated by the communists of the Lublin group. The Western allies admitted defeat over Poland by 'recognising' the largely communist government on 5 July 1945. This meant that Britain and the USA accepted that the communists were in charge in Warsaw. Communist power was strengthened even further in January 1947 when rigged elections were held in Poland. The leader of the London Poles, Mikolaczyk, thought his life was in danger and fled the country.

STAGE 2: THE TAKE-OVER OF ROMANIA AND BULGARIA

After Poland, Stalin's immediate priorities were the control of Romania and Bulgaria. Look at the map; can you work out why these three countries were important to Stalin? As the Red Army swept into Bulgaria and Romania in late 1944 coalition governments dominated by communists were set up. In February 1945, within days of the Yalta agreement, a top Soviet politician, Andrei Vyshinsky, ordered the King of Romania to appoint a new prime minister chosen by Stalin. When the King said that this was not in line with the Yalta agreement, Vyshinsky slammed his fist on the table and shouted at the King. Stalin got his prime minister. By the middle of 1945 communists were in firm control in Romania. Elections took place in Bulgaria in November. These elections were rigged and the communist Fatherland Front won. In September 1946 the communist government in Bulgaria abolished the monarchy. The monarchy in Romania was abolished in 1947.

STAGE 3: THE TAKE-OVER OF HUNGARY AND CZECHOSLOVAKIA

In contrast with Poland, Romania and Bulgaria Stalin did not at first have a clear view of what he wanted for Hungary and Czechoslovakia. He allowed free elections to take place in Hungary in November 1945. The non-communist Smallholders' Party was the most successful party. Fresh elections were held in August 1947. This time the elections were rigged and an exclusively communist government took power. In November all non-communist parties were banned.

The final stage in the take-over came when communists seized power in Czechoslovakia in 1948. Before that the country was ruled by a coalition of communists and non-communists. This was the one country in Eastern Europe with a strong local communist party. There were fair elections in 1946 and the communists won 38 per cent of the vote. The President, Beneš, was a non-communist while Gottwald, the Prime Minister, was a communist. The Foreign Minister, Jan Masaryk, was also a non-communist. There was an economic crisis in the country from mid-1947. The harvest was bad and industry was in trouble. Elections were due for May 1948. The communists were afraid that they would do badly. The communists used armed force to seize power. Many non-communists were arrested and Masaryk was murdered. Rigged elections were held shortly afterwards and the communists won a huge majority. The Soviet take-over was complete.

The war as a triumph for Soviet communism

The Soviet leaders felt that their country had made by far the most important contribution to the winning of the war. The British and the Americans had helped, but Stalin believed, with some justification, that the Soviet Union had cut the heart out of the German army. 10 million Germans, who represented 80 per cent of German losses, died on the Eastern Front. The Soviet leaders believed their country had largely won the war, so they had a right to shape the future of Europe.

Stalin also saw the war as proof that communism worked: in the battle to the death between communist Russia and capitalist Germany, communism had triumphed. This gave a new sense of confidence and determination to the Soviet government.

Never again: the level of the Soviet wartime sacrifice

The Soviet Union suffered much more than the other allies during the war. This made a difference to attitudes after the war. About 15 million Soviet soldiers and civilians had been killed by the Germans. In addition, many people had died because of shortages of food and the other harsh conditions of wartime. As many as 25 million Soviet citizens may have died because of the war. Stalin was determined that this should never be allowed to happen again.

Soviet strategic thinking

How could the Soviet Union ensure that the devastation of the Second World War was not repeated? In 1914 and 1941 Germany had attacked Russia through Poland. In 1945 Stalin thought that sooner or later there could be yet another attack through Poland. To stop this he was determined to control Poland and other East European states. Before the Second World War these countries had been independent. Almost all of them had been governed by right-wing, anti-communist leaders. In Moscow it seemed quite likely that if the countries of Eastern Europe were again allowed to be independent, the states would again become anti-Soviet.

US imperialism?

The USA was by far the wealthiest country in the world in 1945. The Soviet government was convinced that American business leaders were planning to spread their power and increase their profits by buying up companies in other countries and selling American goods wherever they could. In this way the USA could build up a new kind of world empire. American troops would not need to conquer new lands: American capitalism would do it instead. As good communists it was the job of the Soviet leaders to try to stop American businesses from dominating the world. The setting up of a group of friendly communist countries was one way of doing this.

SOURCE A

The devastated landscape of Stalingrad at the end of the war. The Soviet Union suffered far greater damage than any other country.

Stalin's motives

Look at Sources B–F. What can we learn from them about the Stalin's motives at the end of the Second World War? Can you find evidence that:

a Stalin wanted a barrier to stop the Soviet Union from being invaded in the future;

b Stalin did not trust the Americans;

c Stalin believed in communism and thought that every country should be communist.

SOURCE E

A Soviet poster showing Stalin in 1945. The poster celebrates Stalin as the heroic victor of the war.

SOURCE B

Stalin speaking on 9 February 1945:

Victory means, first of all, that our Soviet social system has won. The Soviet social system has successfuly stood the test in the fire of war and it has proved its complete vitality. The Soviet social system has proved to be more capable and more stable than a non-Soviet social system. The Soviet social system is a better form of society than any non-Soviet social system.

SOURCE C

At Yalta, in February 1945, Stalin tried to explain to Churchill and Roosevelt why Poland was so important to the Soviet Union.

Mr Churchill has said that for Great Britain the Polish question is one of honour. But for the Russians it is a question both of honour and security. Throughout history Poland has been the corridor for attack on Russia. It is not merely a question of honour for Russia, but one of life and death.

SOURCE D

In May 1945 Stalin was worried at the end of the war in Europe and felt unhappy at the approach of the new US president, Harry Truman.

The Soviet government is alarmed by the attitude of the US government. The American attitude cooled once it became clear that Germany was defeated. It was as though the Americans were saying that the Russians were no longer needed.

SOURCE F

In March 1946, Stalin replied to Churchill's famous speech about the 'iron curtain':

It should not be forgotten that the Germans invaded the USSR through Finland, Poland, Rumania, Bulgaria and Hungary. The Germans were able to invade because governments hostile to the Soviet Union existed in these countries. As a result the Soviet Union had a loss of life several times greater than that of Britain and the United States put together. Some people may be able to forget the huge sacrifices of the Soviet people but the Soviet Union cannot forget them. And so what is surprising about the fact that the Soviet Union, anxious for its future safety, is trying to see that governments loyal to the Soviet Union should exist in these countries? How can anyone who has not taken total leave of his senses describe these peaceful wishes of the Soviet Union as expansionist tendencies on the part of the Soviet Union?

>> Activity

It has been argued that Stalin took over Eastern Europe as the first stage towards a communist take-over of the world. Does the information in this unit support this explanation? Explain your answer in detail.

The Truman Doctrine and the Marshall Plan

The government of the USA was deeply unhappy at the spread of communism to Eastern Europe. Traditionally American foreign policy was based on isolationism: having as little to do as possible with international politics. The Soviet take-over forced American politicians to think again and to reject traditional thinking.

How did the USA react to the Soviet take-over of Eastern Europe?

After 1945 the USA moved away from isolationism and became active throughout the world. Eventually the USA built up its own 'sphere of interest': a group of pro-American states that included all of the world's richest industrialised countries.

1946: Cold War attitudes develop

Relations between the USA and the Soviet Union deteriorated throughout 1946:

> The Americans were very critical of Soviet policy in Iran. Soviet troops were in the north of Persia, now Iran, at the end of the war. Under wartime agreements they were supposed to withdraw in March 1946. The US government suspected that this was the first step towards a Soviet take-over of part of Iran. They criticised the Soviet occupation at the United Nations. Stalin gave in and withdrew his troops.

> The Council of Foreign Ministers met in Paris in April 1946. The American representative, Byrnes, blocked every Soviet proposal and criticised Soviet policy in Eastern Europe.

> The Soviet navy wished to send ships through the Black Sea Straits and to set up naval bases in the area. Turkey felt threatened by these plans and in August 1946 the US government blocked the Soviet plans. The Americans made it clear that they would use force to resist any Soviet move. American warships were sent to the area to warn off the Soviets.

The crisis of 1947

American policy took shape in the crucial year of 1947. At the beginning of the year there was an economic crisis in Western Europe. The harvest in 1946 was poor and there was food shortage in many places. The winter was unusually fierce and people were cold as well as hungry. In Britain unemployment was soaring and food rationing was more severe than it had been during the war. In Germany people were close to starvation. Millions of refugees had fled to western Germany and this added to the shortage of fuel, food and jobs. In France and Italy discontent led to massive support for the local communist parties; unless conditions improved there was a real possibility that the communists could come to power. By early 1947 it was clear to the US government that their friends in Western Europe could not cope alone. Some Americans had hoped that the return of peace would allow the USA to go back to its isolationist policy. Truman and his advisers realised that this was not possible.

The Truman Doctrine

In February 1947 the British government sent a dramatic message to Washington — Britain could no longer afford to pay for troops in Greece and Turkey. Unless America replaced Britain in Greece and Turkey these countries could easily come under Soviet control. Truman decided to offer American financial help to Greece and Turkey. He went further and declared that American support was available for any people who wanted to fight communism. This became known as the Truman Doctrine. It was based on the idea of containment — the USA would use its wealth and power to stop or contain the spread of communism.

SOURCE A

Truman announced his 'doctrine' in a speech to the US Congress on 12 March 1947.

At the present moment in world history nearly every nation must choose between alternative ways of life. One way of life is based upon the will of the majority, and is distinguished by free institutions, representative government, free elections, guarantees of individual liberty, freedom of speech and religion and freedom from political oppression.

The second way of life is based upon the will of a minority forcibly imposed upon the majority. It relies upon terror and oppression, a controlled press and radio, fixed elections and the suppression of personal freedom.

I believe it must be the policy of the United States to support people who are resisting attempted subjugation by armed minorities or by outside pressures. I believe that we must help free peoples to work out their own destiny in their own way.

Through the Truman Doctrine, the USA had rejected 'isolationism'. America had announced to the world that it would play a leading part in world politics. In Greece and Turkey the doctrine was successful. The communist side was defeated in the Greek Civil War by 1949, and Turkey remained part of the Western pro-American group of countries. Initially, 'the doctrine' was applied in Europe and the Middle East. Eventually, it was extended to the whole world and led to war in Korea and Vietnam.

SOURCE B

A scene from the Greek Civil War: an anti-communist soldier guards communist suspects. Truman intervened to make sure that the communists lost the war. This was the beginning of the Truman Doctrine.

>> Activity

What was the Truman Doctrine? How was the Doctrine different to the traditional American policy of isolationism?

The Marshall Plan

Another strand of American policy emerged in 1947. In Washington there was a belief that communism could only be stopped if Western Europe became wealthy. By the spring of 1947 it was clear that without American help there was little chance of economic recovery.

SOURCE C

Will Clayton, a leading American politician, was sent to Europe in May 1947 to report on conditions.

Millions of people in the cities are slowly starving. Without further prompt and substantial aid from the US, economic and political dislocation will overwhelm Europe.

The USA decided to offer massive economic aid to Western Europe. The project was organised by the American Secretary of State, General George Marshall, and was known as the Marshall Plan. Marshall announced his scheme in a speech at Harvard University in June 1947.

A large amount of American money was made available to those European countries which made an acceptable application. The Soviet Union was, in theory, able to apply for help. However, Stalin saw the plan as an attempt to impose capitalist ideas on European countries. He refused to have anything to do with it. The governments of Poland and Czechoslovkia wanted to join the Marshall Plan but Stalin ordered them not to take part. Stalin was right in thinking that Marshall Plan money would be tied to American-style ideas. The Plan was based on a belief that communism would be much less attractive to ordinary people if they had good jobs and were well paid.

SOURCE D

The American politician, Vandenburg, speaking in 1948, made it clear that the Marshall Plan was part of a strategy to stop the spread of communism.

The Plan is a calculated risk to help stop World War III before it starts. The area covered by the Plan contains 270,000,000 people of the stock which largely made America. This vast friendly segment of the earth must not collapse. The iron curtain must not come to the rims of the Atlantic.

Leaders of 16 West European countries met in Paris between July and September 1947 and wrote a recovery plan. The military governors of western Germany took part. The US accepted the plan and the first American money was transferred. The Marshall Plan was a step towards the division of Germany and this angered the Soviet authorities. Economically, the western area of Germany was now functioning as if it was a separate country from the eastern sector.

The Plan was a great success. Over four years, $13,000 million of help was provided. European countries were encouraged to reduce import taxes and this increased the level of trade. By 1952, when the Marshall Plan officially ended, the countries of Western Europe were well on the road to a period of great economic prosperity. The Plan was also very useful to the USA. By rebuilding Western Europe, America was creating wealthy trade partners who would want to buy large amounts of American goods.

SOURCE E

A Soviet anti-Marshall Plan poster depicting American aid as a menacing influence on the world.

The Soviet response

The Soviet Union organised an international conference in September 1947 in order to condemn the Truman Doctrine and the Marshall Plan. A new organisation was set up to strengthen the links between communist parties in different countries. It was called Cominform (The Communist Information Bureau).

SOURCE F

At the Cominform Conference in September 1947 the Soviet leader, A. A. Zhdanov, bitterly attacked the Truman Doctrine and the Marshall Plan.

The Truman Doctrine and the Marshall Plan are both part of an American plan to enslave Europe. The United States has launched an attack on the principle of each nation being in charge of its own affairs. By contrast, the Soviet Union is tireless in upholding the principle of real equality and independence among nations whatever their size. The Soviet Union will make every effort to ensure that the Marshall Plan is doomed to failure. The communist parties of France, Italy, Great Britain and other countries must play a part in this.

Comecon

Having failed to destroy the Marshall Plan, the USSR created its own economic bloc of countries in Eastern Europe. In January 1949 Comecon (the Council for Mutual Economic Aid) was set up. It was a trading organisation of communist countries but was nowhere near as successful as the Marshall Plan. It did not involve any injection of money into East European countries. Eventually the Soviet Union used it to encourage each country to specialise in different products.

>> **Activity**

1 What was the Truman Doctrine?

2 What was the Marshall Plan?

3 How did the Soviet Union react to the Truman Doctrine and the Marshall Plan?

Communists in Western countries were told to try to wreck the Marshall Plan through strikes. There were very large communist parties in France and Italy. In the winter of 1947–8 communist workers in these two countries organised a series of strikes and demonstrations. This attempt to wreck the Marshall Plan did not work. Despite the strikes, American money flowed into Western Europe and eventually the strikes came to an end.

SOURCE G

Italian soldiers arrest a lorry-load of communist activists during industrial unrest in 1948. The communists were organising strikes in order to wreck the Marshall Plan.

American motives at the start of the Cold War

The American government responded very energetically to the Soviet take-over in Eastern Europe. The Truman Plan and the Marshall Plan signalled a new stage in the developing Cold War.

Why was the US government hostile towards the Soviet Union?

The world's leading nation

The USA was well-placed to play a leading part in world affairs after 1945. It was in excellent economic condition, unlike almost every other powerful country. At the end of the war the defeated nations of Germany and Japan lay in ruins. Several of the 'winners' also faced great difficulties. Britain and France were in debt and were selling very few goods abroad. As a result they could no longer afford to maintain huge armed forces. Much of the Soviet Union was wrecked by the war. By contrast, the rich USA became even richer in the war years. The output of American factories increased by 50 per cent during the war. By 1945 half of all the manufactured goods in the world were made in the USA. One third of all the world's exports came from the USA. Money flooded in and in 1945 the USA held almost two-thirds of all the gold reserves in the world.

As the leaders of the world's richest and most successful country, American politicians were very confident and expected to have a major say in the way the world was run. Leading Americans were extremely proud of their country and believed that American-style capitalism and free trade was the way forward for all other countries. They were, therefore, annoyed by Soviet communists who tried to stop the spread of American business and said that American capitalism was wicked.

SOURCE A

An advertisement of the late 1940s illustrates the relatively high standard of living enjoyed by many Americans. As the elderly couple cook a meal in their comfortable house, their son arrives in his brand-new car. American leaders were very proud of their economic prosperity.

The nuclear monopoly

The USA was not only rich, it was also powerful. With 1,200 major warships and over 2,000 heavy bombers it had the strongest navy and airforce in the world. The American feeling of power was greatly increased when the atomic bomb was produced in 1945. No other country had this immensely powerful weapon. The Soviet Union produced an atom bomb in 1949, but in 1945 Americans thought that it could be 20 years before any other country caught up with their atomic power. American politicians took a more aggressive line towards the Soviet Union because they thought they could use the bomb as a threat. (This overestimated the importance of the atomic bomb. Stalin rightly thought that the bomb was so terrible that the Americans would hardly ever dare to use it.)

SOURCE B

Memories of the 1930s

At the start of 1946 there was a strong feeling in Washington that the US government needed to take a tough line with the USSR. Talks were getting nowhere and Truman became convinced that only the threat of force would stop the Soviets from taking over more land. In January Truman told his advisers that he wanted the USSR to be faced with an 'iron fist'. He added, 'I'm tired of babying the Soviets'.

This hard-line approach was greatly influenced by recent memories. The world had been through great turmoil in the 1930s. In Washington it seemed that the causes of the problem were:

> the rise of evil dictators like Hitler

> the economic crisis of the pre-war Depression.

People in Washington thought that they needed to stop the rise of any more wicked dictators like Hitler. During the war most Americans had a positive view of Stalin. Soon after the war the American Press portrayed him, like Hitler, as a monster and a dictator. The lesson of the 1930s was that appeasement did not work with such people. It would therefore be disastrous if Americans made any concessions to the Soviet Union.

There was also an economic reason for taking a tough line on communism. American politicians were terrified at the idea that there could be another Depression like the one in the early 1930s. Another Depression could only be avoided if American factories were busy. American business was the engine of the world economy and it needed new markets in which to sell its goods. Communist countries were unlikely to buy many American goods. So the spread of communism was a threat to the American economy.

An American atom bomb test. Until 1949 the USA had a monopoly of the atom bomb and this gave the Americans a sense of superiority over the Soviet Union.

George Kennan and the 'long telegram'

One American expert played a crucial part in encouraging a hostile attitude towards the Soviet Union. His name was George Kennan. In February 1946 Kennan sent a famous report to Washington. He was based at the time at the American Embassy in Moscow and his report gave the American government a detailed view of Soviet motives. The report became known as 'the long telegram'. It made a big impact in Washington. The US government accepted Kennan's views and published hundreds of copies of the telegram for its officials to read. Kennan said that the Soviet government was determined to expand and must be stopped. Kennan also developed the idea of 'containment'. The theory of containment was that the USA should use all means, including the threat of force, to stop Soviet power spreading any further. The USA became committed to containment and this remained its policy until the end of the Cold War in the late 1980s.

SOURCE D

A summary of George Kennan's 'long telegram', February 1946:

> Soviet policy is a continuation of traditional Russian policy of hostility towards the outside world.

> Russian leaders today, as in the past, feel threatened and insecure because they know that the West is more advanced. In order to remove the threat, Russian leaders are determined to destroy the Western world.

> Communism has made matters worse. Marxist ideas encourage the Soviet leaders to be absolutely ruthless.

> The Soviet Union will use every method possible to smash democracy in the Western world.

> The Soviet leaders are fanatics and can never be trusted.

SOURCE C

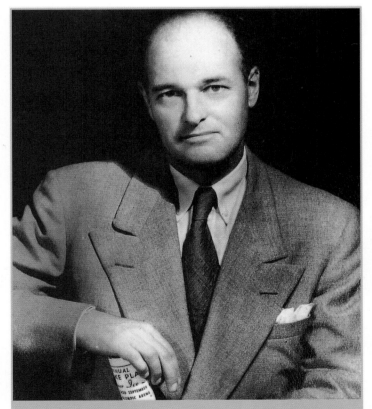

George Kennan. He was a young diplomat based in Moscow in the war. He persuaded many people in the American government of the need for a tough line against the Soviet Union.

SOURCE E

A Soviet poster of the 1940s shows the different ethnic groups of the Soviet Union united by communism. Americans were afraid that Soviet communists wanted to spread their revolutionary ideas throughout the world.

How many different reasons can you find in the following sources to explain why the USA was hostile towards the Soviet Union?

SOURCE F

In 1945 the American ambassador in Moscow commented on the differences between the USA and the Soviet Union.

I am afraid that Stalin does not, and never will, fully understand our interest in free Poland as a matter of principle. It is hard for him to appreciate our faith in principles. It is difficult for him to understand why we should want to interfere with Soviet policy in a country like Poland, which he considers so important to Russia's security, unless we have some ulterior motive.

Averell Harriman

SOURCE G

The US diplomat, George Kennan, in February 1946 said that Soviet leaders wanted to destroy the American way of life.

All Soviet efforts will be negative and destructive in character, designed to tear down sources of strength beyond reach of Soviet control. We have here a political force committed fanatically to the belief that with the US there can be no permanent way of living peacefully together. If Soviet power is to be secure our traditonal way of life must be destroyed and the international authority of our state destroyed.

SOURCE H

Senator E. Johnson made this speech in November 1945:

We can drop, at a moment's notice, atomic bombs on any spot on earth. With vision and guts and plenty of atomic bombs the United States can outlaw wars of aggression.

SOURCE I

President Truman wrote this letter in January 1946:

There isn't a doubt in my mind that Russia intends an invasion of Turkey and the seizure of the Black Sea Straits on the Mediterranean. Unless Russia is faced with an iron fist and strong language another war is in the making. Only one language do they understand: 'How many divisions have you?'

SOURCE J

The American General Eisenhower became President in 1953. In 1951 he commented on American motives.

From my viewpoint, foreign policy is based primarily on one consideration: the need for the US to obtain raw materials and to preserve profitable foreign markets. Out of this comes the need to make certain that those areas of the world where there are essential raw materials are accessible to us.

SOURCE K

William C. Bullitt was a politician and former American diplomat. He made this speech in 1947:

The Soviet Union's assault upon the West is about at the stage of Hitler's manoeuvring into Czechoslovakia. The final aim of Russia is world conquest.

>> Activity

Why was the US government keen to confront the Soviet Union after 1945? In your answer you should mention:

> the wealth and self-confidence of Americans after the war
> the initial monopoly of the atomic bomb
> memories of appeasement
> the influence of George Kennan.

The Berlin Blockade and NATO

In 1948 Stalin tried to starve the people of West Berlin into submission. He failed. The Western allies kept West Berlin supplied through a massive airlift.

What were the consequences of the Berlin Blockade?

Towards a divided Germany

By early 1948 Stalin had control of much of Eastern Europe. The Americans responded by helping to make Western Europe wealthy and pro-American. As part of this process the division of Germany became more and more permanent. The west of Germany had long been the industrial heartland of continental Europe. The US government decided to include western Germany in its plans for a new non-communist Western Europe.

News of a new currency for the west of Germany alarmed Stalin. He saw it as another step towards a divided Germany with the wealthier, larger part of the country closely allied to the USA. Stalin was worried by the idea of a successful, anti-communist government in the west of Germany. In his mind it raised the possibility of another German attack on Russia, as in 1914 and 1941.

In attempting to stop the formation of West Germany, Stalin thought he had one powerful weapon. West Berlin was controlled by the American, French and British forces — but it was a western 'island' deep inside the Soviet sector of Germany. Soviet forces controlled all the land routes into West Berlin. Over 2 million people lived in West Berlin and Stalin could cut off their supplies by simply closing the roads and the railways. As a protest against the currency reforms and the moves towards a divided Germany Stalin decided to put a blockade on West Berlin.

THE EMERGENCE OF WEST GERMANY

> The Marshall Plan for the economic rebuilding of Europe was extended to the western part of Germany but not to the Soviet zone.

> In January 1947 the British and the American governments fused their two zones of Germany into a single administrative unit that was known at the time as Bizonia. In many ways this was the beginning of the establishment of West Germany.

> In June 1948 the Western allies introduced a new currency into their area of control. The new money, known as the Deutschmark, was not used in the Soviet zone.

GERMANY 1945–7

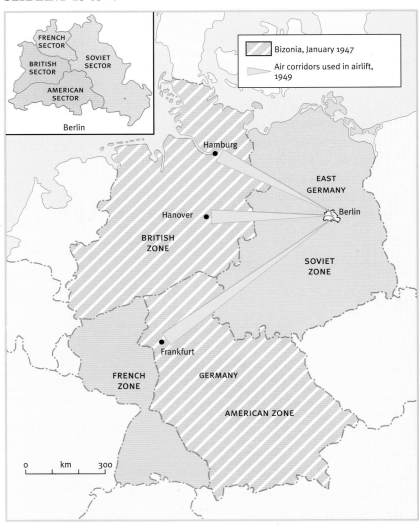

SOURCE A

The blockade began on 23 June 1948 when the Soviet authorities made this announcement:

The transport division of the Soviet Military Administration is compelled to halt all the passenger and freight traffic to and from Berlin at 06.00 hours because of technical difficulties.

The Berlin Airlift

The Western allies were taken by surprise at the start of the blockade. The Americans were initially not sure how to respond. Some advisers thought that the Western powers would have to give way because the 2 million people in West Berlin would starve as long as the roads out of Berlin remained blocked. Another view was that tanks should be used to blast a way through the blockade. The leading American military expert, General Clay, was keen to send his troops down the autobahn towards Berlin. This could easily have led to a full-scale war with the USSR. The government decided on a middle course: not to provoke war by sending troops towards Berlin but to keep the city supplied by aircraft. Never before had a huge besieged city been kept going by an airlift.

SOURCE B

A month after the start of the blockade, Truman ordered General Clay to report to him in Washington to review the Berlin question. In his memoirs, Truman recalled the meeting with Clay on 22 July 1948:

Clay said that the abandonment of Berlin would have a disastrous effect upon our plans for Western Germany. It would also slow down European recovery. The [West] Germans were concerned about the possibility of our leaving Berlin. We should go to any lengths to find a peaceful solution to the situation, but we had to remain in Berlin. He reported that the airlift was more than enough to meet food requirements, but was inadequate to include the necessary amounts of coal.

I asked General Clay if there were any indications that the Russians would go to war. He said he did not think so. What they seemed to be aiming at was to score a major victory by forcing us out of Berlin, either now or after winter weather forced us to curtail the airlift.

I directed the Air Force to furnish the fullest support possible to the problem of supplying Berlin.

SOURCE C

Children from West Berlin watch a US cargo plane bringing in supplies to the besieged city during the Berlin Blockade.

To people in the West, Stalin seemed to be acting with extreme aggression. The attack on Berlin looked like the first step towards a communist march westwards. The Western allies acted firmly in carrying out the airlift. To President Truman it was a test of the new policy of containment: the USSR could not be allowed to take over West Berlin.

>> Activity

Explain in your own words why Stalin decided to impose a blockade on West Berlin.

Stalin ends the siege

Eventually Stalin had to admit that his attempt to starve out West Berlin had failed. In May 1949 the Soviet authorities called off the blockade. The airlift was a triumph for the American and British air forces. During the airlift British and US planes flew nearly 200,000 missions to Berlin. At the end of the blockade the airport in West Berlin was handling an enormous 1,000 arrivals and departures every day. Over 1.5 million tons of food, fuel and equipment was sent in to Berlin. This achievement clearly proved how determined the USA was to resist Stalin. The Berlin airlift showed how far international politics had changed since 1945. Berlin had then been a symbol of defeated Nazism. By 1948 it was a symbol of Western freedom and the struggle with communism.

SOURCE D

Konrad Adenauer, 1949. The blockade strengthened the position of conservative anti-communists like Adenauer. This was the exact opposite of what Stalin wanted when he began the Blockade.

After the blockade: the formation of West Germany

Stalin's attempt to put a stop to the creation of West Germany was a complete failure. The blockade accelerated moves towards a powerful, pro-Western state in much of Germany. As the airlift began, the military authorities in the western zones also organised meetings to work out a constitution for West Germany. The new state was called the Federal Republic of Germany and it was formally founded in May 1949. The Soviet Union responded to this by setting up a new constitution for East Germany. In October 1949 the eastern state was officially established and it was known as the German Democratic Republic.

West Germany held its first elections in August 1949. A political party called the Christian Democrats won the greatest number of seats and dominated the new state. Its leader was Konrad Adenauer, a conservative who hated communism and believed very strongly in linking West Germany to the USA and Western Europe. The development of West Germany under Adenauer was the last thing that Stalin wanted. The idea of a powerful capitalist German state made him feel insecure.

After the blockade: the formation of NATO

The blockade also encouraged the Western allies to form the North Atlantic Treaty Organisation (NATO).

SOURCE E

The North Atlantic Treaty Organisation was set up in April 1949. This is an extract from the treaty.

The Parties to this treaty agree that an armed attack against one or more of them in Europe or North America shall be considered an attack against them all. They agree that, if such an armed attack occurs, each of them will assist by taking such action as it deems necessary, including the use of armed force.

The alliance was dominated by the USA. American influence has been reflected in the fact that every single supreme commander of NATO has been an American. The formation of NATO was a milestone in American foreign policy. Never before had the USA been a member of a peacetime military alliance. The fact that Truman broke with all the traditions of American foreign policy shows how determined he was to stop the spread of communism.

NATO was more than a promise of American help in case of emergency. The alliance was to be supported with large numbers of troops on the ground. In particular, there was a large build-up of NATO forces in West Germany. By 1953, five divisions of US troops were permanently based in Germany.

The Soviet Union felt threatened by this. The sense of threat increased in 1955 when West Germany joined NATO. The Soviet Union responded by setting up its own military alliance in 1955. This was established under a treaty called the Warsaw Pact. For the next three decades NATO and Warsaw Pact forces faced each other and prepared for war.

>> Activity

1 How did the Berlin Blockade end? Was this a victory for the Soviet Union or for the USA?

2 How did the blockade speed up the formation of West Germany?

3 How did the blockade lead to the setting up of NATO?

4 Do you think that Stalin was pleased with the consequences of the Berlin Blockade?

NATO AND THE WARSAW PACT

Legend:
- Warsaw Pact 1955
- Iron Curtain
- NATO
- 1949 date of joining NATO
- communist but neutral

CANADA 1949
ICELAND 1949
USA 1949

SWEDEN
NORWAY 1949
FINLAND
DENMARK 1949
EIRE
NETHERLANDS 1949
BRITAIN 1949
U S S R
EAST GERMANY
POLAND
BELGIUM 1949
LUX. 1949
WEST GERMANY 1955
CZECHOSLOVAKIA
FRANCE 1949
AUSTRIA
SWITZ.
HUNGARY
ROMANIA
PORTUGAL 1949
YUGOSLAVIA
ITALY 1949
BULGARIA
SPAIN 1982
ALBANIA Expelled in 1968
GREECE 1952
TURKEY 1952

0   km   1000

The start of the Cold War

The wartime allies become enemies

Soon after the end of the war the USA and the USSR became hostile towards each other. A period of hostility known as the Cold War lasted until the late 1980s.

YALTA AND POTSDAM

The leaders of the USA, USSR and Britain met twice in 1945 to talk about the world after the war. They had met once before in Tehran, 1943.

Yalta, February 1945

Leaders present: Roosevelt (USA), Stalin (USSR), Churchill (Britain)

Discussed: Poland and the rest of Eastern Europe

Agreed: non-communists to be part of emergency governments

free elections as soon as possible

Outcome: Soviet Union did not allow democracy in Poland

great bitterness caused in the USA

Potsdam, July 1945

Leaders present: Truman (USA), Stalin (USSR), Churchill, replaced by Attlee (Britain).

Discussed: the future running of Germany

Agreed: borders between Germany and Poland wiping out Nazi influence arrangements for reparations

Outcome: USA prevented Soviet Union involvement in the rich Ruhr area of Germany and occupied Japan

The Soviet Union blocked American involvement in Eastern Europe

The Soviet take-over

In 1946 Churchill described how an 'iron curtain' was being put across Europe; the iron curtain divided Soviet-style states in Eastern Europe from democratic, capitalist states in Western Europe. Between 1945 and 1948 the Soviet Union imposed communist governments on several East European countries:

> Poland

> Bulgaria

> Romania

> Hungary

> Czechoslovakia

The communist coup in Czechoslovakia in 1948 particularly angered people in the West.

For the Soviet leader, Stalin, the take-over was a defensive move: an attempt to build up a friendly buffer between the USSR and the Western capitalist states.

For the American leader, Truman, the take-over was an offensive move: the first step in a Soviet attempt to impose communism on all the countries of the world.

A US atomic test taking place in the Pacific Ocean near Bikini Atoll on 25 July 1946.

The American response

Between 1945 and 1949 the Americans developed a policy called 'containment'. This involved using the power and wealth of the USA to try to stop or 'contain' the spread of communism, first of all in Europe and later throughout the world.

CONTAINMENT IN EUROPE

1947: The Truman Doctrine

The American President Truman said that the world was being divided into free, democratic countries and undemocratic communist states. Truman promised help for any people who wanted to resist communism and immediate help to anti-communist governments in Greece and Turkey.

1947: The Marshall Plan

The economy of Europe was in ruins at the end of the war. The Marshall Plan, named after General George Marshall, the US Secretary of State, aimed to re-build the European economy so that it could resist communism. In theory, East European countries could join but the Americans made it clear that communist states were not welcome.

1949: the founding of NATO

The USA took the lead in organising a military alliance of non-communist countries in Europe and North America. It was called the North Atlantic Treaty Organisation. All members agreed to defend each other in case of Soviet attack.

1949: the setting up of West Germany

At the end of the war Germany was divided into the British, French, American and Soviet zones. The city of Berlin was also divided into four zones. At first both the USA and the USSR wanted a unified Germany. When the Soviet Union took control of much of Eastern Europe, America moved towards the setting up of a pro-Western state in the British, French and American zones. West Germany, officially known as the Federal Republic of Germany, was established in May 1949.

THE SOVIET REACTION TO CONTAINMENT

Stalin, in turn, saw American actions after 1945 as aggressive and a threat to the Soviet Union. The Soviet response was as follows:

1948–1949: the Berlin Blockade

West Berlin was an island of democracy and capitalism in the Soviet zone. Stalin was worried by the possibility of a strong West German state. In June 1948 Stalin blocked all road and rail transport with West Berlin. This was a failure. Britain and the USA organised an unprecedented airlift to stop West Berliners from being starved out. The blockade was ended in May 1949. The blockade accelerated moves towards a separate West Germany and the NATO alliance.

1949: COMECON

In January 1949 the Soviet Union tried to answer the Marshall Plan by setting up a trading bloc of communist countries. It was called the Council for Mutual Economic Aid or COMECON.

1949: the setting up of East Germany

After the official establishment of West Germany the Soviet zone of Germany was turned into a separate communist state, officially known as the German Democratic Republic.

1949: the Soviet atom bomb

The USA had a monopoly of atomic weapons after 1945. Stalin ordered Soviet scientists to produce an atomic bomb and in 1949 they succeeded.

1955: the Warsaw Pact

In 1955 NATO was expanded to include West Germany. The Soviet Union created a military alliance of communist countries known as the Warsaw Pact.

Communist China

The civil war

There was a bitter struggle for control of China from 1927 to 1949 between nationalists and communists. The nationalists were led by Jiang Jieshi (Chiang Kai-shek); the leader of the communists was Mao Zedong (Mao Tse-tung). At first the nationalists were the more powerful. By 1934 Jiang Jieshi destroyed the communist forces in the east of the country. Mao Zedong re-organised the surviving communists and led them on a famous Long March north to safety in the region of Yanan. The civil war was interrupted between 1937 and 1945 by a war with the Japanese. In 1945 fighting broke out again. At this point the communists controlled only part of northern China and had a smaller army than the nationalists.

Jiang had American backing. However, his government failed to win the support of the ordinary people. Taxes were high and the government had a reputation for corruption. Most Chinese people lived in the countryside. Mao promised the poor country people a fair share of the land. His soldiers fought a skilful guerrilla war against the nationalist armies. By 1946 Jiang lost control of Manchuria. The communist armies swept to victory in 1948–9. In September 1949 Mao announced that the People's Republic of China was now established. The communists controlled all China, except for the large off-shore island of Taiwan. Jiang Jieshi fled to Taiwan.

A new superpower?

As the state with the greatest population in the world the government of China expected to be taken seriously by other powerful countries. China saw itself as an equal of the Soviet Union and the USA. This view was given extra weight when China exploded its first atomic bomb in 1964.

China and the Soviet Union

The relationship between communist China and the Soviet Union was tense from the beginning. Mao was not impressed by the level of support he had received from Stalin during the years of struggle. The Chinese leadership was not prepared to see the USSR as the senior partner in the communist world. After Stalin's death Mao was angered that the Soviet leaders did not consult him before attacking Stalin's memory. These tensions came to the surface in 1960 when the Chinese criticised Khrushchev for being too friendly towards the West. The USSR ordered home many of the Soviet scientists and engineers who were in China. Between 1968 and 1970 the USSR and China came close to war over arguments about the frontier. The two countries remained on poor terms until the time of Gorbachev in the late 1980s.

Young Chinese read the teachings of Mao near an enormous propaganda poster of the Chinese leader. Mao used young followers, called Red Guards, to strengthen his position during the Cultural Revolution.

The Great Leap Forward and the Cultural Revolution

Mao tried to bring about rapid change in the Chinese economy in 1958. Collective farms or 'communes' were set up in the countryside. New factories were built. This attempt to increase output rapidly was called the Great Leap Forward. It was not successful. Mao tried to increase his power by organising a period of turmoil between 1966 and 1969, known as the Cultural Revolution. Young radical followers of Mao, called Red Guards, toured the country terrorising people in senior positions. Amid the chaos Mao was able to remove many opponents from power.

The Cultural Revolution badly damaged the Chinese economy. It also harmed China's relations with the outside world.

China had a very poor relationship with the USA throughout the 1950s and 1960s. After the Cultural Revolution the two countries began to look again at their relationship. The US president in the early 1970s was Richard Nixon and he was keen to build a good relationship with China. Under Nixon the USA 'recognised' the government of China for the first time. Nixon visited China in 1972.

After Mao

When Mao died in 1976 there was a power struggle between radicals and moderates. The leaders of the radicals became known as the Gang of Four, and included Mao's widow, Jiang Qing. The power struggle was eventually won by the moderates, led by Deng Xiaoping. The Gang of Four were blamed for the chaos of the Cultural Revolution and imprisoned. In the 1980s Deng Xiaoping abandoned many of the ideas of communist economics and encouraged free enterprise and competition. At the same time there was no increase in free speech.

A so-called 'pro-democracy movement' developed among students in the early months of 1989. Demonstrators camped in Tiananmen Square, Beijing (Peking) and demanded free speech and free elections. The students were joined by large numbers of ordinary people. On 3 June the Chinese army moved in and used tanks to clear the square. Many thousands of people were killed. Afterwards, leaders of the pro-democracy movement were arrested and imprisoned. The massacre in Tiananmen Square shocked the world and affected the relationship between China and other countries. After Tiananmen, the government continued with its policy of Western-style economics but little political freedom.

An unarmed protester defiantly stands in the way of the tanks of the Chinese Red Army, Tiananmen Square, June 1989. The Chinese government used great force to smash the pro-democracy movement.

Discussion points

> What impact has Mao Zedong had on China in the twentieth century?

> What has been the relationship between communist China and the superpowers?

> How has communist China developed since the death of Mao Zedong?

The Korean War

The Truman Doctrine stated that the USA would help people to fight against communism. In 1950 the USA showed that this was more than words: US troops went to war to stop the spread of communism in Korea.

How successful was the USA in the Korean War?

THE KOREAN WAR

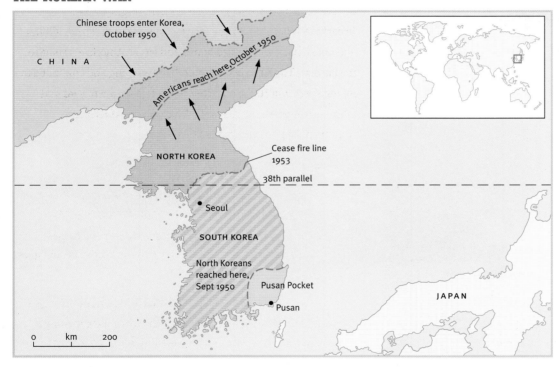

A divided land

The Japanese controlled Korea between 1904 and 1945. At the end of the Second World War Korea was in a situation similar to Germany. Russian forces were in the north of Korea and American troops had landed in the south. Korea became divided in two at the 38th parallel. In 1948 separate Korean governments were set up in the north and south of the country.

A communist, Kim Il Sung, took power in the North. From 1948 the President of South Korea was the anti-communist, Syngman Rhee. He was a corrupt leader and he soon became very unpopular. In April 1950 Rhee did badly in elections. Many of the people of the south voted in favour of unification with the communist state of the north.

Invasion

On 25 June 1950 North Korean troops invaded the South in a bid to re-unite Korea by force. Historians disagree about whether the North Koreans were told to invade by the Russians. Truman believed that the Russians were behind the attack and that it was a test of the US policy of containing communism. The invasion came at a time when many Americans were extremely worried about the challenge of communism. China had recently become a communist state. In September 1949 the Americans found out that the USSR had nuclear weapons. American politicians became convinced that communists wanted to take over the world. On hearing the news from Korea, Truman immediately ordered US forces in Japan, led by General MacArthur, to help South Korea.

Truman asked the United Nations Security Council to back the use of American troops in Korea. At that time the Soviet Union was boycotting the Security Council and was not able to use its veto. As a result the Security Council supported the USA and called on other member states to provide troops. Soldiers from a number of countries fought in Korea, including Britain, Canada, Australia and New Zealand. However, the bulk of the UN forces were provided by the USA.

SOURCE A

General MacArthur, 1949. This US general played a key role in shaping American policy during the Korean War.

The US counter-attack

At first the North Korean attack was very successful. Within four days the Southern capital of Seoul had been captured. The North Koreans conquered all of the country except for a small area in the south around the town of Pusan. In July 1950 MacArthur sent American forces to Pusan and prepared for a counter-attack. The US fight-back began in September. MacArthur organised a successful amphibious attack on the town of Inchon. At the same time US forces broke out of the Pusan area. The counter-attack went extremely well and by 1 October the US troops had reached the 38th parallel, the original border between North and South Korea.

The Americans faced a dilemma. Should they push on and invade North Korea? They now had a chance to go beyond containment and 'roll back' the frontiers of communism. On the other hand, there was a possibility that by invading the North the Americans might provoke China to join the war. MacArthur was keen to go on. Truman approved the change of policy and the US forces crossed the 38th parallel on 7 October. Eventually MacArthur's troops reached the Yalu River, close to the Chinese border. This was the first time since 1945 that Americans had tried to liberate a communist state.

The risk of Chinese intervention

Communist China was a new force in the world. Few people believed that they would risk war with the mighty USA. In early October the Chinese issued a statement that said, 'China will not sit back with folded hands and let the Americans come to the border'. The Americans ignored this warning and continued to march north. On 10 October the Chinese government said that Chinese troops would attack the Americans if MacArthur continued. MacArthur ignored this threat.

SOURCE B

The American view of the dangers of outside help for North Korea was expressed in American magazines of the time.

The danger of Chinese or Soviet intervention if the North Korean Communists are pushed hard to the border is negligible.

Life Magazine, October 1950

If the Chinese should commit their own forces to the struggle in Korea they would do so knowing that they were inviting a general war. That is a price they are not prepared to pay.

The Nation, September 1950

SOURCE C

The communist view was expressed in a Chinese newspaper.

We cannot stand idly by when the American imperialist, a notorious enemy, is now expanding its war of aggression against our neighbour and is attempting to expand the aggressive flames to the borders of our country.

Kung Jen Jih Pao, 13 October 1950

The Chinese intervene

At the end of October Chinese troops went into action and attacked South Korean and American troops. In November the South Koreans and Americans were forced to retreat. Truman and MacArthur were not put off by the Chinese intervention. Britain and France wanted Truman to talk to the Chinese. The advice from these allies was ignored. Instead, MacArthur planned a further push towards the Chinese border. This renewed attack began on 25 November. It went badly wrong. MacArthur made a big mistake: he divided his forces in two and marched north. The Chinese had little difficulty in attacking and destroying many of the US forces. MacArthur had to retreat and the Chinese soon took control of almost all North Korea. Once again it was the turn of the communist forces to push over the border into South Korea. The Chinese offensive continued into the New Year. On 1 January they crossed the 38th parallel, and on 4th January they took the Southern capital, Seoul.

SOURCE D

MacArthur's mistake and retreat was a great blow to the Americans.

There is no doubt that confidence in General MacArthur has been shaken badly as a result of the events of the last few days. Similarly, there is no doubt that the United States leadership in the Western world has been damaged by President Truman's acceptance of the bold MacArthur offensive.

The *New York Times*, 30 November 1950

The success of the Chinese caused great disappointment in America. There were behind-the-scenes arguments about what to do next. General MacArthur recommended extreme action. Truman hinted at a press conference that he might drop the atomic bomb on China.

MACARTHUR'S ADVICE: DECEMBER 1950

> The US should consider all methods to defeat the Chinese; this could include the use of atomic bombs against China.

> The war should be extended to the Chinese mainland in order to cut off supplies to the communist forces in Korea.

> The ultimate aim of the war should be not only the re-capture of North Korea, but also the defeat of communism in China.

The British government was appalled by talk of using atom bombs and invading China. The British Prime Minister, Attlee, flew to Washington and urged Truman to negotiate with the Chinese. Attlee failed to get the Americans to talk to the Chinese but Truman did stop talking about dropping the atom bomb.

SOURCE E

American troops pass through a burning village during the Korean War.

The fall of MacArthur

In February 1951 the Americans launched a further attack on the communist troops. By March the communist forces had been pushed back to the original border, the 38th parallel. At this point MacArthur disagreed with Truman. Truman now abandoned the idea of conquering all of Korea and was considering making peace with China. For a long time there had been tension between Truman and MacArthur. This now reached breaking point. On 24 March MacArthur made a public statement criticising the idea of a deal with the Chinese. Truman was annoyed when he heard this. MacArthur wanted to cross the border again in order to re-conquer North Korea. He sent a message to an American politician explaining his view that America should keep fighting until the Chinese were defeated. Truman was very angry that a general was trying to control the war, instead of obeying his orders, and in April MacArthur was dismissed. This caused a sensation in the United States.

The stalemate

By early summer 1951 the two sides in the Korean War had reached a stalemate. The Chinese launched a huge push south in April and May, but it was not successful. The loss of life on the Chinese side was enormous. In these two months over 200,000 men were killed. Peace talks began in July 1951 but there was no agreed cease-fire. Sporadic but bloody fighting continued. The negotiations soon got stuck over where to draw the border and the exchange of prisoners. As the months passed the situation became similar to the Western Front in the First World War, with both sides dug in to strong defensive positions. This situation continued throughout the second half of 1951 and through the whole of 1952. Soldiers continued to be killed in large numbers on both sides. Between the start of the talks and November 1952, 45,000 American troops were killed or wounded. At the end of 1952 the Americans elected a new President, Ike Eisenhower. The new President took power in January 1953 and he was determined to end the war. An agreement to stop fighting was eventually signed on 27 July 1953.

>> Activity

1 Explain what happened in each of the following phases of the Korean War. For every phase decide whether you think the communists or the anti-communists were more successful.

June 1950 – July 1950

September 1950 – October 1950

November 1950 – January 1951

February 1951 – March 1951

April 1951 – May 1951

July 1951 – July 1953

2 Using all the information in this unit decide whether you think American policy in Korea was successful. Give reasons for your decision.

SOURCE F

Eisenhower. He came to power determined to end the Korean War.

The Cuban missile crisis

Cuba is a large island in the Caribbean. In 1959 a revolution took place in Cuba and Fidel Castro came to power. He introduced a Soviet-style government on the island and he looked to the Soviet Union for support. There was a great uproar in 1962 when the Soviet leader, Khrushchev, placed nuclear missiles on the island.

What happened during the Cuban missile crisis?

The revolution in Cuba was a great blow to America. A communist state had been set up only 90 miles from the USA. In April 1961 the American CIA organised an attack on Cuba. This was carried out by Cuban exiles. Their plan was to land in a remote part of the island and set up a base for guerrilla war against the government of Cuba. They expected that other Cubans would rise up and join the rebellion. The invasion force landed at a place called the Bay of Pigs.

The attack at the Bay of Pigs went disastrously wrong: the Americans had underestimated the strength of the Cuban armed forces and the CIA had misunderstood how popular Castro was. The invasion force was easily defeated by the Cuban government and there was no widespread support for the invasion from among the people of Cuba. The fiasco at the Bay of Pigs was humiliating for the American President, Kennedy.

The struggle for control of Cuba was part of the world-wide Cold War. In early 1962 the Americans placed a number of nuclear missiles in Turkey, within easy range of many cities of the USSR. Shortly afterwards Khrushchev decided to place missiles on Cuba.

THE CUBAN CRISIS, 1962

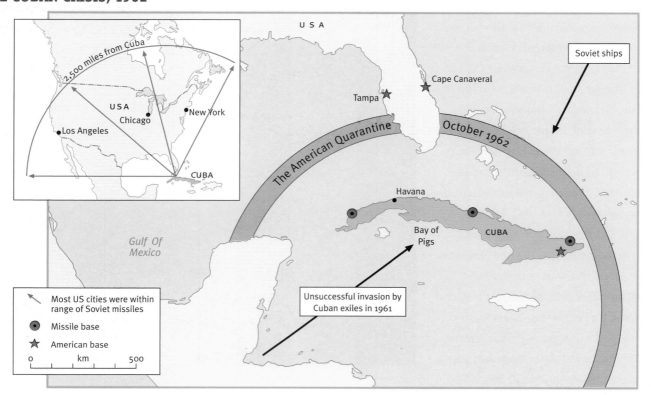

What can we learn from these sources about why Khrushchev placed the missiles on Cuba?

SOURCE A

Khrushchev speaking in December 1962 to the Supreme Soviet (the parliament of the USSR):

Comrades, everyone still remembers the tense days of October when mankind was anxiously listening to the news coming from the Caribbean. In those days the world was on the brink of a nuclear catastrophe. What created this crisis? The revolution in Cuba was met with hostility from the imperialists in the United States of America. The imperialists are frightened of Cuba because of her ideas. They hate the idea that little Cuba has dared go her own way, instead of trying to please American business. American forces have been doing everything they can, from the first day of the revolution, to overthrow Cuba's government and restore their own control. They set up an economic blockade of Cuba. This is inhuman – an attempt to starve a whole nation. Even this was not enough for them. They decided to use force to suppress the Cuban revolution.

We carried weapons there at the request of the Cuban government. Cuba needed weapons as a means of deterring the aggressors, and not as a means of attack. We sent about forty missiles to Cuba. Naturally, neither we nor our Cuban friends thought that this small number of missiles would be used for an attack on the United States. Our aim was only to defend Cuba.

SOURCE B

Fyodor Burlatsky, Khrushchev's assistant, writing in 1992, recalled how the Soviet leader decided to send missiles to Cuba during a visit to Bulgaria in May 1962:

Khrushchev was walking along a beach on the Black Sea with Defence Minister Malinovskiy, who pointed out to him that American military bases with nuclear warheads capable of wiping out the cities of Kiev, Minsk and Moscow in a matter of minutes were located on the opposite shore in Turkey. Khrushchev then asked Malinovskiy, 'And why then can we not have bases close to America? What's the reason for this imbalance?' And right then and there Khrushchev began to question Malinovskiy about whether or not it would be possible to deploy missiles secretly in Cuba. Malinovskiy assured him that the missiles could be deployed without detection.

The crisis

The Soviets tried to move the missiles secretly to the Caribbean. In public Khrushchev stated that 'no missile capable of reaching the United States will be placed in Cuba'. A U-2 spy plane flew over Cuba on 14 October and took photographs of the missile site. On 16 October 1962 President Kennedy was shown the photographs proving that Soviet missiles were on Cuba. The missiles had only recently arrived and would not yet have been in working order. The Americans spent six days secretly discussing and planning how to respond. They did not consult with their allies at this stage. Even the government of Britain, the closest ally, was not told about the missiles until 21 October, shortly before Kennedy made an announcement to the American people.

>> Activity

The Americans considered a range of options:

> a letter of protest to Khrushchev

> bombing the missile sites

> an invasion of Cuba

> a naval blockade of the island.

Imagine that you are Kennedy's adviser. Which of these options would you recommend? Remember you would want to show Khrushchev that you mean business, but you do not want to provoke all-out war with the USSR.

On the edge of a nuclear catastrophe

SOURCE C

Labels on image:
MISSILE TRANSPORTERS
HEAVY EQUIPMENT
12 PROB GUIDELINE MISSILES
5 MISSILE DOLLIES
20' LONG CYLINDRICAL TANKS
MISSILE TRANSPORTERS
OPEN STORAGE

Some of the Cuban missile sites, photographed by an American U-2 spy plane.

Kennedy's response to the news of the missiles was twofold: he decided to get ready for an invasion of Cuba, but first of all to mount a blockade of the island. On 22 October a so-called 'quarantine' was announced – the Americans stated that they would stop and search all ships bound for Cuba. Even at this stage, Khrushchev refused to accept publicly that there were missiles on Cuba. This put the USSR in a difficult position when Kennedy was able to show the world that Khrushchev was lying. Two days later a number of Soviet ships, which probably contained warheads for the missiles, turned back just short of the line of the blockade. This was not the end of the crisis because some warheads were already on the island.

The Americans announced that the missiles must be dismantled immediately or else Cuba would be attacked and invaded. There was a real possibility of a nuclear war breaking out between the USA and the USSR. According to one source, Castro actually suggested to Khrushchev that the USSR should launch nuclear missiles against America to stop the imminent invasion of Cuba. Khrushchev was not impressed by this advice and was horrified to discover that some of his top generals thought it would be better to have a nuclear war than back down. Instead he decided to write an urgent letter to Kennedy. This was sent on 26 October.

SOURCE D

On 26 October Khrushchev sent a letter to Kennedy. It suggested that the missiles could be withdrawn if the USA made a promise not to invade Cuba.

If the assurances were given that the President of the United States would not participate in an attack on Cuba and the blockade lifted, then the question of the removal of the missile sites would be an entirely different question. This is my proposal. No more weapons to Cuba and those within Cuba withdrawn or destroyed, and you reciprocate by ending your blockade and also agree not to invade Cuba.

Before Kennedy had replied to this message Khrushchev sent a second letter on 27 October, with different demands. This second letter demanded that the Americans must take their missiles out of Turkey in return for the removal of the Cuban missiles.

SOURCE E

This an extract from Khrushchev's letter of 27 October.

You are worried over Cuba. You say that it worries you because it lies ninety miles across the sea from the shores of the United States. However, Turkey lies next to us. You have stationed devastating rocket weapons in Turkey, literally right next to us. This is why I make this proposal: We agree to remove the weapons from Cuba. We agree to this and to state this commitment in the United Nations. Your representatives will make a statement that the United States, on its part, will evacuate its similar weapons from Turkey.

The Americans did not know how to respond. The Americans had already considered taking their missiles out of Turkey but Kennedy did not want to be seen to be backing down in the face of Soviet pressure. The American military leaders recommended an immediate air attack on Cuba. Kennedy was unsure. A letter was about to be sent to Khrushchev refusing to do a deal over the Turkish missiles. At this point it was suggested that the Americans ignore the second letter, but reply to the first letter accepting the Soviet proposal that the missiles should be withdrawn in return for an American commitment not to invade Cuba. The President liked this idea and a suitable letter was sent.

The President's brother

Later on the 27 October Robert Kennedy, the brother of the President, went to see the Soviet ambassador. The conversation between Robert Kennedy and the ambassador, Anatoly Dobrynin, was the key to the solution of the crisis. Kennedy gave Dobrynin an ultimatum; he said that if the Soviets did not promise to remove the missiles by the next day the Americans would use force to destroy the missiles. He then made an offer to the Russians – there could be no official deal, but if the Cuban missiles were removed the missiles in Turkey would follow soon after. This message was relayed to Khrushchev, and it was enough for the Russians. On 28 October Dobrynin reported to back to Robert Kennedy and announced that the Russians would withdraw their missiles from Cuba. The crisis was over.

SOURCE F

A few years later, in 1969, Robert Kennedy's account of his crucial conversation with Dobrynin was published.

I said that there could be no arrangement made under this kind of threat or pressure. However, I said that President Kennedy had been anxious to remove those missiles from Turkey and Italy for a long period of time. It was our judgement that, within a short time after this crisis was over, those missiles would be gone.

SOURCE G

Robert Kennedy. The President's brother finally negotiated an end to the crisis with the Soviet ambassador to Washington.

SOURCE I

AFTER THE CRISIS

> The end of the crisis was seen as a victory for Kennedy and a defeat for Khrushchev. The deal over the missiles in Turkey was kept secret so it seemed to the world as if the Soviets had simply backed down. This was good for Kennedy's reputation, but damaging for the Soviet leader. Leading Soviet communists were angry that their country appeared to climb down. This put Khrushchev in a difficult position at home, and contributed to his fall from power in 1964.

> The European allies of the USA were shocked at how little they were consulted during the emergency. It seemed that their opinions was not seen as important by the Americans. The French government of de Gaulle felt this very strongly. As a result de Gaulle eventually pulled France out of NATO and encouraged Western Europe to follow an independent line.

> On the communist side, the Chinese were not impressed by the Soviet performance. They felt that Khrushchev mishandled the crisis and looked cowardly when he removed the missiles. This further encouraged the Chinese to follow an independent line of their own in world politics.

Nikita Khrushchev.

> The most important long-term result of the crisis was that both sides realised the great dangers of direct conflict between the USSR and the USA. Both Soviet and American leaders were shocked at how close they had come to nuclear war. After the Cuban Missile Crisis the Cold War continued but the two superpowers carefully avoided direct hostility. A special telephone 'hotline' was installed so that leaders could communicate easily in any future crisis. The level of tension between the USA and the USSR was never again to be as great as it was in November 1962.

SOURCE H

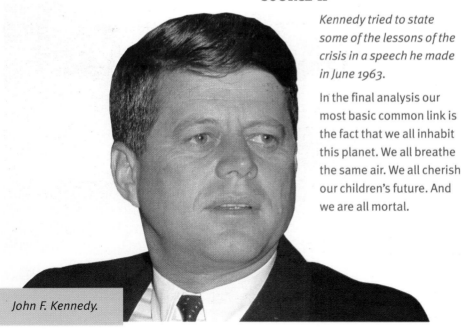

John F. Kennedy.

Kennedy tried to state some of the lessons of the crisis in a speech he made in June 1963.

In the final analysis our most basic common link is the fact that we all inhabit this planet. We all breathe the same air. We all cherish our children's future. And we are all mortal.

>> Activity

Explain in your own words how the crisis:

a appeared to be a victory for Kennedy and a defeat for Khrushchev,

b damaged the relationship between the superpowers and other states,

c led to a period of greater stability in Soviet–US relations.

The Cold War and the Middle East

Israel and the superpowers

Throughout much of the twentieth century there was a bitter argument between Jewish and Arab people over control of the area of the Middle East originally known as Palestine. Until the First World War the territory was part of the Turkish Empire. It was then controlled by the British. After the Second World War the United Nations decided to set up a Jewish state, called Israel, in part of Palestine. As British forces left the area in May 1948, Jewish leaders declared the existence of the new state. Israel was immediately attacked by the neighbouring Arab states of Egypt, Jordan, Syria, Lebanon and Iraq. Fighting came to an end in January 1949 with Israel victorious but this was not the end of the dispute. The two superpowers soon took sides in this conflict. Israel became strongly pro-American, while the Soviet Union became hostile towards Israel.

Suez

There was an upsurge of Arab nationalism in the 1950s supported by the Soviet Union. In 1952 a passionate Arab nationalist called Gamal Nasser took power in Egypt. He turned to the Soviet Union for help in developing the country. In 1956 Nasser seized control of the Suez Canal from the Western powers of Britain and France.

In October 1956 Britain, France and Israel attacked the Suez Canal area. The government of the USA was unhappy about the invasion of Egypt and forced Britain and France to pull out. The Americans got little credit for their actions and radical Arabs increasingly looked to the USSR for assistance. After Suez there was increased Soviet involvement in the Middle East.

War and peace

War broke out again between Israel and the Arab states in 1967 and in 1973. Israel won both these wars and gained control of substantial lands inhabited by Palestinian Arabs. The success of Israel was a blow to the USSR. The Soviets had supplied Egypt and Syria with their weapons but they had lost. Israel was a small country but, with American help, the Israelis had defeated their hostile neighbours. After 1973 the USA was much more successful than the USSR in influencing events in the Middle East. A new Egyptian leader, Anwar Sadat, broke off relations with the Soviet Union and established a good relationship with the USA. With American help and encouragement the states of Egypt and Israel signed a peace treaty in 1979. In the 1980s the Americans tried to bring Jewish Israelis and Arab Palestinians together. After many years of American pressure the Palestinian leader, Yasser Arafat, signed a peace treaty with the Israeli Prime Minister, Yitzhak Rabin, in 1993. By this time the Soviet Union had fallen apart and the Soviet leaders did not play a significant part in the Middle East peace treaty.

US President Clinton encourages Yitzhak Rabin and Yasser Arafat to shake hands in Washington in 1993.

Discussion points

> Which superpower was more successful in influencing Middle East politics?

The Vietnam War

Between 1965 and 1973 US troops fought a disastrous war against communists in South Vietnam. In the end, the wealthiest country in the world was unable to defeat the Vietnamese fighters.

Why did the USA fight and lose the Vietnam War?

Vietnam divided

Vietnam had been a French colony. After the Second World War, Vietnamese nationalists and communists, led by Ho Chi Minh, fought against the French. In 1954 the French decided to pull out and Vietnam was divided in two. Communists took power in North Vietnam. South Vietnam was ruled by an anti-communist leader called Ngo Dinh Diem. In 1959 the communist government of the North decided to encourage a revolution in the South. Southern communists, who had fled North, returned to fight. These forces were known as the Vietcong.

From 1954 South Vietnam depended on aid from the USA. American policy was based on the 'domino theory': the belief that, because neighbouring states are so interdependent, the collapse of one will lead to the collapse of others. The Americans used this theory as a justification of their involvement in foreign states, particularly in South-East Asia, which they felt were likely to be taken over by the communists. In November 1961 President Kennedy began providing wide-ranging support for the army of the South, including some American soldiers as 'combat advisers'. He hoped that with this help Diem would be able to defeat the communist rebels. This did not happen. The Americans became increasingly unhappy with Diem. In 1963 Diem's government further annoyed the USA by clashing with local Buddhists. With American approval, a group of South Vietnamese generals overthrew Diem in a coup in November 1963.

The Gulf of Tonkin Incident

In 1964 regular North Vietnamese forces marched south along what became known as the Ho Chi Minh Trail to support the Vietcong. Without outside help South Vietnam looked doomed. American involvement increased dramatically after a clash at sea between North Vietnam and the USA in August 1964. An American destroyer near the coast of North Vietnam was attacked by North Vietnamese ships. No serious damage was done in this so-called Gulf of Tonkin Incident. However, the new American President, Johnson, ordered the bombing of Northern naval bases in retaliation. Congress passed a resolution giving the President power to 'take all necessary steps, including the use of armed force' in order to defend South Vietnam. After this Johnson felt he had full authority to step up American involvement in the war.

THE VIETNAM WAR

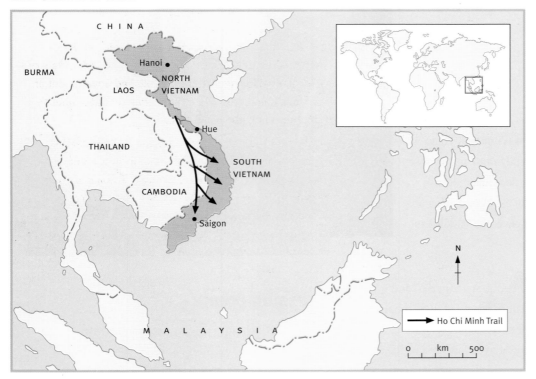

The arrival of US ground troops

By early 1965 American bombers were regularly attacking targets in the North. Johnson did not think that this was enough. He decided that the South Vietnamese needed the help of large numbers of American soldiers on the ground. In July 1965 President Johnson took a fateful step: he agreed to send 180,000 American troops to Vietnam. The number of US troops increased over the next three years until there were 540,000 American soldiers in Vietnam.

SOURCE A

An American B-52 bomber attacks a target near Hanoi, 1966. The US tried to use its massive firepower to force the communists to retreat.

>> Activity

What can you learn from Sources B–D about why the USA got involved in Vietnam?

SOURCE B

Robert McNamara, US Secretary of Defense, March 1964:

We seek an independent, non-communist South Vietnam. Unless we can achieve this objective in South Vietnam, almost all of South-East Asia will probably fall under Communist dominance. Thailand might hold for a period with our help, but would be under grave pressure. Even the Philippines would become shaky, and the threat to India to the west, Australia and New Zealand to the south, and Taiwan, Korea and Japan to the north and east would be greatly increased.

SOURCE C

President Johnson, August 1964:

The challenge that we face in South-East Asia today is the same challenge that we have faced with courage and that we have met with strength in Greece and Turkey, in Berlin, Korea and in Cuba.

SOURCE D

The US government State Department reviewed its policy on Vietnam in February 1965.

South Vietnam is fighting for its life against a brutal campaign of terror and armed attack directed by the Communist regime in Hanoi. This aggression has been going on for years, but recently the pace has quickened and the threat has now become acute. The war in Vietnam is a new kind of war. A totally new kind of aggression has been loosed against an independent people who want to make their own way in peace and freedom. The war in Vietnam is not a spontaneous and local rebellion against the established Government. In Vietnam, a Communist Government has set out deliberately to conquer a neighbouring state.

The people of South Vietnam have chosen to resist this threat. At their request, the United States has taken its place beside them in their defensive struggle. The United States seeks no territory, no military bases, no favoured position. But we have learned the meaning of aggression elsewhere in the post-war world and we have met it. The United States will not abandon friends who want to remain free. It will do what must be done to help them.

The fighting intensifies

The arrival of large numbers of American soldiers stopped the collapse of South Vietnam and strengthened the position of the new South Vietnamese leader, General Thieu. Between 1965 and 1967 there was heavy fighting. The Americans regularly bombed North Vietnam. According to one calculation, more bombs were dropped on North Vietnam than on Germany in the Second World War. American involvement was widely criticised, and many people in the USA were unhappy about the war.

American tactics brought little success. The US forces had the technology to win straightforward battles between tanks or massed infantry. However, the Vietcong and the soldiers of North Vietnam refused to fight this kind of war. Instead they relied on guerrilla tactics: sabotage and sudden ambushes. The American response was to use:

> massive airpower to try to bomb supply lines,

> chemical defoliants to destroy areas of the countryside where communist soldiers might be hiding.

Neither of these methods worked; they simply angered the ordinary people of the Vietnamese countryside and increased support for the Vietcong and Ho Chi Minh.

The Tet Offensive

In January 1968 North Vietnam launched a massive attack at the time of Tet, a religious festival. Communist troops attacked towns all over the country. They struck right in the middle of the Southern capital of Saigon, with attacks on the American embassy. The communists hoped that the Tet Offensive would spark a popular revolution in the South. This did not happen. The losses on the communist side were enormous. About 50,000 communist troops were killed between January and March. The Americans used great force and won back the towns. American guns destroyed the historic centre of the ancient city of Hue, killing many civilians.

What were the results of the Tet Offensive?

The Tet Offensive was a turning-point in the war. Although in the short term it was a failure for the communists, in the long run it helped the North to win the war. The sight of communist fighters in the grounds of the American embassy in Saigon made a mockery of the idea that Americans were close to victory. As a result of the violence of the attack and the clear determination of the communists, many American politicians and people became disillusioned with the war. The anti-war movement in the USA grew in strength. Leading figures in the government began to think that they could not win the war in Vietnam.

SOURCE E

A Vietcong fighter lies dead in the grounds of the US embassy, Saigon, during the Tet Offensive, 1968. This was a turning-point in the war.

>> Activity

Look at the following quotations from the American adviser, Dean Acheson, made before and after the Tet Offensive. What difference is there between the two statements?

SOURCE F

Dean Acheson in November 1967:

We can and will win. We must not have negotiations. When these fellows decide that they can't defeat the South, then they will give up. This is the way it was in Korea. This is the way the Communists operate.

SOURCE G

Dean Acheson in March 1968:

Neither the effort of the Government of South Vietnam nor the effort of the US government can succeed. Time is limited by reactions in this country. We cannot build an independent South Vietnam. The issue is: can we by military means keep the North Vietnamese off the South Vietnamese? I do not think we can.

Johnson bows out and peace talks begin

At the end of March 1968 Johnson admitted that he had failed in Vietnam. Presidential elections were due later in the year; Johnson declared that he would not be seeking re-election. He reduced the level of bombing in the North. He called for peace talks. North Vietnam agreed to negotiate and talks began in Paris in May 1968.

The peace talks got nowhere, but it was clear by the summer of 1968 that the American government was looking for a way out. A new President was elected in November 1968 – Richard Nixon – and he was determined to end the war.

Nixon searches for peace with honour

The challenge for Nixon was to find a way out of Vietnam without humiliation or the clear abandoning of South Vietnam. Nixon tried a number of methods:

1 At the Paris peace talks he tried to persuade North Vietnam that North Vietnamese soldiers should withdraw from the South at the same time as American troops. He threatened a massive attack on the North if they refused to compromise. Nixon was bluffing, and the government of North Vietnam called his bluff. They refused to make a deal but Nixon did not launch an attack.

2 Nixon tried to persuade the USSR and China to use their influence over the government of the North. He told the Soviets and the Chinese that if they helped him over Vietnam the Americans would help them in other areas. This approach did not work. The USSR and China saw no reason to try to help the Americans over Vietnam.

3 Nixon decided to put more of the burden of the war on the shoulders of the government of South Vietnam. He reduced the number of American soldiers and insisted that more of the fighting should be done by South Vietnamese. In April 1969 there were 543,000 American troops in Vietnam. By 1971 the number had gone down to 157,000. This policy of passing responsibility to South Vietnam was known as 'Vietnamisation'.

SOURCE H

A British cartoonist, Nicholas Garland, ridicules Nixon's policy in 1969.
> What point is the cartoonist trying to make?

Atrocities at My Lai

The American war effort was hit by another devastating blow in 1969. It became known that US troops had carried out an appalling atrocity against Vietnamese civilians. On 16 March 1968 American soldiers massacred the villagers of a place called My Lai. The American officer, Lieutenant William Calley, was eventually court-martialled for the murder of 109 civilians. The story of what happened at My Lai horrified many Americans. They had seen their action in Vietnam as a fight against wicked communists. In My Lai all the wickedness was American.

SOURCE J

Murdered women and children at My Lai, 1968.

SOURCE I

In 1969 Time Magazine *reported a series of interviews with American soldiers who had fought at My Lai.*

Varnado Simpson: 'Everyone who went into the village had in mind to kill. We had lost a lot of buddies and the village was a VC [Vietcong] stronghold. We considered them either VC or helping the VC. As I came up on the village there was a woman, a man and a child running away. I told them in their language to stop. They didn't, and I had orders to shoot them down and I did this. This is what I did. I shot them: the lady and the little boy. He was about two years old.

Jay Roberts: 'Just outside the village there was this big pile of bodies. This really tiny kid – he had only a shirt on, nothing else – he came over to the pile and held the hand of one of the dead. One of the GIs behind me dropped into a kneeling position thirty metres from this kid and killed him with a single shot.'

Paul Meadlo: 'We ran through My Lai herding men, women, children and babies into the centre of the village. Lieutenant Calley came over and said, "You know what to do with them, don't you?" And I said, "Yes." and he left and came back about ten minutes later, and said, "How come you ain't killed them yet?" And I told him that I didn't think he wanted us to kill them, just to guard them. He said, "No, I want them dead." So he started shooting them. And he told me to start shooting. I might have killed ten or fifteen of them.'

Protests against the war

News of the atrocities at My Lai fuelled the anti-war feelings of many Americans. The war was shown on American television and this also caused many people to question why their country was fighting in Vietnam. As the peace talks made little progress in Paris there were increasing numbers of demonstrations in America calling for an end to the war.

SOURCE K

The British journalist, John Pilger, described the scene on 25 April 1971 when a huge demonstration of veterans, or former soldiers, protested in Washington against the war.

'The truth is out! Mickey Mouse is dead! The good guys are really the bad guys in disguise!' The speaker is William Wyman, from New York City. He is nineteen and has no legs. He sits in a wheelchair on the steps of the United States Congress, in the midst of 300,000, the greatest demonstration America has ever seen. He has on green combat fatigues and the jacket is torn where he has ripped away the medals and the ribbons he has been given in exchange for his legs.

Along with hundreds of other veterans of the war, he has hurled his medals on the Capitol steps and described them as shit. And now to those who form a ring of pity around him, he says, 'Before I lost these legs, I killed and killed and killed! We all did! Jesus, don't grieve for me!'

Never before in this country have young soldiers marched in protest against the war in which they themselves have fought and which is still going on.

SOURCE L

I WANT OUT

An American anti-war poster. It shows Uncle Sam as a wounded veteran who has had enough of the war. It is a parody of a First World War recruitment poster.

Did Vietnamisation work?

The South Vietnamese forces were not strong enough to defeat the communists. The government of General Thieu lacked the support and loyalty of the Vietnamese people. Thieu had the backing of landlords and Catholic Church leaders but crucially he had little support from the ordinary Vietnamese people in the countryside.

SOURCE M

When Nixon later wrote his memoirs he recognised the weakness of Vietnamisation.

The real problem was that the enemy was willing to sacrifice in order to win, while the South Vietnamese simply weren't willing to pay that much of a price in order to avoid losing.

As part of Vietnamisation the USA stepped up the bombing of the supply lines of the Viet Cong. This had the effect of spreading the conflict into neighbouring countries of Laos and Cambodia. The attacks on these countries did little to stop the supplies to the communist troops but did manage to encourage local communists. Between 1969 and 1973 the US dropped over half a million tons of bombs on Cambodia. This contributed to the support for the ruthless Cambodian communists, known as the Khmer Rouge. Communists won control of Cambodia in 1975. Similarly, the communist force known as Pathet Lao gained support in Laos and took control of the whole country in 1975.

The cease-fire: 1973

The peace talks in Paris dragged on for years without achieving anything. By 1972 the communists felt strong enough to launch another all-out attack on the cities of the South, similar to the Tet Offensive. This attack was more successful than the Tet Offensive but the communists were still not able to conquer the main centres of population. After the offensive of the summer of 1972, neither side could see any hope of victory and the peace talks started to make some progress. At last in January 1973 a cease-fire was agreed and the Americans started to take their troops home.

The fall of the South: 1975

The American forces pulled out soon after the cease-fire agreement was signed. This ended US involvement but it did not end the war. Fighting soon resumed between the communists and the Southern forces. Two years after the agreement in Paris the North launched another major offensive against South Vietnam in March 1975. This time, relying only on South Vietnamese troops and without American air support, the Saigon government was not able to resist. The Vietcong and the army of the North swept victoriously through the South. The war effectively ended on 29 April 1975 when the communists captured the southern capital of Saigon. American TV viewers watched in horror as thousands of south Vietnamese people fought to get on the last US helicopters out of Saigon.

After Vietnam: détente and a loss of confidence

American failure to contain communism in Vietnam led to a deep re-assessment of policy towards the communist world. American leaders had been shocked by their failure in Vietnam. The cost had been enormous: 55,000 dead American soldiers and billions of dollars spent. This huge commitment had achieved nothing. Communist governments had taken power not only in North and South Vietnam but also in the neighbouring states of Cambodia and Laos. In addition, Americans had lost the confidence in their mission as the world's leading nation.

The American President who took the US out of the war was Richard Nixon. Together with his adviser, Henry Kissinger, Nixon developed a new foreign policy for the post-Vietnam world. This became known as 'détente' and it involved striving for agreement and peace with the communist world.

>> Activity

Explain why the USA lost the war in Vietnam. In your answer describe:

a American military tactics,

b the impact of the Tet Offensive,

c atrocities such as My Lai,

d opposition to the war in the USA.

SOURCE N

Desperate scenes as the last US helicopters leave Saigon, just before the communist victory in 1975. A US embassy official punches a Vietnamese man who is trying to board the helicopter.

Nixon in China

Nixon tried to get better relations not only with the Soviet Union, but also with communist China. The world was surprised when Nixon announced in 1971 that he would visit China. Since 1949 the US government had treated China with contempt and had refused to 'recognise' the communist government. The visit took place in 1972 and led to much better relations between the two countries.

SOURCE O

The world was astonished when Nixon visited China in 1972.

Arms control

In dealing with the Soviet Union, Nixon emphasised the need for arms control negotiations. The Strategic Arms Limitation Talks (SALT 1) began in 1969 and led to the signing of an agreement on Intercontinental Ballistic Missiles in 1972. Nixon stated that American policy on nuclear weapons was now one of 'sufficiency', rather than 'superiority': this meant that the Americans wanted enough weapons to defend themselves and were no longer committed to having more than the Soviet Union. Détente also increased trade between the superpowers. In 1972 the US government agreed to supply wheat to the Soviet Union and soon a large proportion of all American wheat was exported to the Soviet Union.

In Europe, détente meant a reduction of tension over the divisions of Germany. In 1974 the USA formally recognised East Germany as an independent country. Détente allowed the two German states to establish better relations with each other.

Détente continued after Nixon's fall from office during the Watergate Scandal in 1974. Brezhnev, the Soviet leader organised a conference on the future of Europe in Helsinki between 1973 and 1975. This produced agreements on ways of avoiding confrontation between East and West and economic co-operation. The Helsinki agreements also committed all parties to respect human rights. Communist countries did very little to honour the pledge on human rights.

The end of détente

The US president, Jimmy Carter (in office 1977–80) attempted to achieve more arms reductions through the SALT 2 talks. These talks were very protracted. Carter annoyed Brezhnev by trying to link cuts in weapons to discussions of human rights in the communist countries. A SALT 2 treaty was finally signed in 1979. This set further limits on the number of nuclear weapons that each side could hold. The SALT 2 treaty was never ratified by the US Congress because the Soviet Union invaded Afghanistan in December 1979. The sending of troops into Afghanistan marked the end of the period of détente. The USA boycotted the Moscow Olympics in 1980 in order to show disapproval for the Soviet nation. In 1981, Carter was replaced by a hard-line President, Ronald Reagan, who rejected détente and who started a new arms race with the Soviet Union. The early 1980s have been called the Second Cold War. Reagan attacked Soviet communism in his speeches and talked of the need to oppose an 'evil empire'. His scientists were instructed to explore ways of giving the USA nuclear superiority by developing ways of shooting down Soviet missiles in space. This project was known as Star Wars, or the Strategic Defence Initiative.

>> Activity

Explain in your own words how American foreign policy developed after Vietnam.

Containing communism

After the communist take-over of Eastern Europe, US governments were preoccupied with the need to stop the spread of communism. This policy was called containment.

The fall of China: 1949

Led by Mao Zedong, communists took power in China in 1949. Communist success in China convinced American leaders that they needed to be more energetic in a worldwide struggle against communism. This led to a huge increase in American spending on defence.

The Korean War: 1950–3

At the end of the Second World War, Korea was divided in two at the 38th parallel – North Korea was communist, South Korea was anti-communist. North Korea invaded South Korea in June 1950. The Americans won UN support for a war against the invading North Koreans. General MacArthur led a fight-back that drove the North Koreans out of South Korea. MacArthur then continued to push deep into North Korean territory. This was going beyond 'containment' and became an attempt to 'roll back' communism.

A massive Chinese army invaded to help the North Koreans in November 1950. The US army was driven back close to the original border in early 1951. There was then a military stalemate. MacArthur wanted to widen the war by attacking China itself. President Truman disagreed and dismissed MacArthur. Peace talks dragged on for two years. The war finally ended in July 1953.

The Cuban Missile Crisis: 1962

Led by Fidel Castro, there was a revolution in Cuba in 1959. Castro introduced communist ideas to Cuba. The US attempted to invade and overthrow Castro, but this ended in disaster at the Bay of Pigs in 1961.

In 1962 Khrushchev, the Soviet leader, placed nuclear missiles on Cuba. American spy planes discovered them and the American President, Kennedy, insisted that the missiles should be removed. There was a real possibility of a nuclear war. Eventually Khrushchev gave way and agreed to remove the missiles in return for a US promise to remove missiles in Turkey. The ending of the crisis was seen as a victory for Kennedy and a defeat for Khrushchev.

Fidel Castro.

Restricting Soviet influence in the Middle East

Both the USA and the Soviet Union tried to influence states in the Middle East. The US encouraged the new Jewish state of Israel, set up in 1948. Some Arabs, including the governments of Egypt and Syria and the Palestine Liberation Organisation (PLO), looked for Soviet help in their conflict with Israel. With American money and weapons, Israel was able to defeat its Arab enemies in a series of wars (1948–9, 1967, 1973). These defeats convinced the Egyptian president, Sadat, to break with the USSR. The US government enabled Israel and Egypt to sign a peace treaty in 1979.

The Vietnam War: 1965–1975

Vietnam had been a French colony before the Second World War. The French pulled out in 1954 and Vietnam was divided between a communist state in the North, and and an anti-communist state in South Vietnam. The leader of North Vietnam was Ho Chi Minh.

After 1958 communist guerillas, known as the Vietcong, helped by troops of the regular army of North Vietnam, tried to overthrow the government of South Vietnam. At first the Americans supplied the South with money and weapons and in March 1965 President Johnson sent US combat troops to Vietnam. Eventually there were 540,000 Americans fighting in Vietnam.

The defeat of the USA

The USA was unable to defeat the Vietcong. Many people in the USA were opposed to the war. In January 1968 the Vietcong launched a massive series of attacks called the Tet Offensive. This was not a military success but it convinced American leaders that they would never win in Vietnam. President Johnson was replaced by Richard Nixon, who was determined to pull out of Vietnam. Nixon tried 'Vietnamisation' – a policy of reducing American troops and trying to strengthen the forces of South Vietnam. In 1973 the US signed a peace treaty with North Vietnam and Americans troops left the country. Vietnamisation did not work – without American forces the government of South Vietnam was overthrown by communist forces in 1975. Vietnam became a single, communist state. After the fall of Vietnam several neighbouring countries also became communist.

After Vietnam: détente

The US presidents of the 1970s – Nixon, Ford and Carter – pursued a policy of 'détente'. This involved establishing peaceful relationships with the two great communist powers: the USSR and China.

Defeat in Vietnam reduced American self-confidence. Further disasters followed:

> The pro-American government in Iran was overthrown in a revolution in 1978. American diplomats were taken prisoner and were held hostage from 1979–81.
> A Soviet army invaded Afghanistan in 1979 to support its new communist government.

Ho Chi Minh.

The end of détente

The new US President, Ronald Reagan, restored some of America's self-confidence in the 1980s. He ended détente. He aggressively challenged the Soviet Union and began a new arms race. This period has been called the Second Cold War. Reagan invested in 'Star Wars' (officially known as the Strategic Defence Initiative). This was intended to be a system for shooting down Soviet missiles in space. The Soviet Union could not compete. Gorbachev came to power in the Soviet Union and established good relations with Reagan. The arms race came to an end and the Soviet Union pulled out of Afghanistan in 1988–9.

Tito and Stalin

Orders from Moscow

After 1945 communists took power in some countries without Soviet help. This happened in Yugoslavia, where a communist leader called Tito led a successful war against occupying German forces between 1941 and 1945. At first, Tito seemed to be highly regarded by Stalin. In April 1945 Tito went on a tour of the USSR and was treated as a great hero. There was, however, an underlying tension between Tito and Stalin. The Yugoslav leader did not see why he should follow orders from Moscow.

Tito, the Leader of Yugoslavia. He successfully defied Stalin.

Tito and Stalin argued in 1948. There were two immediate causes of this rift between Yugoslavia and the USSR:

> Yugoslav foreign policy was at odds with Soviet plans. Tito wanted to control the small neighbouring state of Albania. In late 1947 the Yugoslavs annoyed Stalin by sending their troops into Albania.

> Tito was greatly offended by the way the Soviets recruited agents in Yugoslavia and asked them to report direct to Moscow. Many senior members of the army were asked to become Soviet spies.

'I will shake my little finger'

The conflict between Stalin and Tito was announced to the world in June 1948. Yugoslavia was thrown out of Cominform, the Soviet-led organisation for world communism. Stalin took action to bring Tito into line. Economic sanctions were used – the USSR and other East European states stopped trading with Yugoslavia. Stalin was confident that Tito could be overthrown. At the beginning of the split he said, 'I will shake my little finger and there will be no more Tito'. Stalin hoped that Yugoslav communists would turn against their leader. Tito dealt skilfully with his enemies. Local communists who sided with Stalin were arrested. People in Yugoslavia rallied round their leader.

Tito turns West

Tito believed that the USA and other Western countries would support him in his dispute with Stalin. He was right. Western countries were keen to help Yugoslavia survive the economic blockade. In December 1948 the British provided a $30 million trade deal. Over the next few years the Americans gave considerable financial support. With Western help Tito survived the early days of the split with Stalin. Having failed through other means Stalin began, in 1949, to threaten war. In the early 1950s the West began to give direct military help, as well as money. In 1951 the Americans provided the Yugoslav armed forces with equipment worth $60 million dollars.

Stalin spent his final years making sure that no other East European leaders tried to follow Tito. Some were accused of 'Titoism' and executed. According to some sources Stalin was making plans to have Tito poisoned when he himself died in 1953. After the death of Stalin, the new Soviet leader, Khrushchev, ended the dispute with Yugoslavia in 1955. This was a victory for Tito, who continued with his independent foreign policy.

Discussion points

> Why did Tito and Stalin argue?

> How successful were Stalin's attempts to destroy Tito?

The Red Army in Budapest and Prague

In 1956 the Soviet Union shocked the world by sending troops to overthrow the government of Hungary. A similar invasion of Czechoslovakia took place in 1968.

Why did the Soviet Union invade Hungary and Czechoslovakia?

>> Activity

Imagine that you were working for the United Nations in 1956. You have been asked to write a report on why the Soviet Union invaded Hungary. In your report you should discuss:

> why Hungarians disliked Soviet rule

> how the death of Stalin created a new situation in Eastern Europe

> the impact on Hungarians of events in Yugoslavia and Poland

> how the Soviet Union reacted to changes in Hungary.

Hungary and the Soviet Empire

The Hungarians were a proud nation with a strong sense of identity. Before 1918 they played a key part in the running of the vast Austro–Hungarian Empire. Hungarian nationalists did not like being part of a Soviet Empire after the Second World War.

Stalin's actions increased anti-Soviet feelings in Hungary. Free elections were held in November 1945. The communists got less than 20 per cent of the vote. Stalin ignored the decision of the Hungarian people and imposed a government on the country in which communists had many of the most important posts. In August 1947 another election was held in Hungary. This time the Soviet Union made sure that the

SOURCE A

Cardinal Mindszenty, leader of the Catholic Church in Hungary. As an opponent of Soviet communism he was sentenced to life in prison.

election was rigged so that the communists won. Between 1949 and 1953 Hungary was badly treated by Stalin. Opponents of Soviet power were dealt with ruthlessly. In 1949 the leader of the Roman Catholic Church in Hungary, Cardinal Mindszenty, was sentenced to life imprisonment. Even Hungarian communists were attacked if they showed any signs of disagreeing with Stalin. The leading communist, Laszlo Rajk, was put on trial and hanged in 1949 because he was too independent-minded.

After Stalin

The death of Stalin in 1953 created a new uncertain situation in Eastern Europe. During the Stalinist years, Hungary had been ruled with considerable brutality by Mátyás Rákosi. Rákosi managed to hang on to power after 1953, but he was forced to invite a reformer called Imre Nagy to join his government. The two men got on badly and in 1955 Rákosi got the upper hand and threw Nagy out of the government and the party.

Hungarians were not sure how far the new Soviet leadership would allow Hungary to operate as an independent country. For a number of reasons Hungarians hoped that they might be able to have greater independence:

> The new Soviet leadership was friendly to Tito's Yugoslavia. Yugoslavia had successfully broken away from Soviet control in 1948. People in Hungary thought that other countries could now follow the Yugoslav path.

> Stalin was criticised by the new Soviet leader, Khrushchev, in a famous speech in February 1956. Hungarians hoped that Khrushchev would be very different from Stalin and would be happy with a new, independent Hungary.

> In June 1956 there were anti-Soviet demonstrations in Poland. Khrushchev looked for a compromise. He allowed reforms and he appointed Gomulka, a man who had been imprisoned by Stalin, as the new leader of the Polish Communist Party.

The news from Poland seemed like further proof that the bad old days of Soviet control were over. In fact this was a mistake: the new Soviet leaders still wanted to control the countries of the Warsaw Pact. Hungarians listened to radio broadcasts from the West that criticised communism. Some felt that if Hungary challenged Soviet power they could expect help from the USA. Back in 1948 the Truman Doctrine had stated that the USA would help any people fighting against communism. In practice, the US theory of containment meant that America would only threaten force to stop the spread of communism; countries that were already communist could expect sympathy but no help.

SOURCE B

In 1955 Khrushchev visited Yugoslavia to make friends with Tito. He made a speech claiming that the USSR no longer wished to interfere in other states.

True to the teaching of the founder of the Soviet State, Lenin, the government of the Soviet Union bases its policy towards other countries, big and small, on the principle of peaceful co-existence. We believe in equality, non-interference, respect for sovereignty and national independence. The Soviet Union rejects aggression and believes that any invasion of another state is not to be permitted.

Alarm in Moscow

There was an air of excitement in Hungary in the summer of 1956. People heard the news from Poland. They wanted even more change in Hungary. They talked about Hungary breaking away from the Soviet bloc and becoming a neutral country. This was too much for Khrushchev. He could accept some changes but not Hungarian neutrality. If Hungary left the Warsaw Pact, other countries might follow. The protective buffer of friendly countries built up by Stalin might fall apart.

The Soviet leaders tried to stop the disturbances in Hungary by changing the leadership of the Hungarian communists. Realising that Rákosi was extremely unpopular, the Soviet leadership forced him to resign in July 1956. The new ruler was Ernó Geró. However, Geró was seen as a Stalinist by many Hungarians and the change of leader made little difference.

On 6 October 1956, Laszlo Rajk, the leading victim of Stalinist terror, was re-buried with a state funeral. A huge crowd turned out to show their support for the memory of Rajk and the idea of reform. Further demonstrations called for the removal of Geró and the reinstatement of the popular reformer Nagy. On 24 October Nagy became Prime Minister. Khrushchev had hoped that this would end the disturbances. It did not. Across the country, workers set up revolutionary councils. They demanded a complete end to the Soviet system in Hungary. They called for free multi-party elections, a free Press and for Hungary to leave the Warsaw Pact. Nagy agreed to accept these reforms. At this point Khrushchev decided to invade.

SOURCE C

Laszlo Rajk, on trial for his life. Stalin was afraid that this communist leader would copy Tito and break away from Moscow. Stalin ensured that Rajk was executed.

SOURCE D

The Soviet leader, Khrushchev, expressed his anxiety over Hungary in July 1956.

If the situation in Hungary gets still worse, we here have decided to use all means at our disposal to bring the crisis to an end. The Soviet Union could not at any price allow a breach in the front in Eastern Europe.

SOURCE E

The Soviet Foreign Minister, Shepilov, explained Soviet actions to the General Assembly of the United Nations on 19 November 1956.

We could not overlook the fact that Hungary is a neighbour of the Soviet Union. A victory of the reactionary forces would have converted that country into a new jumping-off ground for an aggressive war not only against the Soviet Union but also against the other countries of Eastern Europe.

>> Activity

1 Look at Source B. Why do you think that Hungarians who wished for independence were encouraged by Khrushchev's speech in 1955?

2 Look at the Sources D and E. What do they tell us about Soviet motives in invading Hungary?

The Soviet invasion

The Soviet forces reached Budapest on 4 November 1956. The Red Army forces comprised 200,000 soldiers and 2,500 tanks. The Hungarians fought against the invaders. At least 3,000 Hungarians were killed (some estimates are much higher). Despite Nagy's desperate appeal (Source G) neither the United Nations nor the USA did anything to help. The powerful Soviet forces took control of Hungary and imposed a new pro-Soviet government.

SOURCE F

Hungarian nationalists engaged in street fighting in Budapest, 4 November 1956.

SOURCE G

When he heard of the invasion, Imre Nagy, the Hungarian Prime Minister, appealed to the United Nations for help.

Reliable reports have reached the government of the Hungarian People's Republic that further Soviet units are entering Hungary. The Hungarian government immediately repudiates the Warsaw Treaty and declares Hungary's neutrality, turns to the United Nations, and requests the help of the great powers in defending the country's neutrality. I request Your Excellency to put on the agenda of the forthcoming General Assembly of the United Nations the question of Hungary's neutrality and the defence of this neutrality by the great powers.

AFTER THE RISING

> The new communist government of Hungary was led by a man called János Kádár. Under Kádár economic conditions in Hungary gradually improved.

> The supporters of the Rising were severely punished. Imre Nagy was executed in 1958.

> The Hungarian Uprising showed East Europeans that they could expect no help from the USA if they rose up against Soviet control. The US policy of 'containment' meant that the Americans would fight to stop the spread of communism but would not interfere if a country was already communist.

> There was a period of uneasy peace in Eastern Europe for the next 10 years. It was not until the mid-1960s that people in the satellite states once again challenged Soviet control. In 1968 the government of Czechoslovakia decided to develop a new form of communism that was much more liberal than Soviet communism.

> Communists around the world were dismayed by the way the Soviet Union used force against the Hungarian people. In Western Europe many communists were disillusioned. In China the leaders became more wary of Moscow.

> The invasion was a blow to the reputation of the United Nations. It did nothing to stop an act of aggression by one member state on another member state.

Czechoslovakia: 1968

Economic problems were a major cause of calls for reform in Czechoslovakia. The country had been economically successful before the Second World War. By the mid-1960s many people were very disappointed with the standard of living under Soviet-style communism. Czechoslovakia had also been a democracy before the war and people resented their lack of freedom of speech under the Soviet system. In 1966 there were student demonstrations and public criticism of the way the Soviet Union controlled the economy of Czechoslovakia. The student protesters called for greater democracy and free speech.

In January 1968 a new communist leader, Alexander Dubček, was appointed. He was determined to improve communism. His plans were described as 'socialism with a human face', and the early months of 1968 have become known as the 'Prague Spring'. Dubček began to introduce a number of reforms:

> the Soviet system of state planning would be altered to give more responsibility to farms and factories,

> trade unions would be given greater freedom,

> more foreign travel to the West would be allowed,

> censorship of the Press would be abolished so that people could say and write what they liked,

> criticism of the government would not be seen as a crime.

At the same time Dubček was still a communist. He did not want to introduce Western-style capitalism. Dubček knew what had happened in 1956. He tried to re-assure the Soviet leaders that his reforms were less radical than those called for during the Hungarian Uprising. He stated repeatedly that he wanted Czechoslovakia to remain a loyal member of the Warsaw Pact. He insisted that changes in Czechoslovakia were no threat to the security of the Soviet Union.

Brezhnev, the Soviet leader, did not accept these assurances from Dubček. He was afraid that once the communist system allowed free speech the country would become chaotic. Brezhnev felt that the Czechoslovak reforms were the first step towards the country leaving the communist bloc and becoming a Western-style country, allied to the USA. He was not prepared to allow this. Czechoslovakia was in an important strategic position. If it was allied to the USA, it would provide a corridor along which American forces could march from West Germany to the Soviet Ukraine. Brezhnev was also under pressure from hard-line communists in East Germany. They argued that if free speech was allowed in Czechoslovakia, people in all other Eastern bloc countries would demand the same rights. This would weaken the power of the communist parties throughout Eastern Europe.

SOURCE H

Dubček during the early days of the Prague Spring.

Help from the USA?

Brezhnev, the Soviet leader, began to plan an invasion of Czechoslovakia. By late July Soviet tanks and troops were massed on the Czechoslovak border. Brezhnev was encouraged by developments in the West. The American government was in crisis in the summer of 1968. There were race riots in the black districts of several cities. The war in Vietnam had gone disastrously wrong for the USA. Brezhnev calculated that there was no possibility of America taking any action to stop the invasion. The Vietnam crisis distracted attention from Czechoslovakia, just as in 1956 the Suez crisis reduced the impact of the invasion of Hungary.

SOURCE I

A letter of warning was sent by the Soviet leadership to the Czechoslovak Communist Party, 15 July 1968.

Developments in your country are causing deep anxiety among us. We are convinced that your country is being pushed off the road of socialism and that this puts in danger the interest of the whole socialist system.

We cannot agree to have hostile forces push your country away from the road of socialism. We cannot accept the risk of Czechoslovakia being cut off from the socialist community of countries. This is something more than your own concern. It is the common concern of all communist parties and states. It is the common concern of our countries, which have joined in the Warsaw Treaty to place an insurmountable barrier against the imperialist forces.

At great sacrifice the people of our countries achieved victory over Hitlerian fascism and won the opportunity to follow the path of socialism. The frontiers of the socialist world moved to the centre of Europe. And we shall never agree to these historic gains and the security of our peoples being placed in jeopardy. We shall never agree to imperialism making a breach in the socialist system of countries.

SOURCE J

Dubček's response to the Soviet threat made matters worse. He invited Tito, the independent communist leader of Yugoslavia, to Prague. Tito arrived on 9 August. To Brezhnev this seemed like a signal that Dubček was moving away from the Warsaw Pact and towards the same independent position taken by Yugoslavia. Dubček also entered into negotiations with the Romanian leader, Nicolae Ceauşescu. A pact of friendship between Czechoslovakia and Romania was signed. The Romanian leader also resented control from Moscow. The closer ties between these two countries seemed like an attempt to undermine Soviet control of the Warsaw Pact.

The Warsaw Pact forces invade

Soviet forces crossed the Czechoslovak frontier on 20 August 1968. They were joined by token forces from East Germany, Poland and Bulgaria. A day later the Warsaw Pact forces were in Prague, the capital of Czechoslovakia. Large-scale loss of life was avoided because the Czechoslovak government decided not to resist the invading army. People took to the streets to protest but there was none of the bloody street fighting that had taken place in Budapest in 1956. The Soviet troops took Dubček to Moscow and ordered him to abandon his reforms. He was finally removed from office in 1969. A pro-Soviet leader called Husák took his place. Soviet power was demonstrated in May 1970 when a Soviet–Czechoslovak treaty was signed. In this the Czechoslovaks were forced to thank the Soviets for the invasion.

Rioting in Prague as Soviet tanks take over the city. In contrast with Budapest, there was relatively little bloodshed in Prague.

THE AFTERMATH OF CZECHOSLOVAKIA 1968

After the invasion Brezhnev said that the Soviet Union was not prepared to let any communist country abandon communism. If a state did try to give up communism, the Soviet Union claimed the right to impose communism by force. This view became known as the Brezhnev Doctrine. The doctrine was finally abandoned in the 1980s.

The way the Soviet Union dealt with Czechoslovakia was less bloody than the treatment of Hungary after 1956. Nagy was executed. Dubček was thrown out of the communist party in 1970. He spent the 1970s and 1980s working as a forestry inspector. However, he kept his life and his freedom.

The government of China was unhappy at the invasion and it led to a further deterioration in relations between the two communist superpowers. The Chinese disliked the way the Soviet Union treated other communist countries. Afterwards, Mao encouraged Yugoslavia and Romania to remain independent of Moscow. There were border clashes between Soviet and Chinese troops in the months after the invasion.

The invasion disillusioned communists around the world. In Western Europe many communists stopped looking to Moscow for guidance. In the 1970s the powerful Italian and French communist parties called for a new style of communism that allowed free speech and free elections.

>> Activity

1 Explain in your own words why Brezhnev decided to invade Czechoslovakia in 1968.

2 Look back at the whole of this unit. What similarities and differences were there between the Hungarian Uprising and the invasion of Czechoslovakia? Think about the following aspects of each event:

> the causes of unrest,

> the aims of the people wanting change,

> the reasons why the Soviet Union found these changes unacceptable,

> the way the Soviet Union invaded,

> the treatment of the leadership after the invasion.

Building the Berlin Wall

In 1945 Berlin was divided into American, British, French and Soviet zones. Berlin itself was deep inside the Soviet zone of eastern Germany. This created a curious situation in Berlin. The American, British and French zones joined together to form a single area known as West Berlin. It became an island of Western capitalism in the middle of the communist sea of East Germany. In 1961 a wall was built to separate East and West Berlin. This became the most famous symbol of the Cold War.

Why was the Berlin Wall built?

> ### BERLIN AND MOSCOW
>
> The existence of West Berlin was very annoying to Soviet leaders in Moscow:
>
> > It was much more prosperous than communist East Germany and was an advertisement for the economic success of Western Europe.
>
> > Western governments used Berlin as a headquarters for their spying activities.
>
> > German people could move freely from communist East Germany to West Berlin. Many decided to flee via West Berlin. Between 1949 and 1960, 3 million East Germans fled to the West through Berlin. These people were often young, talented and well-educated. The communist government could not afford to lose its future managers and leaders.

The crisis over Berlin was not simply about the problems the city posed for East Germany. It was part of the wider Cold War struggle between the USA and the USSR. In the early 1960s both countries had confident, aggressive leaders. The Soviet leader was Nikita Khrushchev and the American leader was John F. Kennedy. Each one was convinced that his side was right and each one was ready to threaten war to get what he wanted.

Khrushchev and the Soviet challenge

Nikita Khrushchev had emerged victorious from the power struggle that followed the death of Stalin in 1953. Khrushchev was confident that Soviet communism would eventually triumph over Western democracy and capitalism. He believed that the communist world was just about to overtake the West in wealth and scientific research. In October 1957 the Soviets launched the world's first ever satellite, called Sputnik. Khrushchev thought that this proved the strength of the communist world. Convinced of the increasing power of communism, Khrushchev decided to extend communist influence in Europe. He chose Berlin as the place for a trial of strength.

SOURCE A

In speeches made in 1958, Khrushchev expressed his view that Soviet communism was overtaking the West.

The launching of the Soviet sputniks first of all shows that a serious change has occurred in the balance of forces between socialist and capitalist countries, in favour of the socialist nations.

January, 1958

We are firmly convinced that the time is approaching when socialist countries will outstrip the most developed capitalist countries in the volume of industrial production.

October, 1958

Khrushchev calls for a neutral Berlin

The crisis that led to the building of the wall started in 1958 when Khrushchev called for the end of the four-power control of Berlin. He set a time limit of six months for the settlement of the future of Berlin. There was a vague threat of war if the matter was not resolved. His own plan was that Berlin should become a neutral free city and Western troops should withdraw. The Western powers were divided about how to react to Khrushchev. The West German leader, Konrad Adenauer, was strongly against any deal. By contrast, The US President, Eisenhower, was ready to negotiate over the future of Berlin. As the deadline approached Eisenhower made it clear that he did not want to risk a war over Berlin. Khrushchev dropped his ultimatum. At a summit meeting in September 1959 Eisenhower said that he was prepared to make concessions on the future of Berlin.

SOURCE C

Eisenhower's views at the 1959 summit:

We must remember that Berlin is an abnormal situation. It has come about through some mistakes of our leaders – Churchill and Roosevelt. There must be some way to develop some kind of free city which might somehow be part of West Germany. Perhaps the UN would become a party to guaranteeing the freedom, safety and security of the city. Berlin would have an unarmed status except for police forces. The time is coming, and perhaps soon, when we would simply have to get our forces out.

The U-2 spy plane incident

So far, Khrushchev had been very successful. Through threatening war he had divided the Western allies and won a promise of change from the US President, Eisenhower. Khrushchev and Eisenhower agreed to meet for further discussions about Berlin in May 1960.

This meeting did not take place. Just before it was due to start, an American U-2 spy plane was shot down over Soviet territory. The pilot, Gary Powers, was taken prisoner and put on trial. Khrushchev demanded an apology. Eisenhower refused to apologise. Khrushchev cancelled the summit meeting. As a result he missed his chance to do a deal over Berlin.

SOURCE B

An exhibition about Gary Powers and his U-2 spy plane, held in Moscow in 1960. The US government was extremely embarrassed by the U-2 incident.

A change of president

Eisenhower retired at the end of 1960. The new President was the young John F. Kennedy. In his election speeches Kennedy said that he was going to be tougher with the Soviets than Eisenhower.

SOURCE D

Extracts from John F. Kennedy's campaign speeches in 1960:

The enemy is the communist sytem itself – unceasing in its drive for world domination. This is a struggle for supremacy between two conflicting ideologies: freedom under God versus ruthless, godless tyranny.

We will mould our strength and become first again. Not first if. Not first but. Not first when. But first period. I want the world to wonder not what Mr Khrushchev is doing. I want them to wonder what the United States is doing.

The threat of war

Kennedy brought a new firm approach to the argument over Berlin. Kennedy and Khrushchev met in Vienna in June 1961. This was unfriendly and unsuccessful. Khrushchev demanded that Berlin should become neutral. He angrily talked about the danger of war if the USA refused to pull out of Berlin. Banging his hands on the conference table, Khrushchev said,'I want peace, but if you want war, that is your problem.' Kennedy ended the conference by saying. 'It's going to be a cold winter.'

SOURCE E

Kennedy and Khrushchev at the summit meeting in Vienna, 1961. At this meeting both sides threatened war.

Afterwards Khrushchev repeated his demands in public and insisted, as he had done with Eisenhower, that the USA must act within six months. At the same time he increased Soviet spending on defence by 30 per cent. Unlike Eisenhower, Kennedy was in no mood to do a deal. At the end of July Kennedy announced a complete rejection of the Soviet demands. He ordered a massive increase in the American armed services: the number of troops was increased by 15 per cent, spending on defence was increased by $3 billion and many new aircraft and warships were ordered. In public speeches both Kennedy and Khrushchev suggested that they were ready for war over Berlin:

SOURCE F

Kennedy made a television and radio speech to the American people on 25 July 1961.

I have heard it said that West Berlin is militarily untenable. Any dangerous spot is tenable if men – brave men – will make it so. We do not want to fight – but we have fought before. We cannot and will not permit the Communists to drive us out of Berlin, either gradually or by force. There is peace in Berlin today. The source of world trouble and tension is Moscow, not Berlin.

SOURCE G

In late July 1961 Khrushchev spoke to an American diplomat and threatened war:

If your troops try to force their way to Berlin, we will oppose you by force. War is bound to go thermonuclear, and though you and we may survive, all your European allies will be completely destroyed.

Behind the angry words it seems that neither side was really willing to start a nuclear war over the future of Berlin.

SOURCE H

On his way back from the Vienna summit Kennedy described his private thoughts.

It seems particularly stupid to risk killing a million Americans over an argument about access rights on an Autobahn or because the Germans want Germany reunified. If I'm going to threaten Russia with a nuclear war, it will have to be for much bigger and more important reasons than that.

Building the wall

While Khrushchev threatened nuclear war, he secretly planned a different solution to the Berlin crisis. The continued uncertainty over Berlin increased the number of East Germans who fled to West Berlin. Every day over a thousand East Germans entered the Western part of the city. In the early hours of 13 August 1961 barbed wire and barricades were erected all around West Berlin. When the people of West Berlin woke up their city was sealed off from East Germany. The barbed wire was later replaced by more substantial barriers; the Berlin Wall was created.

SOURCE I

An 18-year-old builder, Peter Fechter, shot dead behind the East Berlin side of the wall while trying to escape to the West.

WHO GAINED AND WHO LOST FROM THE BUILDING OF THE BERLIN WALL?

> The flow of refugees from East to West stopped almost completely. This allowed the communists to consolidate their control over East Germany.

> Enemies of communism could argue that communism was so awful that people had to be walled in to make sure that they did not run away from communism.

> Between 1948 and 1961 there was a real possibility that arguments about Berlin would lead to a Third World War. This possibility stopped with the building of the Berlin Wall.

> People in East Germany who did not support communism were now trapped. Those who tried to get over the wall were shot.

> The building of the wall was the beginning of a period of calm in Europe. On both sides people accepted that there was no immediate prospect of change and the level of tension went down.

>> Activity

Explain why the Berlin Wall was built. In your answer mention:

> how West Berlin came to exist,

> why West Berlin annoyed Soviet leaders,

> why Khrushchev was keen to confront the USA,

> the different reactions of Eisenhower and Kennedy to Soviet threats.

Solidarity

In 1980 a remarkable new development took place in Eastern Europe. Since the communist take-over in the 1940s Moscow had not allowed any real political opposition to communism in the countries of Eastern Europe. In Poland, in 1980, this changed. A powerful non-communist organisation called Solidarity challenged the government.

What part did Solidarity play in the decline of Soviet power?

The challenge of Poland

With a population of 35 million, Poland was, after the Soviet Union, the largest country in Eastern Europe and there were several reasons why the Soviets had problems controlling Poland:

1   Much of Poland had been ruled by Russia since the eighteenth century. Most Poles were proud of their nation and disliked Soviet communism.

2   The Second World War increased the Poles' hatred for Soviet Russia. Stalin had carved up their country with Hitler in 1939. In 1940 Stalin massacred thousands of Polish Army officers and buried them at Katyn. In 1944 the Soviet Red Army deliberately allowed the Warsaw Rising to fail, with huge loss of Polish life.

3   Most Poles were Catholics. The Catholic Church, which was too well-organised to be broken by the communists, encouraged Polish nationalism. In 1978 a leading Polish churchman became Pope John Paul II.

4   Ordinary Polish people had more power than in other communist countries. Polish farmers successfully held on to their own farms. Among Polish factory workers there was a strong tradition of using strikes against the government. In 1956 and 1970 strikes had forced the communist government to change both its leaders and its policies.

The birth of Solidarity

Polish living standards were poor in the 1970s. The communist government had large international debt. In July 1980 new price rises led to widespread unrest and strikes. Strikers were particularly active at the Lenin shipyards in the town of Gdansk (formerly Danzig). The workers at Gdansk were led by a remarkable man, an electrician called Lech Walesa. He was a brilliant speaker. In August the striking workers set up a new trade union called Solidarity. Unlike all other trade unions in communist states, Solidarity was not controlled by communists. Soon it had 9 million members and was demanding not only better conditions for workers, but also more political and religious freedom. Unrest spread throughout Poland. The communist leader, Gierek, was replaced in September as the communist party tried to find a way out of the crisis. In November, judges in the Polish Supreme Court sided with Solidarity and declared that the union was legal.

SOURCE A

Lech Walesa, the Solidarity leader, speaking at Gdansk, 1980.

Once Solidarity was formed and became a national force, the Polish communist leaders were in an impossible position:

> If they tried to destroy Solidarity they would be despised by the great majority of the Polish people.

> If they accepted the existence of a non-communist opposition force they risked provoking an armed invasion by the USSR.

Send in the tanks?

In December 1980 and March 1981 the Soviet leaders considered sending troops into Poland to impose Soviet power, just as they had done in Hungary in 1956 and Czechoslovakia in 1968. They decided against immediate armed intervention but urged the Polish communists to destroy Solidarity before it got out of control. A new Polish Prime Minister was appointed called Wojciech Jaruzelski. He was a communist and an army general. The Soviet leaders made it clear to him that he must control Solidarity or expect a Soviet invasion.

SOURCE C

Speaking in 1995, Jaruzelski described the pressures that were put on him in 1981.

At first the Soviets gave us an ultimatum: either bring the situation under control or we will cut off supplies of oil, gas and other raw materials. I was summoned three times to the Soviet Union. On the last occasion, in September 1981, I was shown army manoeuvres all along the Polish border. The Soviet army leader, Marshal Ustinov, informed me that what was happening in Poland was intolerable. We had to convince our allies that we would not undermine the Warsaw Pact or allow the state to be de-stabilised. The introduction of martial law allowed us to avoid military intervention.

SOURCE B

General Jaruzelski. The communist leader knew that if he did not control Solidarity, Soviet tanks could invade Poland.

Martial law

Jaruzelski tried to negotiate with Solidarity but the talks were not successful. In December 1981 he took the advice from Moscow and declared a state of martial law in Poland. This meant that the army had emergency powers. The leaders of Solidarity and thousands of its supporters were arrested and held without trial. Meetings and demonstrations were forbidden. Many supporters of Solidarity lost their jobs. In October 1982 the government tried to replace Solidarity with new communist unions.

Jaruzelski's attempt to destroy Solidarity did not work. Walesa was imprisoned but this made him seem even more of a hero. The movement survived underground. No one took the new unions seriously. Communist party members left the party in huge numbers. Almost a year after the declaration of martial law, in November 1982, Walesa was released from prison.

SOURCE E

A British newspaper later summed up the impact of martial law on Walesa while in prison:

Walesa waited, his message to the government the same, 'You will have to talk to us again. Without the public consent, which only Solidarity can deliver, your economic reforms can never succeed.' The claim was the simple truth.

He emerged from prison to a surprising discovery – Poland was not a political wasteland. In addition to the Solidarity underground network there were new groupings producing an extraordinary range of newspapers, journals and books. Far from being snuffed out, the opposition to Communist rule had been broadened and strengthened.

The *Observer*, 'Tearing down the Curtain', 1990

SOURCE D

In 1983 Walesa was awarded a Nobel Prize for his work for Solidarity. In the same year the Pope visited Poland and was greeted with great enthusiasm. He was another symbol of hope for Polish opponents of communism. In 1984, Polish people were outraged to learn that Father Jerzy Popielusko, a priest who supported the union, had been beaten to death by secret police. The continuing support for Solidarity was shown when a quarter of a million people attended his funeral.

Huge enthusiastic crowds turned out to greet Pope John Paul II during his visit to Poland in 1983.

The impact of Gorbachev

In 1985 the political mood in Poland began to change because of the rise to power of Gorbachev in the USSR. By calling for greater freedom in the Soviet Union Gorbachev undermined old-style communism in Eastern Europe. The threat of Russian tanks also began to disappear.

Jaruzelski introduced reforms similar to those being tried in the USSR under Gorbachev. Jaruzelski held a referendum in November 1987 asking for backing for his economic reforms. He failed to win enough votes which was a great blow to his authority. In 1988 Walesa and the still illegal Solidarity organised a nationwide series of strikes against price rises. Walesa called for talks with the government and finally Jaruzelski agreed. As a result of these talks Solidarity was once again legalised and elections were organised for June 1989.

Solidarity triumphs in elections

For the first time since the 1940s free elections were being held in Eastern Europe but the freedom was limited. They were organised so that 65 per cent of seats in the main chamber of the Polish Parliament were reserved for communists. Nevertheless, the elections were a disaster for the communists. So few people voted for them that they looked ridiculous. Almost all leading communists failed to get elected. The Polish people voted massively for Solidarity. In the Polish Senate, the second chamber of the Polish parliament, there were no restrictions and Solidarity won 99 out of 100 seats. Weeks of chaos followed as the discredited communists tried and failed to form a government. Eventually, Jaruzelski agreed that Solidarity could help to form a government. In August, Tadeuz Mazowiecki, a leading member of Solidarity, became the Prime Minister of a coalition government that included both communist and Solidarity ministers. In less than a year Solidarity had gone from being illegal to being the leading part of the government. The remaining communist ministers soon resigned and the Solidarity take-over was complete.

SOURCE F

Bronislaw Geremek was a leading Solidarity activist. He reacted emotionally when in August 1989 Solidarity helped to form a government:

For the first time in 45 years, a Polish government is to be formed, on Polish soil, by non-Communist forces. The monopoly of the Party which ruled Poland against the will of the people has been broken.

>> Activity

1 Explain in your own words why the Soviet Union had always found it difficult to control Poland.

2 Why were the leaders of the Soviet Union worried when Solidarity was set up in 1980–81?

3 How successful was the introduction of martial law?

4 How did Solidarity take power in 1989?

SOURCE G

A Solidarity demonstration in 1989. In that year Solidarity triumphed in elections.

Gorbachev and the fall of the Soviet Empire

Between 1985 to 1991 Mikhail Gorbachev was the leader of the USSR. In 1989 Soviet control of Eastern Europe collapsed. In 1991 the Soviet Union fell apart.

Was Gorbachev responsible for the collapse of communism in Europe?

FOCUS

Look at the following information about the Soviet Union and Eastern Europe before Gorbachev came to power. What were the long-term causes for the collapse of communism?

The standard of living

In the early 1960s, communists had been convinced that communism was better than capitalism and that the communist states would soon produce more goods than in the USA and Western Europe. By the 1980s it was clear that communism had failed to deliver high living standards. Most people in the Soviet Union and Eastern Europe were much poorer than the people of Western Europe. Some basic goods, such as sugar, were rationed. The gap between communist and capitalist economies was growing all the time. The Soviet Union and its allies were not able to compete with the West in the new industries of the 1980s – computers and telecommunications.

By the 1980s Soviet farming had failed. The Soviet Union had rich land at its disposal but it could not produce enough food to feed its people. Many people worked on the land but they were very inefficient. In the 1980s farming employed over 20 per cent of the workforce, compared with 3 per cent in the USA. On average each American farmer produced seven times more food than each Soviet farmer. As a result the USSR had to import millions of tons of grain, much of it from the USA.

SOURCE A

Leonid Brezhnev.

Corruption and the decline of communism

The founders of communism promised a new kind of state based on fairness and equality. Under the leadership of Brezhnev, Soviet communism moved a long way from these ideals and became more corrupt. As a result ordinary people had less respect for communism. It was widely known that the family of Brezhnev was corrupt. Leading communists had luxurious country houses or 'dachas' built for themselves. According to one joke that circulated in the Soviet Union at the time, Brezhnev showed his own mother round a new luxury house that he had just had built; his mother commented 'It's wonderful, Leonid. But what happens if the communists come back to power?'

A second Cold War

With the communist economies in trouble, the cost of the Cold War became more and more unbearable. The price of weapons was constantly increasing. By the 1980s a single bomber cost the same as 200 bombers built during the Second World War. America and its allies could afford these higher costs because their economies were doing well. The Soviet Union could only keep up with the USA by diverting a huge proportion of its national income to defence. People suffered even lower living standards as tanks were built instead of cars and televisions.

The cost of the Cold War began to increase when the US President, Ronald Reagan, came to power in 1981. He rejected the idea of detente and encouraged a policy of confrontation with the Soviets. He took the view that communism was wicked and needed to be approached with great firmness. Reagan increased military spending and challenged the USSR to join a new arms race.

The early 1980s have been called the 'Second Cold War' because there was heightened tension between the USA and the Soviet Union. The competition between the superpowers was symbolised by Reagan's 'Star Wars' project (officially known as SDI: the Strategic Defence Initiative). This project involved research into ways of giving America nuclear superiority by destroying Soviet missiles in space.

War in Afghanistan

Brezhnev made a big mistake in December 1979. Soviet troops invaded Afghanistan to support its communist government. The invasion was widely criticised and lost the USSR many friends. It led to a widespread boycott of the Olympic Games that were held in Moscow. Afghanistan was a Muslim country and the USSR was criticised by much of the Islamic world. The Afghan rebels received help from the USA and the invasion encouraged Reagan to take a tough anti-Soviet stance when he became president in 1980.

The Soviet military action was a failure. The official Afghan army was not strong enough to win alone and once the Soviet forces had become involved it became very difficult to withdraw. With Soviet help the Afghan government controlled Kabul, the capital, and other large towns, but the rebels controlled much of the countryside. More and more Soviet troops were needed to prop up an unpopular government. In the early 1980s there were about 125,000 Soviet troops in the country.

The situation of the Soviets in Afghanistan was similar to that of the Americans in Vietnam a decade earlier. The 10-year war led to the death of about 15,000 Soviet troops. It also damaged the Soviet economy: one estimate is that the war cost the USSR about $8 billion dollars a year. The last Soviet troops finally left Afghanistan in February 1989.

SOURCE B

Soviet troops fighting anti-communist forces in Afghanistan. The war in Afghanistan damaged the international reputation of the Soviet Union.

Andropov and Gorbachev

The ideas of Gorbachev were not completely original. By 1980 there were many younger, idealistic communists who were disgusted by corruption and wanted to reform the system. Several reformers gathered around the head of the KGB, Yuri Andropov. Gorbachev was one of this group. Brezhnev died in 1982 and Andropov became the new Soviet leader. Within a few months he became desperately ill and he died in February 1984. Although he was not in power long, Andropov introduced some policies that were later developed by Gorbachev:

> He called for an end to the arms race, and offered to reduce the Soviet stockpile of weapons in return for American reductions.

> He attacked corruption at home.

Andropov made a number of offers to Reagan. One of these was revolutionary – this was a plan to abandon the Brezhnev Doctrine and to promise never again to invade other Warsaw Pact countries. Reagan did not take this offer seriously and it came to nothing. Although Andropov had many original ideas he did little to provide more freedom for the people of the Soviet Union. As the KGB Chairman from 1967–82 he had played a key role in the persecution of dissidents, nationalists and different religious groups. After the death of Andropov, the new leader of the Soviet Union was Konstantin Chernenko. He had little interest in reform. Like Andropov, Chernenko did not live long enough to have much impact. He died in 1985 and his replacement as General Secretary was the reformer Mikhail Gorbachev. He introduced policies of 'glasnost' or 'openness' and 'perestroika' or 'economic restructuring'.

One critical difference between Gorbachev and Andropov was in the way glasnost gave new freedom to the people of the Soviet Union. This was a radical change. Control of ideas had always been a central part of the Soviet system. Under glasnost, people were told an increasing amount about the atrocities committed by the government when Stalin had been in power. Thousands of political prisoners were released. The leading dissident Andrei Sakharov was released in 1986.

THE GORBACHEV AGENDA

> The economy was failing. The communist system needed to be reformed but not replaced. This would be done by a process called 'perestroika' or 'restructuring'.

> Perestroika would require a new honesty on the part of people in the Soviet Union. Free speech should be allowed. There should be a new spirit of 'glasnost' or 'openness'. There should be an end to the persecution of the dissidents.

> Corruption must be stamped out.

> A key cause of the economic problems was the amount of money being spent on defence. To reduce this the Soviet Union should:

pull out of Afghanistan

negotiate arms reductions with the USA

stop interfering in the affairs of other communist countries.

Another distinctive feature of the Gorbachev leadership was the energy and imagination with which he pursued the idea of disarmament with the US president, Reagan. Unlike Andropov he was able to persuade Reagan that he genuinely wanted an end to the Cold War. The two men met, face-to-face, at a series of summit meetings. The main focus for these discussions was arms control. The result was a major disarmament treaty in 1987. Both the USA and the Soviet Union agreed to remove medium-range nuclear missiles from Europe within three years.

Withdrawal from Afghanistan

As soon as he was in office, Gorbachev began to explore ways of ending the war in Afghanistan without destroying the communist government in that country. In February 1988 he announced publicly that the Soviet army was going to pull out of Afghanistan. The withdrawal began in May 1988. By February 1989 the last Soviet troops had left.

Failure at home

Gorbachev had many triumphs in foreign policy but he was less successful at home. By encouraging free speech, Gorbachev simply brought problems out into the open. He wanted to make the Soviet system of centrally planned production more efficient. This did not happen. The levels of corruption and inefficiency in the economy were too great. The managers of the Soviet economy saw the reforms as a threat to their jobs and they blocked the changes.

>> Activity

1 What similarities and differences were there between the policies of Andropov and those of Gorbachev?

2 What can you learn from Sources C and D about the motives of Gorbachev?

SOURCE C

Gorbachev 1987:

I want to put an end to all the rumours in the West, and point out once again that all our reforms are socialist. We are looking within socialism, rather than outside it, for the answers to all the questions that arise. Those who hope that we shall move away from the socialist path will be greatly disappointed.

SOURCE D

In 1992, after he had lost power, Gorbachev tried to make sense of his years in control:

I knew that an immense task of transformation awaited me. Engaged in the exhausting arms race, the country, it was evident, was at the end of its strength. Economic mechanisms were functioning more and more poorly. Production figures were slumping. Scientific and technical developments were cancelled out by an economy totally in the hands of the bureaucracy. The people's standard of living was clearly declining. Corruption was gaining ground. We wanted to reform by launching a democratic process. It was similar to earlier reform attempts.

SOURCE E

Gorbachev and Reagan, 1987. The two men established a warm personal relationship and agreed to substantial disarmament.

The end of the Brezhnev Doctrine

Another foreign policy breakthrough came in December 1988, when Gorbachev spoke at the United Nations. He announced huge cuts in the Soviet armed forces. Gorbachev also made it clear that the Brezhnev Doctrine was now abandoned: the countries of Eastern Europe could do what they liked. There would be no more Soviet tanks rolling into Prague or Budapest.

SOURCE F

Gorbachev, speaking to the United Nations on 7 December 1988:

Force or the threat of force neither can nor should be instruments of foreign policy. The principle of the freedom of choice is mandatory. Refusal to recognise this principle will have serious consequences for world peace. To deny a nation the choice, regardless of any excuse, is to upset the unstable balance that has been achieved. Freedom of choice is a universal principle. It knows no exception.

SOURCE G

1989: year of revolution

When it became clear that the Soviet Union was no longer ready to use force to control its Empire, there was rapid change. In May 1989 the Hungarian government opened the frontier with Austria; there was now a gap in the Iron Curtain. In June free elections were held in Poland. Solidarity won and in August led a new non-communist government. Gorbachev expressed support for a peaceful hand-over of power. The rolling back of communism in Eastern Europe had begun. Many young East Germans made their way to Hungary and passed though Austria into West Germany. This made a nonsense of the Berlin Wall.

In October 1989 Gorbachev visited East Germany for the celebration of the fortieth anniversary of the state. Behind the scenes Gorbachev explained to East German leaders that he had no intention of using Russian force to stop reform. A month later, on 10 November, the Berlin Wall was torn down. The most famous symbol of the Cold War had been destroyed. On 17 November a series of massive anti-communist demonstrations took place in Czechoslovakia. By early December the Czechoslovak communist government had collapsed. On 21 December a revolution began in Romania. The Romanian dictator, Ceauşescu, was executed on Christmas Day. Throughout Eastern Europe there was no popular support for communism and, without the threat of Soviet tanks, communism fell apart. In 1990 the two halves of Germany were re-united and a single pro-Western state was established.

The collapse of European communism was symbolised by the fall of the Berlin Wall, November 1989.

The last days of the USSR

After 1989 Gorbachev was in a difficult position. His plan to reform communism had failed. Communism had been rejected by Eastern Europe and different nationalities demanded independence from the Soviet Union. The call for independence was strongest in the Baltic republics of Latvia, Lithuania and Estonia. In Russia itself, the heart of the USSR, many people demanded an end to communism. On 4 February 1990, 250,000 people demonstrated in Moscow against communism.

With his plans in ruins Gorbachev responded by drawing back from reform and trying to make an alliance with old style, hard-line communists. On May Day 1990, demonstrators humiliated Gorbachev by shouting at him in public during the traditional communist march.

The rise of Yeltsin

Boris Yeltsin became the leader of the reformists. He had been a communist boss in the city of Moscow until he was dismissed in 1987 by Gorbachev because of his radical views. In May 1990 Yeltsin was elected President of Russia. The USSR was divided into separate republics and Russia was the largest of them. A month later Yeltsin left the communist party and joined forces with those who wanted to destroy Soviet communism. Gorbachev was losing control of events.

In the autumn of 1990 Gorbachev tried to stop the disintegration of the USSR by using force against nationalists in the Baltic republics. At the same time Gorbachev appointed more old-style communists to key positions of government. This new hard line from Gorbachev was not a success. He began to lose many of his long-standing friends and supporters. In December 1990 the Soviet Foreign Minister, Eduard Shevardnadze, resigned and complained of a move towards dictatorship. This was a great blow – Shevardnadze had been one of Gorbachev's allies for many years.

The fall of Gorbachev

The struggle for control of the USSR came to a head in 1991. Yeltsin attacked the power of the communist party in the daily life of Russian people. He banned the party from operating at all places of work. The Russian Parliament that Yeltsin controlled became more powerful and challenged the central government of Gorbachev. Gorbachev did not know which way to turn. In August 1991 a group of hard-line communists tried to seize power. They arrested Gorbachev and declared a state of emergency. The coup was opposed by Boris Yeltsin and it soon collapsed. After the coup, the authority of Gorbachev was damaged. In December 1991 the individual Soviet republics became independent and Gorbachev resigned as Soviet leader. The Soviet state, born in the 1917 revolution, no longer existed.

SOURCE H

Boris Yeltsin at the time of the 1991 coup. Yeltsin took power in Russia as the Soviet Union fell apart.

>> Activity

Explain the part that Gorbachev played in the collapse of communism in Eastern Europe and the Soviet Union. In your answer discuss:

a the long-term causes of the crisis for communism,

b the personal contribution of Gorbachev.

The Soviet Empire 1948–91

The split with Tito

The Yugoslav communist leader, Tito, liberated Yugoslavia from German control without help from Moscow. He argued with Stalin and refused to take orders from Moscow. In 1948 Yugoslavia was expelled from Cominform, the international grouping of communist parties. The Soviet Union imposed a trade ban on Yugoslavia but they survived due to support from the USA. Stalin dealt ruthlessly with other East European countries between 1949 and 1953. He was worried that they might try to copy Tito. Leading communists with independent ideas were imprisoned or executed.

TURMOIL IN THE COMMUNIST WORLD AFTER STALIN

> After Stalin's death in 1953 people in Eastern Europe hoped for more freedom from Soviet control.

> The new Soviet leader, Khrushchev, established friendly relations with Yugoslavia in 1955. Hungarians hoped to copy Yugoslav independence.

> In 1956 unrest in Poland led to reforms and concessions by the communist government. This encouraged Hungarians to demand reforms.

The Hungarian Uprising

In October 1956 unrest in Hungary led to the appointment of a new Prime Minister, the communist reformer, Imre Nagy. People demanded that Hungary should leave the Warsaw Pact and become neutral. Nagy agreed but in November 1956 Soviet troops invaded Hungary and imposed a new pro-Soviet government. There was fierce street fighting in which thousands of people were killed. Nagy was arrested and later executed. The USA did nothing to help the Hungarians: people in the West were preoccupied with the Suez crisis.

The Prague Spring

Economic problems caused unrest in Czechoslovakia in 1967. A new communist leader, Dubček, took power in January 1968. He introduced democratic reforms while remaining communist. In August 1968 Soviet troops invaded Czechoslovakia to end the reforms. Dubček lost his job in 1969 and a pro-Soviet government was put in place. Afterwards the Soviet leader, Brezhnev, announced the 'Brezhnev Doctrine': the Soviet Union would use force to keep communists in power in any country.

1956 AND 1968 COMPARED

> In both cases the Soviet Union used force to end reforms in East European countries. New pro-Soviet governments were imposed.

> The Hungarian government wanted to break with the Soviet Union, leave the Warsaw Pact and become neutral. The Czechoslovak government wanted much more democracy at home but promised to stay in the Warsaw Pact.

> In both cases the USA did nothing to help. The West was preoccupied with Suez in 1956 and Vietnam in 1968.

> The Hungarians fought against the Soviet invasion – thousands were killed. The Czechoslovak people offered non-violent resistance. The Hungarian leader, Nagy, was executed; the Czechoslovak leader, Dubček, lost his job but remained alive and free.

The Berlin Wall

Between 1958 and 1961 there was a dispute between the Soviet Union and the USA over Berlin. The Soviet leader, Khrushchev, said that Western forces should leave the city and that it should become neutral. The US president, Eisenhower, was prepared to compromise but he was replaced in 1961 by President Kennedy. Kennedy refused to compromise and both leaders publicly threatened war over Berlin. In 1961 the crisis was resolved, and the threat of immediate war disappeared, when a wall was built around West Berlin to stop East Germans fleeing the communist state.

Poland and the rise of Solidarity

Shipyard workers in Gdansk went on strike in 1980 in protest against rising prices. They were led by Lech Walesa and formed a new non-communist trade union called Solidarity. Millions of workers joined Solidarity. The Soviet government considered invading Poland in order to crush the union. To avoid this the Polish communist leader, Jaruzelski, banned Solidarity in December 1981. He declared martial law and imprisoned Solidarity leaders without trial but failed to destroy the union. Solidarity did well in elections in 1989 and formed a non-communist government.

SOVIET COMMUNISM IN DECLINE

The Soviet Union was in crisis by the early 1980s:

> The economy had failed to match the economies of America and Western Europe.

> The arms race further reduced living standards.

> There was widespread corruption.

> The Soviet Union was fighting a disastrous war in Afghanistan.

The second Cold War

After the Vietnam War the USA pursued a policy of detente with the Soviet Union. This involved peaceful co-existence and some arms reductions. Ronald Reagan became president of the USA in 1981 and he ended détente and began a new arms race with the USSR.

Gorbachev

Mikhail Gorbachev, a reformist communist, took control in the Soviet Union in 1985. He wanted to improve the Soviet Union by 'perestroika' – 'restructuring' or reforming the economy – and 'glasnost' – greater 'openness' and freedom of speech. His reforms undermined the position of old-style pro-Soviet leaders in other countries. He renounced the 'Brezhnev Doctrine' of interference in other countries.

The whole of communist Europe was swept with revolution in 1989. One by one, the communist authorities were overthrown. The Soviet Union led by Gorbachev did nothing to stop this process. The Berlin Wall was torn down in November 1989. In 1991 the Soviet Union fell apart. After a failed communist coup in August, the republics that made up the USSR declared their independence. Gorbachev resigned. Russia became a separate state ruled over by Boris Yeltsin.

Crowds outside the Reichstag celebrate the reunification of Germany, 3 October 1990.

BRITISH HISTORY
1906–1918

What was Britain like in 1900?

Britain in 1900 included England, Scotland, Ireland and Wales. It was one of the wealthiest states in the world, although about a third of British people were poor, and it had an empire that stretched across one fifth of the world's land mass. The Industrial Revolution is the key to understanding why Britain was in this position.

Britain was the first country to industrialise from about 1750 onwards. New machines were invented to quicken and increase production; water wheels, steam power and then electricity replaced horses and muscle power; money was invested in new businesses; and the growing population at the time both supplied the workers for the new factories and increased demand for mass produced goods. These factors combined together to spur Britain's economy and change dramatically the lives of the people on these islands.

New cities sprung up, linked together first by canals and then, after the 1840s, by the faster railway system. By 1900 nearly 80% of British people lived in urban districts with populations of 10,000 or more. They were connected by 18,680 miles of railways and the improved road system and could communicate by using the telegraph, the newspapers and penny postage. In 1902 the Post Office opened its first telephone exchange and by 1910 Britain had 122,000 telephones. Industry was linked with trade. Railways and canals connected the new centres of manufacturing like Leeds, Sheffield, Newcastle and Birmingham with ports like London, Bristol, Cardiff and Liverpool. To these ports came raw materials from the colonies; cotton from India, for example. From these ports British manufacturers sent finished goods to all corners of the empire and beyond.

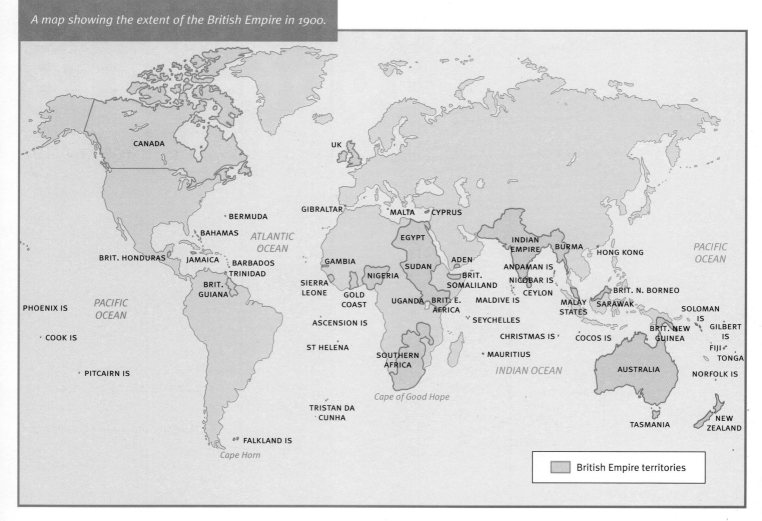

A map showing the extent of the British Empire in 1900.

British Empire territories

The harvest in progress. A photo of rural life in 1899. The numbers of those working on farms had declined dramatically during the nineteenth century.

Pressures building for change

The growth of these new cities and large towns was unplanned. Increasing numbers of workers in small areas resulted in cramped and unhealthy living conditions; working conditions had improved but were not much better. Daily contact and large numbers meant workers could meet, discuss and organise themselves to act as groups rather than as individuals. One result was the development of trade unions in various parts of the country and these gave the workers more influence in trying to improve pay and conditions. Easier communication meant that some of the unions developed into national organisations: workers acted together to educate themselves, discuss new political ideas, write pamphlets and build up their own funds from membership subscriptions. They also had a powerful weapon to use against their employers: the strike.

Better communication and improved literacy rates helped to open people's minds to new ideas about how society should be run and what role men and women should play. The press was the single, most important means of communication. In newspapers, magazines, pamphlets and journals, writers undermined common attitudes and beliefs: women demanded the right to vote in national elections; politicians went abroad and wrote about the social reforms in countries like Germany and proposed similar schemes in Britain to remedy social ills, and socialists demanded that the gap between the rich and the poor should be closed. Not everyone was convinced by these fresh ideas. Traditional views remained fixed in the minds of many: know your place and defer to and respect those in power.

Discussion points

> Why was the development of cities and large towns (urbanisation) a crucial factor in creating pressures for change in Britain?

> What possible social and economic benefits would there be for a government that introduced social reforms to help the sick, the poor and the unemployed?

> Why would the British government want to defend the empire against rivals?

Weavers at work in a factory in Lancashire, c.1900.

Who ruled Britain in 1900?

New economic and social pressures for change were opposed by a minority of the upper and middle classes who ran the political system. Power in 1900 was in the hands of relatively few wealthy men. Queen Victoria had some influence but very little power. Only 28.5% of the adult population could vote and these were all men; even fewer were qualified to become Members of Parliament. Elected MPs from across the country sat in the House of Commons to debate and pass new laws. But the process did not stop there. The bills (as the proposed laws were called) were then discussed and voted on by the House of Lords – mostly unelected landowners. If the Lords rejected the bill there was nothing that the House of Commons could do about it. As David Lloyd George, a future Prime Minister, put it in 1909: how could 'five hundred ordinary men, chosen accidentally from among the unemployed' override 'the judgement of millions of people who are engaged in the industry which makes the wealth of the country?'

British society

British society was, in many ways, divided along lines of class and gender. Class was determined by family background, property ownership and education. The class system produced huge inequalities. At the top of society in terms of wealth, power and influence was the aristocracy or upper class. Their wealth was usually inherited and derived from owning large areas of land. They lived a life of leisure and some families, like the Stanleys, the Russells and the Cavendishes had sent representatives to the House of Lords for generations. Nearly all of them were natural supporters of the Conservative Party who enjoyed a majority in the unelected second house despite making up only a tiny proportion of the population.

Next came the middle class. These were professionals (doctors, lawyers, accountants), owners of small businesses like shops or factories, or tenant farmers. They were able to vote in elections and a few who were wealthy enough decided to become MPs. The political loyalties of the middle class tended to be divided: some supported the Conservatives while others joined the Liberal Party.

At the bottom was the working class. A minority of working class people were reasonably well off by 1900, but the majority lived close to the poverty line. A promise of a better future for the working class came in the form of a new political party that claimed to represent their interests. In 1900 the Labour Representation Committee was established – in 1906 it changed its name to the Labour Party. In the years before 1900 those few working class people who had the vote had supported the Liberal Party; but disappointment with the lack of substantial change resulted in the creation of the Labour Party.

Men's attitudes to women and women's attitudes towards themselves ensured that in 1900 British society was divided as much by gender as it was by class. Women of all three classes were firmly under the influence of men. Women had no political power because they could not vote in general elections or become Members of Parliament. Trade unions were also male-dominated. Although middle and working class women worked in a range of occupations it was not until 1882 that married women were allowed to own their own property. Although there were signs of improvement, these were very slow in coming and many women believed that one way to accelerate change was to win the vote and make Parliament take more notice of their demands.

A middle class family painted by Sir William Orpen in 1907.

A photograph of a street in Whitechapel, London, 1900.

Table 1

Land in the British Isles held in estates of over 1000 acres, 1880.

Country	Number of owners	% of total land area
England	4,736	56.10
Wales	672	60.78
Ireland	3,745	78.40
Scotland	1,758	92.82
Total	10,911	66.14

Table 2

The size and social composition of British Cabinets, 1895–1919.

Year	Party	Cabinet size	Aristocrats	Middle class	Working class
August 1895	Conservative	19	8	11	0
July 1902	Conservative	19	9	10	0
December 1905	Liberal	19	7	11	1
July 1914	Liberal	19	6	12	1
January 1919	Coalition	21	3	17	1

Discussion points

> What inequalities were there in 1900?

> Why do you think so many people accepted these inequalities?

> To what extent do these inequalities still exist today?

Poverty in Britain at the beginning of the twentieth century

Towards the end of the nineteenth century and the beginning of the twentieth century several surveys about the poor were carried out in Britain. In 1886 Charles Booth began a systematic investigation into the number of poor in London. Booth surveyed London's poor over a number of years and, between 1889 and 1903, filled seventeen volumes with his evidence and conclusions. While Booth was surveying London, Seebohm Rowntree began investigating the poor in the much smaller city of York. In 1901 his findings were published under the title *Poverty: a study of town life*.

How much poverty was there in Britain in 1900?

SOURCE A

A working class family in the East End of London, c.1900.

SOURCE B

Booth's main conclusions from his survey of London's poor.

Booth calculated that 21 shillings (£1.05) a week for a family was enough to maintain a minimum standard of health whilst paying out for food, clothing and shelter and to make adequate provision against the possibility of sickness, accident and unemployment in the future.

30% of people are below the poverty line.

38% of working class people are below the poverty line.

SOURCE C

Rowntree's main conclusions from his survey of York's poor.

Rowntree calculated that for two adults and three children 21 shillings and 8 pence (approximately £1.08) each week was enough income to avoid poverty.

10% of people living in York are in 'primary poverty'.

15% of working class people are in 'primary poverty'.

18% of people living in York are living in 'secondary poverty'.

28% of working class people are in 'secondary poverty'.

(Primary poverty was when people did not waste money but income was still insufficient; secondary poverty was a condition where income was sufficient to maintain health but not enough to provide security against unemployment, old age or illness.)

Rowntree concluded that: 'the proportion of poverty in London is equalled in York. We are faced with the startling probability that between 25% to 30% of the urban population are living in poverty.'

SOURCE D

An extract from a letter from Booth to Rowntree, 25 July 1901. This is in response to Rowntree's comments in Source C.

Our totals (of those in poverty) may be correctly compared, and the comparison, as you have shown is very close. At this I am not surprised. I have long thought that other cities, if similarly tested, would show a percentage of poverty not greatly differing from that existing in London.

SOURCE E

Rowntree produced this diagram of the poverty cycle. It shows the stages during a lifetime when poverty increased and decreased.

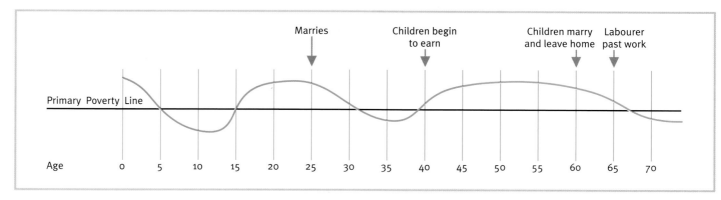

Young children increased the demands upon their father's wage and so the first experience of poverty often came early in life. Adolescence and the opportunity to start earning eased this pressure but marriage, and their own children soon pushed young workers back towards the poverty line. Relief came as their children became self-sufficient but in time earnings began to reflect the onset of old age and declining strength.

SOURCE F

In 1912 and 1913 A. L. Bowley and A. R. Burnett-Hurst carried out a survey into poverty. These are their conclusions.

6% of the people in Stanley (in the north-east of England) were poor.

9% of the people in Northampton (in the Midlands) were poor.

15% of the people in Warrington (in the north-west of England) were poor.

29% of the people in Reading (in the south-east of England) were poor.

SOURCE G

An extract from a history book, British Labour History, 1815–1914 by E. Hunt, published in 1981.

How much reliance can be placed on the results of the early poverty surveys? Few of the results can be accepted with complete confidence. Booth relied heavily upon information from school attendance officers. So families with children of school age were over-represented in his sample although he thought they were typical of the population as a whole.

Some food experts nowadays think that Rowntree over-estimated the amount of food a working class family needed to be healthy. When people from the middle classes asked them, the working classes often said that they earned less than they did. Rowntree's survey was undertaken at a fairly prosperous time, his definition of the family's minimum necessary expenditure on items other than food was mean.

Activities

1 Study Source A. How can you tell that this family is not rich?

2 How useful would this photograph be to a historian investigating the causes of poverty?

3 Study Source B. What questions would Booth's investigators have to ask the family in order to decide whether or not they were poor?

4 Study Sources A, B and E. At what stage in the poverty cycle is the family shown in Source A?

5 The authors of Sources F and G have challenged the conclusions of Booth and Rowntree that similar levels of poverty might be found in most British towns. They have also found errors in the way that Booth and Rowntree carried out their surveys. Does this mean that the evidence from Booth and Rowntree is not reliable?

6 How much poverty was there in Britain? Try to use all the sources in your answer to this question.

Lloyd George and the Liberal social reforms

In 1906 the Liberal Party won a landslide victory at the polls and had a massive majority in the House of Commons. The leader of the Liberal Party at the time was Henry Campbell-Bannerman and his cabinet included talented politicians like David Lloyd George and Winston Churchill. In the five years following the Liberal victory a series of social reforms were made law that aimed to address poverty and ill-health by supporting the young, old and unemployed.

David Lloyd George, Chancellor of the Exchequer between 1908 and 1915. He was responsible for munitions during 1915–16 and was then Prime Minister between 1916–22.

Social reforms were nothing new. During the nineteenth century the government of the day had acted in response to the worst effects of the Industrial Revolution. In 1833, 1844, 1847 and 1867 Factory Acts were passed to limit the hours worked by women and children, and to ensure that no child under the age of nine was employed. The Public Health Act of 1875 compelled local authorities to improve sanitation and to appoint a Medical Officer of Health. In 1870 the Education Act created 2,500 local school boards to provide elementary education for the children of the poor; the school leaving age was set at eleven in 1893 but raised to twelve in 1899.

These and other changes are examples of where the state had already intervened in people's lives before the 1906 election. What was different about the 1906–11 reforms was that so much was packed into so short a time and that to pay for all the new legislation new taxes had to be raised and the rich would have to pay. The power of the House of Lords to reject bills passed by the Commons was about to be challenged.

The Conservative Party had a majority in the House of Lords and they considered the Liberal reforms too expensive: the country could not afford to pay for pensions and insurance whilst Britain was falling behind in the naval arms race with Germany. Furthermore, many Conservatives considered the state should only play a strictly limited role in people's lives and the new reforms would go beyond that. Above all else the Lords did not want to pay more tax and lose their power.

In 1909 David Lloyd George, the new Chancellor of the Exchequer, presented his People's Budget to the House of Commons. In his financial proposals for the country ordinary people would pay the same amount of tax, but those who earned more than £3,000 per year would pay about 1% more. Those who earned more than £5,000 per year would pay an extra 2.5%. Increases in land tax and death duties were also proposed.

THE PHILANTHROPIC HIGHWAYMAN.

Mr. Lloyd-George. "I'LL MAKE 'EM PITY THE AGED POOR!"

A cartoon from Punch, *5 August 1908 showing Lloyd George as an armed highwayman.*

The House of Commons passed the People's Budget but the Lords rejected it. A long and bitter struggle ensued. Lloyd George asked an audience at Oxford 'whether this country is to be governed by the king and his peers [lords], or by the king and his people?' The Duke of Beaufort remarked that he would like to see Lloyd George and Winston Churchill in the middle of a pack of twenty hunting dogs. The House of Lords was nicknamed 'Mr Balfour's poodle' by Lloyd George – Balfour was leader of the Conservative Party. The Lords only conceded when the king threatened to create enough Liberal peers to pass the budget. The House of Lords lost its right to veto money bills but could still delay other legislation for a period of two years.

RICH FARE.

The Giant Lloyd-Gorgibuster : "FEE, FI, FO, FAT,
I SMELL THE BLOOD OF A PLUTOCRAT;
BE HE ALIVE OR BE HE DEAD,
I'LL GRIND HIS BONES TO MAKE MY BREAD."

A cartoon from Punch, *28 August 1909 showing Lloyd George as a giant about to slay the rich.*

Table 1

Date	Act	Main purposes of the new law
1906	Workmen's Compensation Act	Required employers to pay compensation for injuries sustained at work from unsafe or unhealthy conditions. This covered workers who earned less than £250 per year.
1906	Trades Disputes Act	No union could be sued for damages as a result of losses incurred during strike action.
1906	School Meals Act	Tried to ensure that children of the poor were given one good meal each day. Local authorities were not compelled to provide meals but could use money raised from local taxes (rates) to provide meals. This became compulsory in 1914.
1907	Education Act	Set up the Schools Medical Inspection Service to give free medical examinations and basic treatment for school children.
1908	The Children Act*	Children under the age of 16 forbidden to go into pubs or smoke cigarettes. No child under the age of 14 could be put in prison. There were penalties for parents who neglected their children. Children were forbidden from doing unsuitable work. Special schools for disabled children started in 1908.
1908	Old Age Pensions Act	Introduced pensions of 5 shillings (25p) per week for single people over 70 whose income was less than £26 per year; and 7 shillings and 6 pence (37.5p) a week for married couples earning less than £39 per year.
1909	Trade Boards Act	The Factory Acts in the nineteenth century were extended to apply to tailoring and lace making, where long hours, poor conditions and low pay were usual.
1909	Labour Exchanges Act	1 Labour Exchanges were set up to help the unemployed find jobs. 2 The government established a development fund at the disposal of local authorities for the reduction of unemployment by public works.
1910	Education Act	Tried to cut down the number of children leaving school and going into dead-end jobs by providing them with some vocational training.
1911	National Insurance Act	There were two parts to the Act. 1 A compulsory health insurance scheme was set up. Each worker paid 4 pence a week, the employer 3 pence, and the state 2 pence. The scheme entitled each worker to 10 shillings a week sickness benefit during absence from work through illness. The scheme applied only to those workers earning less than £160 per year. 2 The Act introduced limited insurance against unemployment for those in the building, engineering, shipbuilding and iron and steel making industries.

The Children's Charter*

The Children Act of 1908 is sometimes known as the Children's Charter. Other parts of the Charter detailed what parents were expected to do for their children regarding their care, medical attention, abstention from alcohol and cigarettes, and the prevention of injuries or burns. The Children's Charter also established juvenile courts for cases involving children; borstals were started to train youngsters in 'better habits' rather than resorting to prison; and probation officers were trained to stop children re-offending.

A Conservative Party poster criticising the Children Act of 1908.

Discussion points

> To what extent does the Children's Charter of 1908 mirror parental responsibilities and children's rights today?

> Study the two cartoons and the poster. Why do you think there was so much opposition to most Liberal reforms yet the Children Act of 1908 was passed easily by both Houses of Parliament?

> Do the Liberal reforms represent a turning point in state provision for the poor, the sick and children or is the period 1906–11 part of a trend stretching back into the nineteenth century?

Social reform 1906–11

Ever since the Liberal reforms were introduced historians have argued about the reasons why they were implemented. Some of the arguments have arisen because historians have taken different approaches to the key question: why were the reforms introduced? One approach has been to treat all the reforms together as a single big change (Table 1); the second approach has been to take each reform in turn and see them as individual solutions to particular social problems (Table 2).

Why did the Liberal government introduce reforms to help the young, old and unemployed?

Table 1

Year	Historian	Interpretation of why the Liberal reforms were introduced
1930	Slater	Several factors: the increasing number of middle class and working class voters put pressure on politicians to make changes; the impact of feminism; the birth rate was falling and so children were more highly valued as national assets; and the shock on learning about the poor physical condition of army recruits fighting in the Boer War.*
1932	Halévy	Concern about the empire and social reform were linked. The changes were made because politicians were worried that Britain was falling behind Germany and the USA and needed to catch up. The wealth of a country was dependent upon the health of its people.
1967	Thompson	The Liberal government was worried about the popularity of the new Labour Party and so it passed the reforms to ensure the support of the working class at election time.
1975	Hay	Other countries, facing similar social problems, adopted similar reforms to the Liberals. The reforms were a response by governments in capitalist societies to the effects of economic growth and industrialisation.

CONCLUSIONS OF RECENT RESEARCH CONDUCTED BY HISTORIANS

1 Democratic pressures from working class voters seem to have had little impact on the thinking of politicians who initiated the social reforms.

2 Social reform was not an issue during the 1906 election campaign for the leaders of any political party; some individual Liberal party candidates did campaign for it.

3 The impact of the Boer War (1899–1902) on attitudes is very difficult to separate from the impact of other health concerns that arose before the beginning of the war.

The Boer War 1899–1902*

The war was fought between the British and the Boer descendants of Dutch settlers in South Africa. The significance of the war in terms of social reform concerns the men who came forward as recruits to fight there. 40% of them were rejected as physically or medically unfit; this figure was as high as 60% in Leeds and Sheffield. The men were undernourished and many were living on a diet of bread, tea and margarine. Reports on the health of these soldiers shocked the public and politicians of all parties. These reinforced the conclusions of Booth and Rowntree in their surveys of London and York.

Discussion points

> Look at the conclusions from recent research. Which interpretations in Table 1 now seem to be less justified?

> Why do interpretations of history change over time?

Table 2

Why were there social reforms specifically for children?	Many politicians, especially Liberals and Conservatives were worried about the young because they believed that healthy children were an asset to society. Healthy children would improve national efficiency – a fit population would lead to an efficient and prosperous nation. Pressure from the Civil Service was also needed to ensure Parliament passed the Education Act of 1907. A leading civil servant, Sir Robert Morant, Permanent Secretary of the Board of Education, wanted to use medical inspection of schoolchildren to highlight preventable diseases and to link this with treatment. It was his persistence that convinced the Liberal Cabinet.
Why were there social reforms specifically for the old?	The Liberal government was persuaded by humanitarian arguments and the powerful evidence from Booth and Rowntree's surveys which suggested that the majority of the working class found it impossible to save enough money to provide for old age. The government was further influenced by a pressure group, the National Committee of Organised Labour on Old Age Pensions.
Why were there social reforms specifically for the unemployed?	Unemployment had been an issue since the 1880s when it had reached very high levels. Some writers saw it as the root cause of crime, begging and prostitution. Broader public concern was heightened by the riots involving unemployed workers in 1886–7. The economic trade depressions in 1892–5, 1903–5 and 1908–9 all produced high levels of unemployment.
	The Liberals came to power with no party commitment to tackle unemployment. Labour MPs and trade unions tried to pressure the government; and then, in the first nine months of 1908, the Liberals lost seven by-elections to the Conservatives and unemployment figures reached their highest peak since 1886. With the death of the Liberal Prime Minister Campbell-Bannerman in April 1908, Lloyd George and Winston Churchill became more important figures in the Liberal government and some historians argue that it was Churchill's drive and initiative that led to the National Insurance Act.
Why were there social reforms relating to health?	The health insurance scheme was designed to complement the provision for the unemployed. Rowntree had uncovered a low standard of health amongst the working class. Some enlightened employers pressured the government to do something because they understood the benefits of a healthy workforce. The 1911 Act did not attempt to tackle the causes of ill-health but Lloyd George tacked onto the insurance scheme the right to treatment for tuberculosis in sanatoria and some money for medical research.

Activity

Using Table 1 and Table 2 make a list of causal factors under the following headings to explain why reforms were introduced 1906–11.

Reforms affecting:	What factors made the reforms possible? Long-term factors	What factors made the reforms likely? Medium-term factors	What factors made the reforms happen when they did? Short-term/trigger factors
Children			
Old			
Unemployed			
Sick			

SOURCE A

Written by Winston Churchill in 1901 when he was an MP but not a government minister.

I have been reading a book by Mr Rowntree called *Poverty* which has impressed me very much ... it is evident from the figures that the American worker is a stronger, larger, healthier better fed and consequently more efficient animal than a large proportion of our own population ... I see little glory in an empire which rules the waves, and is unable to flush its sewers.

SOURCE B

Lloyd George speaking as a Member of Parliament in 1890.

What are the real causes of poverty among the industrial classes? Old age, bad health, the death of the bread-winner and unemployment. When Bismarck [German Chancellor in the 1880s] was strengthening the German Empire, one of his first tasks was to set up a scheme which insured German workers and their families against the worst evils arising from the accidents of life. And a superb scheme it is. It has saved a huge amount of human misery among thousands of people.

SOURCE C

Lloyd George, Chancellor of the Exchequer, speaking in public in 1909.

Help for the aged and the deserving poor – it is time it was done. It is a shame that a rich country like ours – probably the richest in the world – should allow those who have toiled all their days to end in poverty and starvation.

SOURCE D

Lord Curzon remarked in 1910.

We can hardly take up our morning paper without reading of the physical decline of the race ... beaten in cricket, then in polo!

SOURCE E

Social reforms in other countries.

Year	Country	Type of reform
1880s	Germany	Health insurance, accident at work insurance, old age and disability pensions
1898	New Zealand	Old age pension scheme

SOURCE F

A graph comparing steel production between Britain, Germany and the USA between 1870 and 1900.

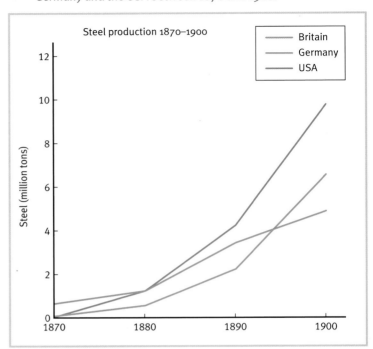

SOURCE G

A graph comparing output of coal in Britain and Germany between 1870 and 1910.

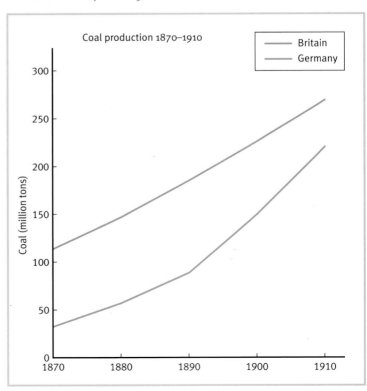

SOURCE H

From a history book by J. R. Hay, 1975.

Some reforms were a response to a particular specific electoral situation as was the case with the decision to proceed with labour exchanges and unemployment insurance in 1908–9. But this isn't a complete explanation. Lloyd George and Churchill looked beyond individual pieces of legislation towards the creation of a society in which the worst ravages of poverty would be eliminated. They thought the reforms would stop people voting Labour and support the Liberals instead, contribute to the efficiency of the British economy by preventing the physical and mental deterioration of the workers, and provide a measure of social justice which would attract working class votes without alienating the middle classes.

Activities

1 Study sources A, B and C. Can you see any connections with the idea of national efficiency?

2 Sources A, B and C are statements by politicians. Can we trust sources like these in determining their motives?

3 Study sources E, F and G and use your own knowledge. How far do they support the judgements expressed in Sources A, B, C and D?

4 Study Source H and use your own knowledge. Which parts of Hay's interpretation can you find evidence to support? Which parts are less easily justified from the evidence you have?

5 Look back at your table that explains the causes of the reforms. Do Sources A to H support your previous conclusions on the long-, medium- and short-term factors explaining why the reforms were introduced?

How effective were these reforms?

There is no doubt that taken together the Liberal reforms are an impressive series of laws. However, both Lloyd George and Winston Churchill did not see their reforms as final solutions to the problems of ill-health, poverty and unemployment; instead the changes were temporary provisions to help the very poor. So, how effective were the reforms?

Undoubtedly, old age pensions were very popular and effective. In the first year of operation (1909–10) about 570,000 pensioners made weekly visits to their local post offices to draw their money. However, it was only provided for those over the age of 70 and life expectancy at that time was 52 years for men and 55 years for women. Furthermore, the weekly payment of 5 shillings was reduced if money was still being earned.

Sickness insurance was compulsory for everyone earning up to £160 per year. Sick workers were entitled to 10 shillings a week and free medical care from a doctor. About 15 million people were covered by the scheme. The government's scheme only provided insurance for the worker but did not cover family members such as partners and children. Hospital treatment was not included and neither was dental nor eye care.

Unemployment insurance helped about 2.5 million people in the building, shipbuilding, engineering, and iron and steel industries. There were millions who were not covered. The benefits themselves were small and were not enough to live on. Benefits were kept low to avoid encouraging people to stay unemployed. Workers who were dismissed for misconduct lost their right to unemployment benefit.

The provision of free school meals by local authorities worked well in many parts of the country. However, in a few places it caused some resentment because of what was seen as unnecessary means testing of those parents who claimed them on behalf of their children.

In conclusion, the Liberals' reforms were never intended to establish anything like the modern welfare state. They were conceived of only as a safety net for the most needy in society. Universal rights to healthcare and social security were not established by the reforms, nor were they intended to do so. Indeed, some of the reforms discriminated between different types of poor people. Many people at this time divided the poor into two: the 'deserving poor' who were judged to be thrifty and sensible with the little money they had; the 'undeserving poor' who were judged not to deserve the support of the state because they did not make enough effort to stand on their own two feet. For example, unemployment benefit was withdrawn if a worker's bad behaviour led to dismissal. Some say that, by 1914 the Liberals had created a 'social service state' but not a 'welfare state' to deal with the effects of economic growth and industrialisation, and in having these reforms Britain was far from unique.

Table 1

This shows the percentage changes of the causes of death comparing the 1890s with the year 1912.

Causes of death*	Figures for 1912 compared with the average for the 1890s
Measles	Down by 16%
Scarlet fever	Down by 66%
Whooping cough	Down by 40%
Diphtheria	Down by 57%
Tuberculosis	Down by 32%
Pneumonia	Down by 15%
Bronchitis	Down by 45%

*The death rate from all causes declined by 27% and infant mortality fell by 38% between the 1890s and 1912.

Table 2

Date of survey	Title	Conclusions
1924	Has poverty diminished?	A. L. Bowley repeated his survey of four British towns that he had carried out in 1912 and 1913. He concluded that poverty had fallen. The improvement since 1913 is very striking. The proportion of families in poverty in 1924 was little more than half that in 1913.
1920s	The new survey of London life and labour	Llewellyn Smith conducted his survey in the 1920s and published his findings in 1934. He tried to make a comparison with Booth's survey. Llewellyn Smith concluded that poverty had declined by about two-thirds.
1935–6	Progress and poverty	Rowntree repeated his 1899 survey of York. Using the same criteria for judging poverty he found that 6.8% of the working class were living in primary poverty; this compares with 15.5% in his first survey.

A photograph showing unemployed men queuing for their benefit payment after the National Insurance Act of 1911.

Discussion points

> Do Tables 1 and 2 suggest that the Liberal reforms were effective in helping the young, the old and the unemployed?

> What other factors aside from the reforms could explain the changes outlined in Tables 1 and 2?

> Other surveys of poverty were conducted in the 1930s. Why would they be of limited value to the historian studying the effects of the Liberal reforms?

Votes for women: the movement for female suffrage

What role did women play in nineteenth century Britain?

Over a hundred years ago attitudes towards women were very different from today. Joseph Ashby, the agricultural reformer, came from a labouring home, of which his daughter writes:

> Their mother would teach them, always by action and sometimes by words, that girls and women find it best to submit to husbands and brothers. Their duty was to feed them well, to run their errands and to bear for them all burdens save physical ones ... Of course the main source of these attitudes was father's head! Independence would be 'false, foolish, destructive of women's best and holiest qualities.'

It was a man's world. It said so in the Bible. Eve was created from one of Adam's ribs and woman was the source of temptation, as Adam had found out. Attitudes such as these might surprise us now, but they very much influenced the way men and women behaved in the nineteenth century.

What was the situation in 1900?

By 1900 women had achieved many improvements in their social and economic rights as you can see in Table 1 – but only after individuals had spent years struggling for change. In employment and education there were still many inequalities. Most women

On the campaign trail: Mrs Emmeline Pankhurst, leader of the suffragettes and her daughter, Christabel Pankhurst.

Table 1

The gains made by women in terms of their social and economic rights.

1839	Custody of Infants Act	Gave divorced and separated mothers access to their children.
1857	Matrimonial Causes Act	Allowed a deserted wife to keep her own earnings; a wife separated from her husband could take legal actions on her own behalf.
1870, 1882, 1884	Married Women's Property Acts	Allowed married women to own property on the same terms as those who were unmarried; a woman in terms of her legal status was no longer regarded as chattel but as an independent and separate person.
1886	Guardianship of Infants Act	Allowed women to become the legal guardians of their children in the event of the father's death.
1886	Married Women (Maintenance Act)	Required a man who deserted his wife to pay her maintenance.

either worked at home, or as servants in the homes of the wealthy, or in factories and workshops. The minority of educated women had new opportunities in the professions of teaching, medicine and clerical work, but they were barred from being lawyers or architects. Men were paid more – in some cases men earned double for the same work.

From about 1850 onwards some women came to the conclusion that unless they could gain the right to vote (suffrage) in national elections they would always be second-class citizens or worse. To win the vote MPs had to be persuaded to change the law.

Campaigners for the vote did not always agree on the tactics they should use to convince Parliament to change the law. Two main groups emerged: the suffragists, led by Millicent Fawcett, and the suffragettes, led by Emmeline Pankhurst. The main difference between them was their tactics: the suffragists used only peaceful means of persuasion; the suffragettes were more militant and used direct action. The antis (those who wanted to deny women the right to vote) formed their own organisation called the Anti-Suffrage League. Its leader was Mrs Humphry Ward.

Table 2

The gains made by women in terms of their political rights.

1869	Municipal Franchise Act	Entitled unmarried female property owners to vote in local elections; in 1888 this was extended to include the right to vote in the newly created county council elections.
1894	Parish and District Councils Act	Extended right to vote in parish and district council elections to married women who owned property and allowed women to be elected to those councils.
1907	Qualification of Women Act	Right to become borough and county councillors.

Mrs Humphry Ward, leader of the Anti-Suffrage League.

July 1913 in Hyde Park, London. Millicent Fawcett addressing a crowd.

What were the arguments against giving women the right to vote?

There were a number of reasons why people did not want women to have the vote. At first most of public opinion was against the idea of giving women the vote. In the early years of the movement many treated the campaign as a joke and plenty of women opposed the suffrage movement: Mary Kingsley and Gertrude Bell were two of the best known. However, by 1914 many of the arguments voiced by the antis seemed ridiculous and the debate had more or less been won, even though Parliament had not yet given women the right to vote.

1 Women were inferior. They could never enjoy full rights of citizenship because they could not fight to defend their country or the British Empire, unlike men.

2 Scientists during the Victorian period had allegedly 'proved' that women's brains were smaller than men's. This meant they were less intelligent and more emotional so they could not be trusted with the vote or the power they would enjoy if they took over Parliament. This so-called scientific view of women was linked to a view that saw women at the mercy of their reproductive cycle. Menstruation made women fickle, childish and unlikely to be able to make rational judgements on political issues.

3 It was God's wish that men should rule over women. In the book of Genesis in the Bible it was said that Eve was created from the rib of Adam and so was subject to his command.

4 Men and women fulfilled different roles in society. The role of men was to feed and protect their families and to run the government and political system; the role of women was to run the home and bring up children. Each gender possessed the talents and temperament needed to carry out these functions.

5 Women had no need of the vote because men represented women's views in Parliament indirectly. Male MPs were husbands and fathers and so they understood women's interests and concerns.

6 Giving the vote to women would send a dangerous message to the colonies. People in all parts of the empire would demand the vote and this would eventually lead to independence.

What were the arguments in favour of giving women the right to vote?

Those who campaigned for the right to vote voiced a range of arguments to support their case.

1 The middle class female suffragists complained it was unjust and illogical to disenfranchise women who were holders of property and payers of rates and taxes. This argument became more forceful each time the franchise was changed to give more men the vote, as in 1867 and 1884. More and more wealthy women saw men less wealthy than themselves obtain the vote. After the extension to the franchise in 1884 some 30,000 Englishwomen farmers saw many of their male agricultural workers use their newly-acquired right to vote when they could not.

2 In many of her speeches Millicent Fawcett argued her case on grounds of individual human rights and equality before the law; the vote, she said, would complement the gains made in other areas (Tables 1 and 2). Women had made remarkable progress during the nineteenth century in public service, education and the workforce, it was time the political system recognised this and made women part of the developing democracy.

3 Giving women the vote would benefit the whole community. The vote would allow women to protect themselves and others in British society against neglect or oppression by politicians and remove obstacles in the way of a fair day's wage for a fair day's work. Sweated labour existed throughout the country. It was believed that the granting of the right to vote would lead to an improvement in pay, conditions and the life of working class women. Millicent Fawcett used this argument regularly in order to deflect criticism that votes for women was merely the concern of a selfish and unrepresentative minority of women.

4 Those who wanted female suffrage were able to point to women's considerable political experience at local level. Contrary to anti-suffragist fears there was no evidence that women's voting in local government elections had led to any ill effects. Women had not disrupted elections, nor had they become obsessed with politics and neglected their families. They had responded well to the challenge. In the Conservative, Liberal and Labour Parties there were women's groups who had helped the parties organise themselves at election time. In New Zealand women had been given the vote in 1893 without any negative impact.

5 Britain claimed to be one of the world's great civilised powers; those in power applauded the work of women who went abroad on civilising missions. So, why should women not contribute to politics?

The suffrage movement did not actually campaign for all women to have the vote, only some women. The reason for this was that the aim of both the suffragists and the suffragettes was for women to possess equal rights with the male electorate, but not all adult males could vote. So, if women were granted equal rights with men, this would automatically exclude a large section of the female population. There were socialist campaigners who argued that the campaign should not exclude any female but these views were not shared by the leadership of the suffrage movement. In their view if they could persuade MPs to accept limited suffrage for women and make it a success, then there was a greater chance that this could be extended in the years to come.

A poster produced in 1912 for the suffrage movement.

Discussion points

> Why did many women not join the suffrage campaign?

> Which of the arguments in favour of giving women the right to vote contain evidence which could be used to discredit the arguments of the antis?

> Which arguments in favour of female suffrage is the poster supporting? Which arguments of the antis is it challenging?

Votes for women: the campaigns

The suffrage movement included people with a wide range of views even though they were united in their purpose of gaining the vote for women. Mostly, the women and men were middle class; they had the time and money to spend on the campaign. In the early days of the movement in the 1850s there was no national organisation, only local groups. But in 1890 the National Union of Women's Suffrage Societies (NUWSS) was formed to amalgamate the local organisations into one. Its leader was Mrs Millicent Fawcett.

What tactics did the campaigners use?

The NUWSS (the National Union of Women's Suffrage Societies) – the suffragists

By the end of the nineteenth century the women's suffrage movement seemed to be united and strong. If you look at the map you will see there were about 400 NUWSS branches all over Britain. In 1910 membership had grown to 21,571, and by 1914 it was 53,000. The NUWSS leadership believed that winning the vote for women should be achieved using peaceful methods of persuasion. Millicent Fawcett explained why in 1911: 'I wanted the NUWSS to show the world how to gain reforms without violence, without killing people and blowing up buildings and doing the other silly things that men have done when they wanted the laws altered.'

Tactics

The NUWSS used a variety of peaceful methods: leaflets were distributed; processions were organised; petitions were signed; meetings were held with politicians of all parties to argue the case for women's suffrage. At election times they helped any candidate who supported it. In spite of all these efforts the franchise was not extended to include women. Millicent Fawcett was unconcerned by the lack of progress: she said that her movement was like a glacier; it might be slow-moving but it was a powerful force and unstoppable.

The WSPU (Women's Social and Political Union) – the suffragettes

Some women lost patience with the non-violent strategy of the NUWSS. The tactics were not producing results. By 1900 women's suffrage had been rejected fifteen times since it was first put before Parliament in 1867. The press reported little of the campaign and the public took little interest. In 1903 Emmeline Pankhurst and her daughter, Christabel, formed a breakaway group; they were called the suffragettes. Whereas the NUWSS had campaigned only for the vote, the WSPU also wanted better working and living conditions for women. 'Deeds not words' was the motto of the new organisation.

Tactics

The suffragettes chose direct action to make their point. They produced clever posters, organised demonstrations, broke windows, chained themselves to railings and set fire to postboxes. They fought police when they were arrested and went on hunger strike when imprisoned. They may have broken the law many times over but this militant action won massive publicity. The WSPU was particularly successful in London where thirty-four branches sprang up compared with fifty-four in the rest of the country. Half a million people attended their meeting in London in June 1908. The suffragettes worked together with the Labour Party.

Suffrage propaganda

All suffrage groups used propaganda to promote their cause. Apart from posters and newspapers, music, poetry and films were used to make a political point. Goods were made using the suffragette colours and at the 1908 FA cup final the WSPU flew a kite with 'votes for women' written on it.

How did the Liberal government react to the suffrage movement?

The Liberal government response to any illegal activity was to use the full force of the law. When the WSPU began to use illegal methods, the government reacted by denying women the usual democratic forms of protest: the government refused to accept petitions or to meet campaigners; they banned meetings in public places and censored the press to try and silence the WSPU. The London Commissioner of Police, acting on government orders, refused to allow suffragettes to hold meetings in any London parks. The government even raided the homes and offices of WSPU members and eventually forced Christabel Pankhurst to flee to Paris.

Some suffragettes who broke the law were sent to prison. There, they were treated harshly. They were locked in separate cells and contact with the outside world was restricted. Some suffragettes responded by going on hunger strike. At first hunger strikers were released, but then the government introduced force-feeding for women who consistently refused to eat. Over a thousand women suffered in this way: they were force-fed through the nostril or the mouth. There was great uproar at this. On 25 April 1913 as a result of the bad publicity, the Prisoners Temporary Discharge for Ill-Health Act was passed. This allowed the release of persistent hunger strikers from prison to give them time to regain their strength. As soon as they were better they were sent back to prison. This law was nicknamed the 'Cat and Mouse Act' because of the way the government played with women's lives as a cat does with a mouse.

Parliament debates female suffrage

As you can see from Table 1, time and time again from 1907 to 1913 bills were put before Parliament which would have given limited suffrage to women, but all failed. The main reason was that the Liberal Cabinet was so badly split that it was unable to give the proposals wholehearted support. Herbert Asquith, the Prime Minister, was against it; Winston Churchill was unsure and Lloyd George was in favour. In 1910 the WSPU suspended its militant campaign to see if there could be a compromise. The failure of the bills greatly angered the WSPU and they reverted to militant action. During 1913 and 1914 they increased their campaign of direct action; race courses and golf courses were vandalised with 'votes for women' being burnt into the turf. Telephone wires were cut. Railway stations, sports pavilions and empty houses were bombed.

By the outbreak of war in 1914 the public were becoming increasingly tired of the suffragettes' campaign of direct action and the antis were having considerable success in disrupting their meetings. The Cat and Mouse Act took away from the suffragettes what had previously been a useful source of public sympathy. With each successive debate in Parliament fewer and fewer MPs supported female suffrage.

Table 1

The Liberal government and votes for women.

1907   Women's suffrage bill rejected by the House of Commons.

1908   Women's suffrage bill passed by the House of Commons on first reading.

1909   Women's suffrage bill passed by the House of Commons on second reading but Prime Minister Asquith failed to support it, so the bill was rejected.

1910   First conciliation bill passed on first reading but the government failed to grant any more time for discussion, so it was rejected.

1911   Second conciliation bill passed on first reading but Asquith said he preferred to support an extension to male suffrage, which would not include an amendment for women.

1913   Franchise bill introduced to extend the suffrage for men, but an amendment to include women was rejected by the Speaker of the House of Commons because he said it changed the nature of the bill.

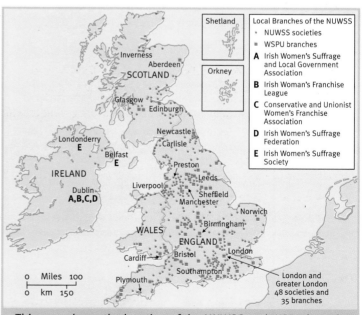

This map shows the location of the NUWSS and WSPU branches in Britain and Ireland in 1914.

How effective were the activities of the suffragists and the suffragettes?

Both the suffragists and the suffragettes wanted the same thing but went about achieving it in different ways. Was either approach effective? Was one more effective than the other? It is important to note that history books often over-emphasise the violence of the suffragettes. The WPSU did not break with the past when they made use of direct action to promote their cause; they were building upon what had gone before. Violent action did not replace peaceful protest: throughout this period before the war in 1914 both the suffragists and the suffragettes continued to use petitions, to lobby MPs and to demonstrate. Nevertheless, by 1914 neither strategy had worked.

In one sense neither the NUWSS nor the WPSU was successful because by the beginning of the war in 1914 women still had not won the right to vote — even after fifty years of campaigning! But did the campaigns bring female suffrage any closer or make it less likely? Did the direct action of the suffragettes help or hinder the cause?

SOURCE A

A suffragette poster laying the blame on Prime Minister Asquith for Parliament not granting female suffrage.

SOURCE B

A suffragette poster printed in 1910.

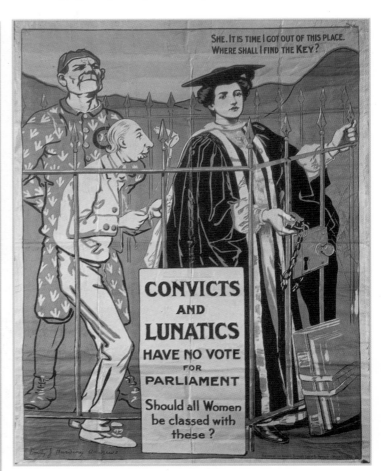

A suffragette poster printed in 1905.

A suffragette poster printed in 1913 during the period of more militant activity. A thousand women went on hunger strike in prison.

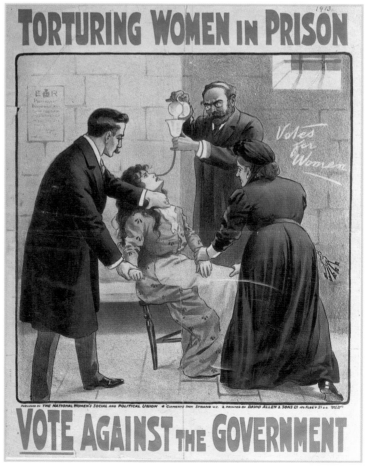

SOURCE E

From a history book, The Changing Role of Women, *by Paula Bartley, 1996.*

Historians have sometimes argued that the militancy of the WSPU destroyed support for votes for women because it alienated sympathetic members of the public and MPs and because it gave the Liberal government an ideal excuse to deny women the vote. This is not so. The long peaceful campaign waged before 1905 had not persuaded the House of Commons to extend the suffrage; and even in 1910, when the WSPU suspended its direct action and used peaceful tactics women were still not granted the vote.

The suffrage movement was unsuccessful in persuading the majority of women to join the struggle for the vote. In the early part of the twentieth century there were approximately 17 million women in Britain and only a small percentage of them belonged to the suffrage movement. However, by 1914 the female suffrage issue had become the foremost political question and it attracted the support of large numbers of men and women. Between 1906 and 1914 many thousands pledged their time and money to the suffrage campaign. After 1907 over twenty new women's suffrage societies were formed; by 1914 there were fifty-six societies with a total membership of 300,000. In 1908, 1910 and 1911 demonstrations attracted 100,000 each time.

SOURCE F

Votes in Parliament on the first reading of bills extending the franchise to women between 1909 and 1914:

March 1909: majority of 34 in favour.

June 1910: majority of 110 in favour.

May 1911: majority of 167 in favour.

March 1912: majority of 14 against.

May 1913: majority of 48 against.

SOURCE G

Lloyd George speaking during the debate on the bill to grant female suffrage in May 1913.

Haven't the suffragettes the sense to see that the very worst way of campaigning for the vote is to try and intimidate or blackmail a man into giving them what he would gladly give otherwise?

SOURCE H

Part of a speech by Herbert Asquith in the House of Commons 1917. Asquith had been Prime Minister between 1906 and 1916.

Why have I changed my views [about female suffrage]? How could we have carried on the war without them? There is hardly a service in which women have not been as active as men. And let me add that, since the war began, we have had no recurrence of that campaign [of violence].

SOURCE I

Written by Mrs Fawcett to The Times *when suffragette leaders were in prison, 1906.*

I hope that the more old-fashioned suffragists will stand by their comrades who in my opinion have done more (to advance the cause of women's suffrage) in twelve months than I and my followers have been able to do in the same number of years.

SOURCE J

Part of a book called My Own Story *by Emmeline Pankhurst, founder of the WSPU. It was written in 1914.*

What good did all this violent campaigning do us? We have often been asked that question. For one thing our campaign made women's suffrage a matter of news – it had never been that before. Now the newspapers are full of us.

The argument of politicians and the suffragists has always been that once public opinion swings our way then without any force at all women will be given the vote. We agree that the public must be educated, but in 1906 there was a very large section of the public who were in favour of women's suffrage. But what good did that do the cause? We called upon the government to give us the vote but they didn't. So, now we will fight for our cause.

SOURCE K

A comment in the Daily Mirror, *1906.*

When the suffragettes began their campaign they were mistaken for featherheads. Their proceedings were not taken seriously. Now they have proved they are in dead earnest, they have frightened the government, they have broken the law, they have made votes for women practical politics.

SOURCE L

A photograph taken in 1910 in Dundee, Scotland. It shows the arrest of a suffragette.

A suffragette being arrested.

SOURCE M

From a history book, People, Power and Politics, *by Bob Ellis, 1992.*

The militancy of the WSPU made it difficult for the Liberal government to grant the vote to women because as Asquith later said they were 'unwilling to yield to violence what we refused to concede in argument'. The government was not alone in condemning the tactics, many women deplored their violence. It was women and not men who organised the first anti-suffrage groups which in 1910 were amalgamated into the National League for Opposing Woman Suffrage.

Activities

1 Study Sources A to D. Explain in your own words the 'message' of each poster.

2 In spite of all the posters and other forms of propaganda women were not granted the vote by 1914. Does this mean that the posters were ineffective?

3 Study Sources E, F and G. In what way do Sources F and G seem to contradict Source E. Can you explain this apparent contradiction?

4 Should we trust what Emmeline Pankhurst says about the effectiveness of the suffragettes in Source J? Use Sources I and K to help you.

5 Compare Sources E and M, both written by historians. Both studied the speeches made by Asquith and Lloyd George and yet have reached different conclusions about the effect of the suffragette violence, why?

6 'If the suffragette movement had been less militant and more peaceful women would have been given the vote by 1914'. How far do the sources show this statement to be true?

The outbreak of war and British society

When Britain declared war on Germany on 4 August 1914 it was the first war against a European power since the end of the Crimean War in 1856. It was also the first time Britain had been involved in a war threatening the British Isles since the final defeat of Napoleon at Waterloo in 1815.

How did people react to the outbreak of hostilities?

Popular attitudes: recruitment and propaganda

Immediately war was declared, war fever swept across Britain. One eye-witness in London recalled what it was like:

> Parliament Street and Whitehall were full of people highly excited and rather boisterous. All were touched with war fever. They regarded their country as a crusader – setting right all wrongs. Cries of 'Down with Germany' were heard. Later in the evening the enthusiasm culminated outside Buckingham Palace. The cheering grew into a deafening roar when King George appeared on the balcony. Later a hostile crowd gathered outside the German Embassy and smashed windows.

Today we find it hard to understand why the vast majority of British people felt like this and why thousands of young men would want to join up voluntarily. Two words, 'honour' and 'duty', are helpful here. Many felt duty-bound to go to the help of Belgium after the German invasion. Britain had guaranteed Belgian neutrality in the 1839 Treaty of London, and the Germans had torn this to shreds when they marched over the frontier. Women felt it was their duty to send men off to the war, especially as the popular view of fighting at this time saw war in terms of cavalry charges and heroic deeds. In addition, the newspapers all said it would be over by Christmas. All of these beliefs were important, but the key factor that prevented people thinking more calmly about what the war might mean for them was the feeling of patriotism, fighting for the honour of Britain and her empire. In many minds the Great War was a conflict between civilisation (the Allied Powers) and barbarism (the Central Powers).

Why did people volunteer to fight in the war?

SOURCE A

A soldier in the Great War recalls how he was affected by a show he went to see shortly after war was declared:

I went with a friend of mine to Shepherd's Bush Empire to see the big show there. At the end they showed the Fleet sailing the high seas and played 'Britons Never Shall be Slaves' and you know, one feels that little shiver run up the back and you know you've got to do something. I had just turned seventeen at the time and on Monday I went to enlist.

SOURCE B

Lord Chandos joined up in 1914. He wrote this after the war.

We were all swept along by patriotism. It did not occur to us to ask whether it was right or wrong.

SOURCE C

Part of an interview with Private George Morgan, Ist Bradford Pals after the war.

We had been brought up to believe that Britain was the best country in the world and we wanted to defend her. The history taught us at school showed that we were better than other people and now all the news was that Germany was the aggressor and we wanted to show the Germans what we could do.

SOURCE D

Personal memories of Alfred Blake, who joined up.

I had a dead end job in a dead end town. Here was a chance to see the world, and boys like me hadn't the money to travel then.

SOURCE E

Part of an interview with William Brooks in 1993 about his experiences during the First World War.

Once war broke out the situation at home became awful because people did not like to see men or lads of army age walking about in civilian clothing, especially in a military town like Woolwich. Women were the worst. They would come up to you in the street and give you a white feather or stick it in the lapel of your coat. A white feather is a sign of cowardice.

It got so bad it wasn't safe to go out. So, in 1915 at the age of seventeen I volunteered. Once you applied you were given a blue armband with a red crown to wear. This told people that you were waiting to be called up, and that kept you safe, or fairly safe, because if you were seen to be wearing it for too long the abuse in the street would soon start again.

SOURCE F

From a history book, War in Britain, *by Fiona Reynoldson, 1988.*

Friends joined up together. Often they formed pals battalions (about a thousand men). Footballers joined together. Artists joined together. Friends from the same town joined together.

SOURCE G

A photograph of new recruits being measured at Marylebone in 1914.

Activities

1 Study Sources A, B and C. What motives inspired these men to join up?

2 Study Sources D, E and F. What other motives for joining up are suggested in the sources?

3 Study Sources A to F and use your knowledge. What evidence is there that some of the volunteers were pressured to join up rather than do so voluntarily?

4 Study Source G. What other sources would you need to use with this photograph to discover the motives that drove these men to join up?

5 'Pressure rather than patriotism made men enlist in the armed forces in 1914'. Use all the sources and your knowledge to say how far you agree with this statement?

Army recruitment

At the outbreak of war Britain had about five and a half million men of military age available for service; another half a million coming of age each year. Within days of the outbreak of the war an increase in the armed forces of half a million men had been authorised. On 15 September another half million was agreed followed by a million in November. To start with, all the government had to do was to channel the flood of patriotic feeling and to cope with an overwhelming number of recruits. By early 1915, however, there was some slackening of recruitment that worried the government given the losses on the Western Front; by the middle of 1915 casualties had risen to 380,000 including 75,000 dead. The government had to do something to increase the numbers coming forward.

How effective was government propaganda in recruiting soldiers?

At the beginning of the war one of the physical requirements to get into the army was that a volunteer had to stand five feet eight inches tall; this was reduced to five feet five inches on 11 October 1914 and in November to five feet three inches. A Parliamentary Recruiting Committee commissioned over a hundred different posters to persuade men to enlist; by the autumn of 1915 fifty-four million posters had been issued. Postcards were used in the same way. Propaganda themes ranged from avenging German atrocities in Belgium and the appeal of helping those already fighting in France to the threat of lasting shame for those who ignored the call to arms. In January 1915 posters appeared aimed directly at women; married men were goaded with the question from their children: 'Daddy, what did you do in the Great War?'

Numbers of recruits fell to 71,000 in September 1915. In that same year the National Registration Act revealed that almost two million men were still available and had not yet come forward, so the government decided it was time to compel men to join up. Conscription was introduced in May 1916.

In spite of opposition, conscription was accepted by the majority of the public. But the results were disappointing. The number of those enlisting fell to 40,000 a month; the numbers excluded on grounds of ill-health or war work exceeded expectations.

SOURCE A

A table showing the total number of men joining the armed forces for each year of the war.

Year	Number joining armed forces
1914	1,186,357
1915	1,280,000
1916	1,190,000
1917	820,646
1918	493,562

SOURCE B

A recruitment poster, dated 1915. Scarborough had been bombed earlier on in the war.

SOURCE C

A recruitment poster 'Women of Britain say GO!'

SOURCE D

Lord Kitchener was used in this recruitment poster, dated 1915. He was a military commander during the Boer War in South Africa. He was thus well-known when Asquith appointed him Minister of War in August 1914.

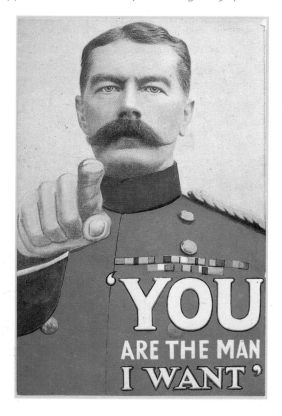

SOURCE E

From a history book, The Deluge, by Arthur Marwick, 1965.

Given the patriotic attitudes of the press, preachers and popular writers there was no need for the government to have complete control of opinion. The popular press were following current attitudes rather than leading them, but the patriotic rubbish printed remained the invention of the proprietors and editors rather than governments.

SOURCE F

A headline from the Daily Mail during the early stages of the war.

REFUSE TO BE SERVED BY AN AUSTRIAN OR GERMAN WAITER.
IF YOUR WAITER SAYS HE IS SWISS ASK TO SEE HIS PASSPORT.

Activities

1 Study Sources B, C, D, and use your knowledge. What was the target audience for each poster in terms of age and gender? Why were these posters produced in 1915 and not any earlier? Does Source A help you assess the effectiveness of these posters in attracting more men to join up?

2 Study Sources E and F and use your knowledge. Why do you think the Daily Mail gave the sort of advice to be found in Source F?

3 'Between 1914 and 1916 men joined up willingly, government propaganda had no impact on their decision'. How far do the sources and your knowledge show this to be true?

Conscientious objectors

The new conscription law contained get-out clauses for conscientious objectors – they were nicknamed 'conchies'. These were pacifists. Many were Quakers, a Christian religious group whose beliefs did not allow them to enlist and fight. Tribunals were set up to hear the cases of those who thought they should be exempted from joining up. 10,000 gained exemption: 7,000 worked as non-combatants and the remaining 3,000 were sent to Home Office labour camps. Many applied for exemption but were rejected and ended up in France. There, they faced court martial for not obeying orders. Many were not well treated. In 1918 when a new franchise law was passed by Parliament, they were disqualified from voting for five years. By the end of the war seventy-one conchies had died in prison or as a direct result of their bad treatment in captivity; thirty-one others had gone mad.

What happened to those men who did not join up after May 1916?

SOURCE A

A government propaganda poster aimed at conscientious objectors.

Daddy, what did YOU do in the Great War?

SOURCE B

From a speech by Lloyd George, Minister of Munitions.

I do not think the conchies deserve the slightest consideration. With regard to those who object to the shedding of blood it is the traditional policy of this country to respect that view, and we do not propose to depart from it. I shall only consider the best means of making their lot a very hard one.

SOURCE C

A photograph of conscientious objectors working on Dartmoor, April 1917. The caption on the back of the photo said: they are here seen supposedly tilling the soil, but they spend much of their time 'on leave' or 'strolling on the moors, smoking, reading and talking'.

SOURCE D

Part of a diary entry written by the Reverend A. Clark for 11 July 1916.

Richard Arnold asked to keep his farm man called Wells because: a) 'Wells is the man who looks after my sheep. If he were taken away I must sell my sheep and then there would only be one flock in the parish; and b) Wells has four young children and if he were killed the country would have a long time to keep them.'

SOURCE E

John Graham, a Quaker leader, wrote this during the war.

The conscientious objector seemed to hold aloof from the hard and dangerous work of defending their country ... He seemed to be merely a shirker ... The women he knew cut his acquaintance. His mother and brother often jeered at him at home. Shirker, coward, dog, these were the words they were thought to deserve.

SOURCE F

Howard Marten described what it was like to be in the hands of the army as an objector.

We were placed in handcuffs and locked in cells and tied up for two hours in the afternoon. Then we were confined to our cells for three days on 'punishment diet' – four biscuits a day and water. Often the days seemed endless. There were eleven of us in one cell that measured 11' 9" by 11' 3".

Some objectors were tortured to make them obey army orders. They tried to break Gray's will by throwing a live bomb at his feet after removing the pin and demanding that he throw it when ordered. Gray stood perfectly still and calm when the bomb was hissing at his feet and the officer who threw it ran for cover.

After successive days of worsening treatment ... Gray was stripped naked, a rope tightly fastened around his abdomen and he was pushed into a filthy pond and held under the water eight or nine times in succession. The pond contained sewage. Gray eventually gave in and obeyed army orders after his will was broken.

SOURCE G

This is a letter that was published in the Manchester Guardian. *This newspaper was one of the very few which supported the conscientious objectors. The letter caused such a scandal that the author was immediately taken away from the army camp and handed over to the civil authorities. James Brightmore's letter was written on the cover of a cigarette packet and smuggled out by a friendly soldier.*

My dear _____,

This is the best stuff I can find to write what may be my last letter. Everything has been taken off me. I have been bullied horribly and sentenced to 28 days' solitary confinement. I have been confined to a pit. The bottom is full of water, there is no room to walk about and sitting is impossible. The sun beats down, and through the long day there are only walls of clay to look at. Already I am half mad.

Goodbye,

James Brightmore.

SOURCE H

Part of a story told by a conscientious objector after the war.

I learnt that the only people from whom I was to expect sympathy were the soldiers, not the civilians. When I was waiting in the guard-room five men bustled into the room, and the door slammed on them. They were all in a rage. Their language was incredible. I gathered they were all soldiers who, for some reason or another, were under arrest.

Finally, they noticed me in my corner. They stopped swearing and one of them walked up to me.

'What are you in here for, mate?'

'Well, you see, I am a Quaker, and I refused to join the army, because I think that war is murder', I said.

The man took a step backwards. The room was very silent.

'Murder?' he whispered. 'Murder? It's *bloody* murder'.

Then we were friends. We only had a little while together, because the men were soon marched away and I never saw them again. As they went, they came up to me, and shook me by the hand.

'Stick to it, matey! Stick!' they said, one after another.

Activities

1 Study Source A. How can you tell this poster is aimed at pacifists and conscientious objectors?

2 Study Sources B and C. To what extent does Lloyd George's attitude towards conscientious objectors agree with that of the author of the caption on the back of the photograph?

3 Study Sources B and D. How would Lloyd George have responded to the claim for exemption from Richard Wells? Would his response in private be any different from a public response?

4 Study Sources B, F and G. Would Lloyd George have agreed with the treatment of Marten, Gray and Brightmore?

5 In Source F the soldiers treated the conscientious objectors very badly, but in Source H the soldiers encouraged the objector not to give up. How would you explain this contradiction?

6 Why would the government not want many letters, like the one by James Brightmore, to be published?

7 'Conscientious objectors were badly treated.' Using the sources and your own knowledge say whether you agree with this statement?

Daily life during the war – the home front

How did the war affect Britain?

The First World War affected men and women, young and old in ways that no war had ever done before. In previous conflicts the war had only a limited impact on daily life back home. In 1914–18 things were very different; the Great War was the first total war. To fight the Central Powers the government made laws that compelled all British people to be active citizens in fighting the war, whether man, woman or child. Air raids and bombardments from the seas meant that Britain's own soil and civilian population were not safe – for the first time ever civilians were killed. Other major differences included the expansion of the workforce to involve many women, and government control of industry in order to secure the necessary supplies for the war. Alongside this extension of government powers came a huge growth in government bureaucracy and officialdom. Britain between 1914 and 1918 was a nation at arms.

The historian A. J. P. Taylor summed up the dramatic changes that affected the daily lives of British people during the war:

To begin with the government wanted to give the impression that as far as they were concerned it was 'Business as Usual' and little would change. This was because they did not want to induce any panic amongst the civilian population and because they thought the conflict would be short and over by Christmas. Morale at home could be best maintained, the government judged, by preserving the habits of peacetime.

Daily life during the war

DORA – the Defence of the Realm Act, 1914

Right at the beginning of the war the government realised it was going to have to take control over aspects of people's lives that it had never touched before. The purpose of the first DORA in 1914 was to ensure public safety and the defence of the realm. Initially, this meant preventing information leaking out that might help the enemy and protecting the vital centres of communications such as railways, docks and harbours. Those who broke the law were to be tried by

> Until August 1914 a sensible, law-abiding Englishman (and woman) could pass through life and hardly notice the existence of the state, beyond the post office and the policeman … All this was changed by the impact of the Great War. The mass of the people became, for the first time, active citizens. Their lives were shaped by orders from above, they were required to serve the state instead of pursuing exclusively their own affairs. Five million entered the armed forces, many of them under compulsion. The Englishman's food was limited and its quality changed by government order. His freedom of movement was restricted; his conditions of work prescribed. Some industries were reduced or closed, others set up just for the war period. The publication of news was censored. Street lights were dimmed. The sacred freedom of drinking was tampered with: licensed hours were cut down, and the beer watered by order. The very time on the clocks was changed. From 1916 onwards every Englishman got up an hour earlier in the summer than he otherwise would have done, thanks to an Act of Parliament. The state established a hold over its citizens.

court martial. Further extensions to the Defence of the Realm Act enabled the government to put in place a series of regulations governing food control, air raid precautions and press censorship.

Air raids

The first Zeppelin bombing raid on Britain took place on 19 January 1915; 119 people were killed during the raid on Scarborough. Although during the war 1,500 were killed and 3,000 injured, the air raids had little impact. They did not destroy factories, ships and docks. The reason for this was that dropping the bombs from the Zeppelins was very haphazard; often the crews did not even know where they were.

Government control of food: rationing

Much of Britain's food came from other countries. To begin with, the government wanted just to act as a buyer of food for the armed forces and to bring in more controls when a particular shortage occurred. However, shortages caused by U-boat sinkings (the Germans had imposed a submarine blockade around Britain in February 1915) and the huge demand from the armed forces caused prices to rise. Rather than move straight to rationing the government tried other methods: in 1917 price controls were put on meat. But by the end of the year, the shortages were so serious that the government was forced to take control of the slaughter and purchase of farm animals and the wholesale meat trade. Posters were put up to encourage people to economise and allotments were made available so people could grow their own food. None of these measures was enough to prevent the shortages.

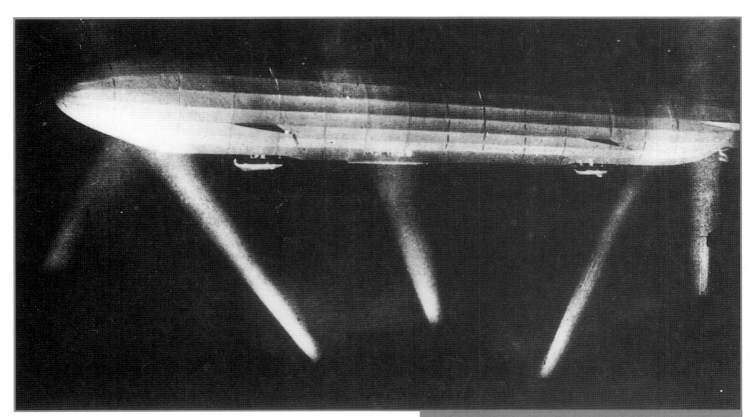

A German Zeppelin, caught in searchlights during a bombing raid. Zeppelins proved to be vulnerable as British airmen successfully shot down several in flames.

Concern over food supplies increased in 1917 because a report indicated that rising prices was a major cause of recent strikes. Alongside this, the queues for certain foods were lengthening during the winter of 1917–18. In the end a system of rationing was introduced. By April 1918 meat rationing applied to the whole country. Tea, sugar, butter and margarine were the other items that could be bought with a ration card and coupons. Bread and potatoes were not rationed but were subject to price controls. The amount of food you could buy depended on your job and gender: manual workers got more than office workers and teenage boys more than girls. Table 1 shows the amount of rationed food allowed for one adult each week.

Table 1

Food	Amount allowed
Jam and marmalade	113 grams
Tea	56 grams
Bacon and ham	340 grams
Lard	56 grams
Butter and margarine	113 grams
Sugar	226 grams

Rationing actually continued into the years after 1918 because there were still shortages of essential items and because it helped reduce the threat of labour unrest. Milk rationing was started after the armistice in November 1918, while the Ministry of Food stopped rationing meat, butter and sugar in October 1919. The rationing system was largely successful during the war. Although shortages existed and there were queues, the situation never developed into a crisis and on the whole people thought it was a fairer way of sharing out the food. There was never anything in Britain to compare with the shortages in Germany or Austria.

Controlling drink

Before the outbreak of war an evening's drinking was a very important leisure activity for many people. Once the conflict started the government became worried about the effects of alcohol on recruits in case they were to come on parade or on to a ship suffering from heavy hangovers. Lloyd George spoke of a small minority of workmen whose drinking was 'doing us more damage in the war than all the German submarines put together'. The government was determined to act.

Part of the Defence of the Realm Act in 1914 enabled licensing authorities in England and Wales to impose restrictions on the times alcohol was permitted to be sold. In London a new closing time of 11 p.m. was introduced on 4 September; it became 10 p.m. on 19 October. The Liberal government put further pressure on drinkers when the price of beer was put up from 3 pence to 4 pence a pint in the budget; later budgets increased the taxes on spirits.

Before taking further steps to control the excessive consumption of alcohol the government investigated the bad time keeping of some workers in key industries. Heavy drinking, it was discovered, was the main cause of lateness at work. This was all the evidence the government needed. It set up the Central Control Board in 1915 to take over control of licensing from authorities where excessive drinking was common. In fourteen areas there was to be no alcohol for sale before midday and throughout the afternoon after 2.30 p.m. Everywhere incidences of drunken behaviour declined. By March 1916 the regulations applied to twenty-seven areas and 30 million people; by March 1917 they applied to 38 million people out of the population of 41 million.

Other measures included reducing both the strength of beer and its production. All of these measures put together brought about a much-needed change in one of the most important social habits of British people. Drunkenness by the end of the war was a limited and manageable problem. In 1914 average weekly convictions for drunkenness in England and Wales totalled 3,388 each week; by the end of the war they had fallen to 449. Scottish figures reveal the same decline. Female drunkenness fell too. Drink was no longer a vital part of some people's days and nights.

Government control of industry

During the war the government took control of industries that were the key to winning the war: steel, shipbuilding, coal mining and the railways. Doing this ensured that raw materials, food and vital supplies got to places where they were most needed.

In 1915, Lloyd George became Minister of Munitions and he was determined to increase production of vital munitions. To achieve this he introduced 'dilution'. This meant that semi-skilled and unskilled workers were able to work in jobs which skilled workers usually did. The unions and the skilled workers objected to Lloyd George's plans. However, he won them over with the promise that the changes in the workplace would only last for the duration.

Discussion points

> Why did the government not tell the public at the beginning of the war to expect hardship?

> The Defence of the Realm Act enabled the government to intervene in people's lives in ways that had never happened before. Compare the wartime government role with that of the government today. Which aspects of state intervention are similar and which are different?

A government poster encouraging people to be careful with their food. Sometimes the public had to endure shops running out of food, but in other countries the civilian population suffered greater hardship and worse shortages.

Women and the war effort

How did women contribute to the war effort?

In August 1914 when war broke out, both the suffragists and the suffragettes immediately stopped their campaigns for women's suffrage because they saw it as their duty and because the war might offer opportunities for women to show those who opposed them just what women were capable of. Mrs Fawcett said in August 1914: 'Let us show ourselves worthy of citizenship, whether our claim is recognised or not'.

The WSPU followed her lead. Shortly after the war began they placed their funds and organisation at the government's disposal. Lloyd George, Minister of Munitions, worked with the WSPU to recruit women into the workforce. The NUWSS formed and financed the Scottish Women's Hospitals Units. These employed all female teams of doctors, nurses and ambulance drivers to work in the front line. By 1915 five units were operating in Corsica, France, Salonika and Serbia. The NUWSS also set up maternity and children's hospitals for refugees and sanatoria for tuberculosis sufferers.

When men joined up and went off to war many women stepped into their jobs as well as taking up new jobs that were created by the need to manufacture munitions. The government's propaganda machine produced posters to encourage women to join the war effort.

Voluntary Aid Detachments (VADs)

Fifteen thousand young women joined the VADs during the war. They were not paid so only women from well-off families could afford to volunteer. Vera Brittain commented that their expectations of the work were not matched by reality: they 'came to the hospital expecting to hold the patients' hands and smooth their pillows while regular nurses fetched and carried everything that looked and smelt disagreeable.' What they found was very different: long hours and caring for men who were badly wounded and in great pain. For many upper and middle class women it was their first opportunity to leave the shelter of their homes and become independent.

The first VAD unit left for France in October 1914; the following year the VAD General Section was created. This gave women the opportunity to become cooks, clerks and accountants instead of nurses.

Women's Army Auxiliary Corps (WAAC)

This organisation helped to run the army while the men were off fighting in France. By the end of the war some 8,000 women had joined and were supporting the army abroad and in Britain they numbered 31,000. When the drivers, messengers, telephonists, storekeepers, cooks and typists joined the front line women took their places; in the navy (Women's Royal Naval Service) and in the air force (Women's Royal Air Force) similar organisations were set up.

Women at the home front: farms and factories

Women of all classes contributed to the war effort in Britain. Upper class women advised the government on health and employment and led food economy campaigns. Lady Londonderry, for example, became Colonel in Chief of the Women's Volunteer Reserve. In 1915 many upper and middle class women joined the Land Army. On the farm, these women were expected to look after animals, plough, plant and harvest. It was tough, physical work done in all weathers.

A recruiting poster to persuade women to join the Land Army.

Unlike most upper and middle class women working class women had to work anyway, whether there was a war on or not. Many were exploited in domestic service or sweated labour; the war offered them a way out, at least for the duration. At railway stations women became porters, ticket collectors and guards. Women drove buses, swept chimneys, delivered coal, swept the streets and put out fires.

Munitions

It was women's contribution to the munitions industry that received the greatest publicity. The Woolwich Arsenal employed just 125 women in 1914. By 1917 the figure was over 25,000. In munitions factories fourteen-hour days were common and conditions were dangerous. The workers made bullets, filled shells and assembled detonators. Many suffered from TNT poisoning. Their skin turned yellow, hence their nickname, 'canary girls'. 37% of the workers in

Woman worker in a munitions factory during the First World War.

Table 1

The main jobs of women working on the home front, 1914–18.

Job	Number of women working in 1914	Number of women working in 1918
Munitions	212,000	974,000
Transport	18,200	117,200
Agriculture	190,000	228,000
Industry	2,178,000	2,970,600
Domestic service	1,658,000	1,250,000

the Woolwich Arsenal suffered from stomach pains and nausea, swelling of hands and feet and skin rashes. Explosions at these factories often killed women; in the factory at Silvertown in the East End of London several were killed in 1917.

What had women achieved by 1918?

By the time the Armistice was signed in November 1918 women had shown that they could do almost every job, including the most skilled and the most arduous. Many middle class women for the first time had enjoyed some degree of independence with their own income and a new environment outside the home. Wider employment opportunities helped to liberate working class women from the hardships and constraints of the slums. Many escaped from the poorly paid sweated labour and domestic service jobs to take better-paid work in munitions factories.

How did men feel about women in the workplace?

Most men thought that women were weak and incapable of working machinery. Male workers were scared that women would be paid the same wages and undermine their position in the workplace. A government report in 1919 commented that 'in every industrial district without exception there was continuous opposition from men to the introduction of women. In some cases the men went on strike; in other instances the men just refused to instruct women or tried to restrict what they could do or just discredited their work'. In particular, skilled workmen were afraid for their jobs. Lloyd George, Minister for Munitions, wanted women to do skilled jobs to avert the labour shortage, but this was resented by the unions. They argued that this 'dilution of labour' cut across the traditional status of skilled work and routes into such jobs. Eventually, the practice of 'dilution' was accepted by the trade unions concerned, but only as a temporary measure until the end of the war and only after the government agreed to protect the wages of skilled workers.

Discussion points

> Why did the suffrage movement suspend its campaign to win women the vote?

> What effects do you think war work had on women's view of themselves?

> After the war many women left their jobs and went back to what they did before 1914. Why was that?

British propaganda during the First World War

To think of propaganda as telling lies to make people believe something is too simple. Propaganda can be the outright lie, but it is more likely to be the half truth, or the truth taken out of its context, or indeed a mixture of all three. Propaganda had several purposes in the war. Firstly, it was needed to whip up emotions against the enemy; secondly, the government used it to maintain friendly relations with neutrals and allies; and thirdly propaganda was produced to arouse the neutrals against the enemy. Between 1914 to 1916 the government scarcely needed to produce any propaganda against Germany, such was the number of preachers, politicians and pressmen who did the job of encouraging hatred so effectively. However, by mid-1916, when war weariness was setting in, the rate of government propaganda activity increased.

How was propaganda used in the First World War?

The British government took different approaches to influencing opinion at home and abroad. At home its censorship and propaganda were directed towards influencing mass opinion but abroad the government focused exclusively on those in power or those who were close to them – the political elite.

To begin with two bodies, the Admiralty and the War Office, both acted as censors. The result of this double handed grip on information control was that the papers had hardly any war news to report at all. This forced them into spreading rumours, telling atrocity stories and conducting a witch-hunt against spies and aliens. For example, the *Daily Mail* was guilty of reporting an entirely fictitious naval battle off the coast of Holland. Eventually, the government set up an Official Press Bureau which presented information about the war to the newspapers and to which editors were supposed to submit all controversial articles. Aside from sanitising the news from the battlefield, the government propaganda machine became involved in the promotion of recruitment to the forces and the war industries, and the encouragement of thrift in the purchase of food.

Propaganda in the cinema

Film (albeit silent film) presented the propagandists with a new medium to use in manipulating opinion. As early as 1914 the Cinema Division of the government's Department of Information had created short length cartoons such as the 'Bully Boy' series to ridicule the Kaiser (German emperor). In 1915 films were produced for foreign consumption. By 1916 more effective use was made of the three thousand cinemas that were attracting large weekly audiences. One film that attracted large numbers was called *The Battle of the Somme*. During the film, carefully crafted scenes were shot before the battle actually started; they convey only a faint idea of what the fighting must have been like.

To what extent was the propaganda effective?

The Department of Information succeeded in encouraging anti-German feeling and disguising the full horrors of the war. Official reports, press coverage and film material usually tended to promote the good side of the war and conceal as much as possible of its ghastly reality. It was little wonder that servicemen on leave found the civilian view of the war way out of touch with their first-hand experience.

SOURCE A

Lord Northcliffe's comments at a private dinner party on 8 November 1917. Northcliffe owned the Daily Mail *and the* Daily Mirror.

We're telling lies, we daren't tell the public the truth, that we're losing more officers than the Germans, and that it's impossible to get through on the Western Front. You've seen the newspaper journalists shepherded by General Charteris. They don't know the truth, they don't speak the truth and we know they don't.

SOURCE B

From a history book, British Society, *by John Stevenson, 1984.*

The use of propaganda can clearly be seen as yet one more ratchet on the wheel whereby the state took greater control over people's lives. It not only told them what to do, where to work, what to eat and how to spend their leisure, but also what to think. Most important of all the propaganda denied
its citizens access to the diversity of information which, because it might have hindered the war effort, might also have led them to question whether the war was worth fighting.

Pictures like this were censored so British citizens were not aware of the grim realities of war.

SOURCE C

Lloyd George's comments in December 1917 on hearing a description of the fighting from the war journalist, Philip Gibbs.

I listened last night to the most impressive and moving description from him of what the war on the Western Front really means. Even an audience of hardened politicians and journalists were strongly affected. If people really knew, the war would be stopped tomorrow. But, of course, they don't know and can't know. The journalists don't write the truth and the censor wouldn't pass the truth. What they send is not the war, but just a pretty picture of the war with everybody doing gallant deeds.

Activities

1 Study Sources A, B and C. To what extent to they agree about the degree to which battlefield news was censored?

2 What did Lloyd George mean when he said, 'but, of course, they don't know and can't know'?

3 A historian has speculated that if 'television cameras had existed and had been allowed anywhere near the trenches to record the harsh realities of the Western Front, the war would never have lasted as long as it did'. Do you think this is correct?

The sinking of the *Lusitania*, May 1915

During the war the USA was, at first, neutral but both Britain and Germany were keen to persuade it to enter the war on their side. Winston Churchill was in charge of the navy at this time and he wanted the USA to help Britain win the war.

Who was to blame?

In the first few months of the war the USA sold supplies of food and armaments to both sides. In February 1915 the German submarines set up a blockade around Britain to strangle Britain's trade with other parts of the world.

The *Lusitania* was a passenger ship sailing from the USA to Britain in May 1915. On 7 May, just off the coast of Ireland, the German submarine U-20 torpedoed and sank the British liner. This was done without warning, ignoring the usual procedure of allowing the crew and passengers of unarmed ships to escape in their life boats before their ship was sunk. Nearly 1,200 people were drowned, including 118 from the USA. Who was to blame for the sinking of the *Lusitania* and how did the British government use the incident for its own propaganda purposes?

SOURCE A:

A drawing of the Lusitania *going down from* The Illustrated London News, *June 1915.*

A CRIME THAT HAS STAGGERED HUMANITY: THE TORPEDOING OF THE LUSITANIA

DRAWN BY CHARLES DIXON, R.I. FROM MATERIAL SUPPLIED BY SURVIVORS

SOURCE B

From the Daily Mirror, 8 May 1915.

LUSITANIA TORPEDOED BY GERMAN PIRATES

The Daily Mirror

CERTIFIED CIRCULATION LARGER THAN ANY OTHER PICTURE PAPER IN THE WORLD

No. 3,600.   SATURDAY, MAY 8, 1915   16 PAGES   One Halfpenny

THE HUNS CARRY OUT THEIR THREAT TO MURDER : FAMOUS CUNARDER SUNK OFF THE IRISH COAST.

May 8, 1915   THE DAILY MIRROR   Page 5

THE LUSITANIA TORPEDOED BY GERMAN PIRATES

Cunard's Mammoth Liner That Cost £1,250,000 Sunk in Eight Minutes—1,918 Souls on Board.

DASH OF RESCUE SHIPS IN REPLY TO "S.O.S." CALL—MANY LIVES SAVED

SOURCE C

Extracts from a booklet published in October 1915 by Cunard, the company which owned the Lusitania.

On 1 May she left New York for Liverpool ... Before sailing, threatening statements were published in the American press by the Germans foretelling the sinking of the liner.

On 7 May the Irish coast was sighted ... without the slightest warning she was struck by a torpedo between the third and fourth funnels. There was evidence of perhaps a third and perhaps a fourth torpedo was fired and the great ship sank within twenty minutes. The doomed liner's SOS was answered and 764 lives were saved.

This is the foulest act of wilful murder ever committed on the high seas and resulted in the loss of 1198 innocent people. It was only to be expected that the enemy would attempt to justify its evil work by proclaiming that the vessel was armed. The Lusitania was never actually in government service. Another German lie exposed!

SOURCE D

Part of a statement issued by the German government, May 1915.

The German Ambassador warned Americans against sailing on the Lusitania. Does a pirate act thus? Does he take pains to save human lives? Nobody regrets more than we Germans the hard necessity of sending to their deaths hundreds of men. Yet the sinking was a justifiable act of war, just like the bombing of a fortress. The sinking was necessary because she was equipped for fighting, and especially because we had to protect our brave soldiers from death by war supplies from the USA.

SOURCE E

Part of a history book, Lusitania, *by Colin Simpson, 1972. He had studied the original drawings of the alterations made to the ship.*

Under strict secrecy the Lusitania entered dry dock on 1 May 1913 ... Revolving gun-rings were mounted on the rear deck so that two 6 inch guns could be installed. Other decks were adapted to take four 6 inch guns on each side.

SOURCE F

Part of a letter written by Winston Churchill in 1914.

We need to entangle neutral ships with the German submarines, and the ships we most need to involve are the Americans'.

SOURCE G

Part of a history book, Lusitania, *by Colin Simpson, 1972.*

Looming large on the map in front of Churchill were the *U-20*, the British cruiser *Juno* and the *Lusitania*. Shortly after noon the Admiralty [naval headquarters] signalled the *Juno* to abandon her mission of escorting the *Lusitania* to Liverpool. The *Lusitania* was not informed that she was now alone and every minute getting closer to the *U-20*.

SOURCE H

Part of an article published in the Sunday Times, *15 August 1982.*

The *Lusitania* was built for Cunard in 1906, financed by a massive government subsidy. Cunard, in return, agreed to build her so she could be converted into an armed cruiser ... She had special mountings built into her decks which could take 6 inch guns. There is no available evidence that the guns were fitted. But the Germans believed they were hidden just below deck and could be brought out in a matter of minutes. During the war on almost every voyage from America she was stuffed with war materials. On her last voyage there is convincing evidence that apart from five million rounds of ammunition, she carried a large quantity of explosives.

Activities

1 Study Sources B, C and D. To what extent do the sources agree on what happened and who was to blame?

2 Study Source E. Does Source E help you to decide which of Sources B, C or D is more reliable in finding out what happened and who was to blame?

3 Study Sources F, G and H. On the basis of the evidence now available to you which of the Sources B, C or D would you call propaganda?

4 'The blame for the sinking of the *Lusitania* should be shared equally between the Germans, the British and the USA'. To what extent is this judgement justified?

**How did the British government make use of the sinking of the *Lusitania*
for propaganda purposes against the Germans?**

Government propaganda relating to the sinking of the *Lusitania* was primarily aimed at the political elite in the USA. The propagandists working for the British government knew that those Americans in positions of power were far too clever to be taken in by any blunt and crude propaganda stunt. A more subtle approach was needed: the USA was neutral and the hope was to encourage her to join the Allied Powers. When the *Lusitania* sank, drowning over a hundred American citizens, it was an opportunity too good to be missed for the British to exploit. So, when the Germans said that the *Lusitania* was carrying munitions the claim fell on deaf ears partly because of a brilliant propaganda campaign.

The British obtained a copy of the commemorative medal (Source A detail) struck by a private German craftsman. The British Department of Information decided to produce a boxed replica of the medal. About 300,000 replicas of the *Lusitania* medal were eventually sold with profits going to the Red Cross.

SOURCE A

This is a photograph of the one of the forty-four commemorative medals that were struck by a private German craftsman soon after the sinking of the *Lusitania*. One side reads 'The great steamer *Lusitania* sunk by a German submarine, 7 May 1915'. The inscription at the top reads, 'no contraband'. The other side of the medal shows Death selling tickets in the Cunard office under the motto 'business before everything'.

SOURCE B

A British government leaflet accompanying the boxed replica of the German medal.

This medal has been struck in Germany with the object of keeping alive in German hearts the recollection of the glorious achievement of the German navy in deliberately destroying an unarmed passenger ship, together with 1198 non-combatants, men, women and children. The picture seeks to suggest that if a murderer warns his victim of his intention, the guilt of the crime will rest with the victim and not with the murderer.

SOURCE C

British government poster published soon after the sinking of the Lusitania *with the medal struck by Germany in the bottom left-hand corner.*

SOURCE D

A summary of the findings of the Bryce Report into alleged German outrages. It was published within days of the sinking of the Lusitania. *The report printed unchallenged testimonies of Belgian refugees.*

Belgian refugees claimed they had seen or heard of the raping of women, children and babies; heads and women's breasts being cut off, the bayoneting of children and the nailing of a child to a farmhouse door.

Activities

1 Look at Sources A, B and C. What impression of Germany's naval forces is conveyed by each source?

2 Why is the message in Source A different from that conveyed by Sources B and C?

3 Why was the target of the *Lusitania* propaganda the American political elite?

4 The USA did not join the war on Britain's side until April, 1917. Does this mean the propaganda campaign following the sinking of the *Lusitania* was a complete failure?

5 Do you trust what Source D says about German atrocities?

6 The historian, Philip Taylor wrote, 'We are unable to track the precise impact of any propaganda campaign.' Why is it so difficult for the historian to do this?

Women's suffrage

In 1918 the war ended. For some women 1918 was a year of double celebration. Not only was the war over but women over thirty were enfranchised. Why did some women finally win the struggle for the vote?

Why were some women given the vote in 1918?

In 1915 the government had realised that the old voting system was not going to work. It required that voters had to have lived in the same place for twelve months before an election. This meant that soldiers would not be able to vote. The law had to be changed. A Speaker's Conference was set up to discuss proposals for reform. Women seized the opportunity for a bigger change that included votes for women. They put pressure on the government to include female suffrage in the new law. There was no violence this time; instead, meetings were organised between politicians and suffrage leaders. One key difference, compared with the prewar situation was that Asquith was no longer Prime Minister; in 1916, the job was taken by David Lloyd George.

A law was finally passed in 1918 but it only gave the vote to women over thirty. Why did the law change in 1918 and why was the vote given only to older women? Some historians argue that the work done by women during the First World War was the key factor in winning the right to vote; others say that it was the fact they had demonstrated their loyalty as citizens of the British state. It is important to bear in mind that in other countries women had won the right to vote at different times. In France, Britain's ally during the 1914–18 conflict, it was 1944 before the franchise was extended to women.

SOURCE A

Part of a speech by Herbert Asquith in the House of Commons in 1917. Asquith had been Prime Minister from 1908 to 1916 when he had opposed giving women the vote.

My opposition to women's right to vote is well known. However, for three years now the suffragettes have not started that horrible campaign of violence. Not only that, they have contributed to every service during this war except that of fighting. I therefore believe that some measure of women's suffrage should be given.

SOURCE B

From a history textbook called Votes for Women 1860–1928, *written in 1998.*

A very simplified view would see the vote as a reward for loyal wartime service. However, careful study shows how little changed from the war, not how much. In the newspaper reports of the time women workers received a warm welcome; but in farms, hospitals and factories they were greatly resented. This reflects most men's attitudes towards women at the time. Men felt happiest if women became nurses, providers of refreshments for the troops and brought up fighting men of the future. Politicians themselves agreed with the idea that the woman who had brought children up successfully had performed a service for the government that could be rewarded by giving the vote to such loyal citizens. The age limit of 30 was agreed by politicians because these women seemed to be more sensible and more likely to vote the same way as their husbands.

SOURCE C

A government poster put up during the war to encourage women to work in munitions factories.

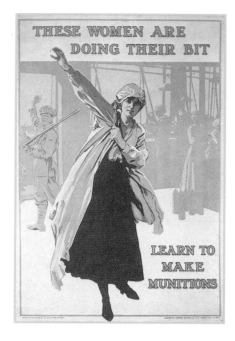

THESE WOMEN ARE DOING THEIR BIT

LEARN TO MAKE MUNITIONS

SOURCE D

Part of the obituary in the Guardian *of Millicent Fawcett, founder and leader of the NUWSS, 6 August 1929.*

Had there been no militancy and no war, the emancipation of women would have come, although more slowly. But without the faithful preparation of the ground over many years by Millicent Fawcett and her colleagues, neither militancy nor the war could have produced the crop.

The first female MP, Lady Astor.

SOURCE E

From a history book called the First World War in British History *written in 1995.*

In 1918 the vote was granted to women aged over 30 years. This can be explained partly as the result of a fifty year campaign during which some, at least, of the fears about women's enfranchisement had been allayed, and partly as a by-product of the decision to grant a vote to all adult men by the Speaker's Conference of 1916–1917. One of the reasons the politicians imposed a 30 year age requirement was their fear that the younger women might attempt to run their own candidates.

Activities

1 Study Sources A and B. Can you explain the contradictory attitudes towards women in these sources?

2 Study Source C. Many women who worked in munitions factories did not win the right to vote in 1918. Why not?

3 Study Sources D and E. To what extent do they agree on the reasons why women got the vote?

4 'Women over thirty were given the vote in 1918 because men thought it was safe to do so'. Study all the sources and use your knowledge. Is this an accurate statement?

The end of war and the beginning of peace: 1918

By 1918 British attitudes towards Germany had been coloured by the war, the propaganda and the allegations of atrocities. 'Hang the Kaiser' was a popular slogan at the time of the Armistice. Many British people blamed him for starting the war. Now that the fighting was ended and attention was turning to the Paris peace conference starting in January 1919 at Versailles, many people simply had one thing on their mind: revenge. Did everybody in Britain share the clamour for revenge and hate the Germans?

A painting by Franz Lesshaft. Peace – public celebrations.

What was the attitude of the British people at the end of the war towards Germany?

SOURCE A

Sir Edward Geddes, Member of Parliament, speaking in public soon after the Armistice.

Germany is going to pay. I personally have no doubt that we are going to get everything out of her that you can squeeze out of a lemon and a bit more. Not only all the gold Germany has got but all her silver and jewels shall be handed over. All her pictures and libraries shall be sold to the allies and the proceeds used to pay the indemnity. I would strip Germany as she stripped Belgium.

SOURCE B

Prime Minister Lloyd George in Parliament the day after the Armistice.

We must not let any sense of revenge, any spirit of greed, any grasping desire override the fundamental principles of righteousness. The mandate of this government at the next election will mean that the British government ... will be in favour of a just peace.

SOURCE C

A photograph taken in November 1918 at Brackley, Northamptonshire. The two effigies are the Kaiser and his son.

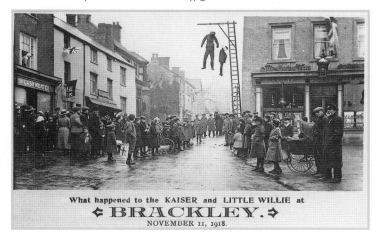

What happened to the KAISER and LITTLE WILLIE at
← BRACKLEY. →
NOVEMBER 11, 1918.

SOURCE D

A poster produced by the British Empire Union. This organisation wanted to protect Britain's trade with the rest of the empire.

SOURCE E

A summary of the narrative of a silent film, Once a Hun, always a Hun, that was shown in British cinemas towards the end of the war.

Two German soldiers are first shown in a ruined French town meeting a woman with a babe in arms. The soldiers strike them to the ground. The scene changes. The two soldiers gradually merge into two commercial travellers now in an English village after the war. They enter a shop and show the shopkeeper a pan. At first the shopkeeper is impressed, but his wife appears, looks at the pan and reveals the 'Made in Germany' inscription underneath. She calls in a policeman who orders the Germans from the shop. The final words on the screen point up the message, 'there can be no trading with these people after the war'.

SOURCE F

A cartoon from Punch magazine, February 1919.

GIVING HIM ROPE?

Activities

1 Study Sources A and B. To what extent do they agree about how Germany should be treated?

2 Study Sources C, D, E and F. What do these sources suggest about the British public's attitude towards Germany at the end of the war?

3 Do these sources suggest anti-German attitudes were common in Britain at the end of the war?

4 Lloyd George was unable to take a lenient approach towards Germany at the Paris peace conference. Use the sources from this unit to explain why this happened.

Review: British society 1906–18

BRITAIN IN 1906

At the beginning of this period Britain was experiencing the consequences of the Industrial Revolution – urbanisation, widespread poverty and inequalities. Alongside these pressures ran changes in technology and education. British people were increasingly literate and more easily able to communicate with others across the country. Traditional ideas and attitudes were challenged by the decline of religious belief.

CONTINUITIES AND CHANGES

> During these twelve years many changes took place but not all of them were long lasting. The government's powers increased significantly during the First World War, but the state withdrew from many of its wartime activities in the post-1918 period. Likewise, the changes in women's employment during 1914–18 were only temporary as those men who survived returned to their old jobs and the industries that had sprung up because of the war declined.

> Britain became more democratic during these years. Even though the class structure remained the same the power of the House of Lords was curtailed. It could no longer delay money bills that had been passed by the House of Commons. Furthermore, in 1912 MPs were paid salaries for the first time, thus encouraging the less well-off to stand as candidates. Not only was power shifting towards the House of Commons, but the expanded electorate after 1918 included some women. However, women voters and the presence of female MPs did not signal a substantial change in male chauvinist attitudes.

> The poor were better off in 1918 than at the beginning of the century. Growing numbers of workers were joining trade unions. The Liberal reforms passed between 1906 and 1911 offered selective support for the sick, the unemployed and the poor. The Children's Charter was a significant event for young people, too.

> The effects of the Great War loomed large in postwar Britain: nearly 1 million men died, countless others injured, the economy drained of resources and Germany, one of Britain's best trading partners lay shattered in the middle of Europe. During the twenty years after 1918 some people, who were duped by the government's censoring of the reality of war, joined groups to campaign for a peaceful world. Among them were many women, who, for the first time were part of the democratic process.

GERMANY
1919–1945

The Weimar Republic

War and revolution

In 1918 Germany began to crack under the strain of war. Shortages, power cuts, inflation and anti-war demonstrations were bad enough, but then a lethal virus swept across Europe: influenza. Thousands of soldiers and civilians died. With the German army in disorder, General Ludendorff announced in the Reichstag (the German parliament) that Germany was in grave danger of defeat. A peace must be made soon before Germany lost on the battlefield.

President Wilson offered an armistice on condition that Germany became more democratic. In particular, he wanted the Reichstag to have greater power and the Kaiser to have less. At first the Kaiser would not budge. Then, on 28 October 1918, sailors at Kiel refused to put to sea to fight the British. From this point on, Germany descended into chaos. The government in Berlin lost control and could not stop the ordinary civilians and soldiers seizing power. Between 4 and 6 November, mutineers seized control of the ports of Rostock, Cuxhaven and Lübeck. Revolution then spread inland. In Saxony and Bavaria, socialists established republics. Lacking the support of his army generals, the Kaiser fled to Holland on 10 November, never to return again. In his place came not a hereditary monarch or emperor but an elected politician: Friedrich Ebert, leader of the Social Democratic Party.

The new democratic Germany

After the Armistice had been signed, Friedrich Ebert had two tasks: to hold democratic elections so a new government could be formed and to hammer out a new constitution detailing how the German people would be ruled. Elections in January 1919 did not produce a clear winner. The Social Democratic Party gained the most seats but had to join up with two other parties in order to form a government with a majority in the new parliament. Coalition governments were to be a feature right through the period 1918–30.

Politicians decided that Berlin was not a calm enough place in which to settle the details of the new constitution so they met in a small town called Weimar. Within six months the constitution was ready. Germany was, at least on paper, a democracy like Britain, France or the United States.

Period of crisis, 1918–23

During this five-year period, the newly formed Weimar Republic survived some serious crises. From both the left and the right came putsches (revolts), assassinations and anti-government propaganda. The economy, already weakened by the war effort, was further damaged by demands for reparations from the Allies and by terrifying inflation. And always the Weimar governments were baited about the 'stab in the back' and the punishing Treaty of Versailles which they had signed.

INFLATION

The price of bread in Berlin in German marks.

1918	0.54	1923	January	250.00
1921	3.90		June	3,465.00
1922	163.50		September	1,512,000.00
			November	201,000,000,000.00

ECONOMIC PROBLEMS

> 1918   2.4 million Germans killed. 70% of the cost of the war met by loans.

> 1921   Government prints more money to pay for the reparations.

> 1923   Government prints more money to pay the wages of workers on strike in the Ruhr.

ATTEMPTS TO TAKE POWER

> 1919 (January): the Spartacist revolt. A group of Communists tried to take control of Berlin. Ex-soldiers, the Freikorps, were let loose and killed the leaders.

> 1920 (March): the Kapp Putsch. Wolfgang Kapp led the Freikorps in an attempt to take control of Berlin. The workers came out on strike, bringing the city to a standstill. Kapp was arrested.

> 1923 (November): the Beer Hall Putsch (or Munich Putsch). Adolf Hitler, with the support of some leading army figures, tried to take over Munich. The police and army restored control. The leaders were arrested and put on trial for treason.

IMPLEMENTATION OF THE TREATY OF VERSAILLES

> 1919 French, British and US troops move into the Rhineland.

> 1920 The peace treaty comes into force.

> 1921 Reparations total decided: £6,600 million.

> 1922 (December) Germany defaults on her reparation payments.

> 1923 (January) French and Belgian troops enter the Ruhr to take goods from Germany to maintain reparation payments. The German workers come out on strike and refuse to co-operate with the French.

> 1923 (September) Stresemann calls off passive resistance in the Ruhr.

> 1923 (November) New currency introduced: the Rentenmark.

A French soldier guarding a train full of German coal from the Ruhr. In 1923, the French invaded to take goods back to France for reparation payment.

Period of recovery, 1924–29

What brought stability and recovery to Germany was a huge loan from the United States in an agreement called the Dawes Plan. This £40 million loan, combined with a new currency to replace the one so devalued by inflation, revived the German economy. Much of this short-term loan was used by the government on housing and public works. Unemployment figures fell. Prosperity was further enhanced when reparations were cut as part of the Dawes Plan and cut again by the Young Plan in 1929. Germans were finally enjoying good times, and support for politicians on the extreme left and right who wanted radical change dwindled away at election time.

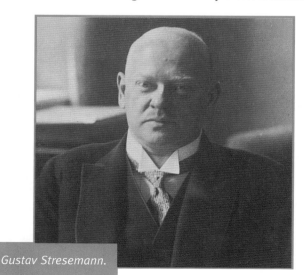

Gustav Stresemann.

One politician who was popular during this period was Gustav Stresemann, the German Foreign Minister. He combined stability on the domestic front with success abroad. In 1925 Germany signed the Locarno treaty. The next year she was allowed to join other countries on an equal footing at the League of Nations. Germany signed the Kellogg–Briand Pact in 1928. These two agreements marked Germany's reintegration into the family of European powers. The following year Britain and France agreed to withdraw their troops from the Rhineland, five years ahead of the schedule laid down by the Treaty of Versailles.

In 1928, the Weimar Republic was celebrating its tenth birthday. The young democracy had weathered many storms and Germany was once more respected abroad. Nothing, it seemed, could spoil Stresemann's apparent success and Germany's revival since the years of crisis.

Discussion points

> Why do wars sometimes bring about revolutions like the one in Germany in 1918?

> In which year was the existence of the Weimar Republic most in danger?

The Spartacist revolt

Historians do not only describe events, they interpret them. One label they often use is 'revolution'. Is this a justifiable interpretation of events in Germany in 1918–19?

Was there a revolution in 1918–19?

The chaos in Germany in 1918 saw the power of central government in Berlin break down as Workers' and Soldiers' Councils took control in most towns and cities. The rulers were no longer trusted and ordinary people were enjoying the taste of power. Then the Kaiser abdicated and a republic was declared in Berlin by Ebert, the leader of the Social Democratic Party (SPD), the moderate socialists. In December 1918, a national congress of Councils met in Berlin. Since most of the delegates were moderate socialists, they supported Ebert's proposal to hold elections for a National Assembly. But the revolutionary socialists (Spartacists) disagreed: an election would mean that upper-class and middle-class Germans would still run Germany and the workers would lose out.

The Spartacists refused to let their chance of creating a socialist Germany slip away. In January 1919, Karl Liebknecht and Rosa Luxemburg led an armed uprising in Berlin to snatch power from Ebert. From Ebert's point of view, Germany needed law and order more than it needed socialism. He could not rely on the army because it had dissolved after the Armistice so instead he used the Freikorps, bands of ex-servicemen who hated socialism in any shape or form. Brutally, they crushed the Berlin revolt. Liebknecht and Luxemburg were murdered. The surviving Spartacists saw this as treachery: the moderate socialists had betrayed the working class. This split on the left was to prove very costly. When German democracy started to crumble after 1930, the workers were unable to unite in order to save it.

SOURCE A

Demands made by the Spartacists on 7 October 1918.

The struggle for real democracy is not about a National Assembly and the vote; it is concerned with the real enemies of working people: private property, control over the army and justice. We demand the transfer of power to Workers' and Soldiers' Councils; the nationalisation of all property, and the reorganisation of the army so that ordinary soldiers have power.

SOURCE B

From a speech by Max Cohen, a member of the SPD, the moderate socialist party led by President Ebert.

The will of the people can only be reflected in a National Assembly elected by every German. The Workers' and Soldiers' Councils can only express the will of some of the people not all of them.

Ebert used force to crush the Spartacist revolt because he was so scared of Germany collapsing into chaos. This had happened in Russia after the 1917 socialist revolution. His fear prevented him from supporting the Workers' Councils. If he had worked with them, together they could have introduced democratic reforms in the civil service, the army and the judiciary. As it was, the 'old guard' survived; only the Kaiser himself was swept away.

Freikorps use bales of paper as a barricade during fighting outside newspaper offices in Berlin, 1919.

>> Activities

1 Look up the word 'revolution' in a dictionary. Do the events in Germany in 1918–19 deserve the label 'revolution'? If so, why?

2 Compare developments in Germany with other events which historians call revolutions. For example, what similarities and differences are there with the Russian revolutions in 1917?

3 One historian has labelled developments in Germany in 1918–19 a 'half-finished revolution'. How far do you agree with this interpretation?

Democracy in Weimar Germany

In August 1919 the new republic adopted a new constitution so that the country could be run as a democracy.

How democratic was the Weimar Republic?

The parliament

A new parliament (Reichstag) was established with members elected by Germans over the age of 20. Voting took place in secret and the number of seats a political party won in the Reichstag was dependent upon the proportion of votes cast. Called 'proportional representation', this system never produced a majority of seats for any one party; coalitions had to be formed.

The President

A President was elected separately so that he could act as a check on the Reichstag's power. He held office for seven years. His powers included the ability to appoint and dismiss the government. He could dissolve the Reichstag and, under Article 48, he could announce a 'state of emergency' to preserve law and order in a crisis. Under these circumstances he could assume enormous power by setting aside the Fundamental Rights (a series of articles focusing on the rights of the individual).

SOURCE A

The main features of the pre-1919 German constitution.

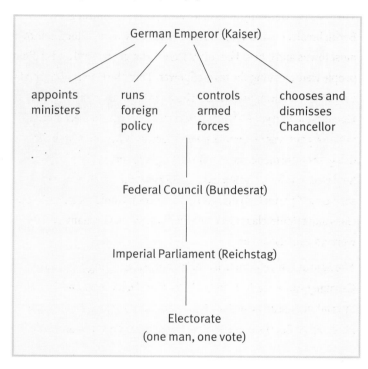

Federal government

The Weimar constitution established a federal system of government. This means that the power to make and enforce laws was shared between the central government in Berlin and the 18 state (Länder) governments. For example, Berlin had control over taxation and religion; the Länder governments had control over the police, courts and schools.

In addition to these provisions on the running of government, there were 56 articles setting out the rights of individual Germans.

SOURCE B

Personal freedom is guaranteed. No-one can be arrested unless they have broken the law.

The home of every German is a place of safety for him. The authorities cannot enter it without proper cause.

Every German has the right to express his opinion freely by word, writing, printed matter or picture.

All Germans have the right to hold peaceful meetings.

All Germans have the right to form unions and societies.

Property is guaranteed.

Some of the 56 articles and Fundamental Rights in the Weimar constitution of 1919.

SOURCE C

This map shows most of the 18 German Länder in 1919 after the Treaty of Versailles.

Map labels: Oldenburg, Mecklenburg, East Prussia, Prussia, Brunswick, Hanover, Thuringia, Hesse-Darmstadt, Saxony, Palatinate, Baden, Bavaria, Württemberg, Prussian Land

>> Activities

1 Describe the differences between the pre-1919 constitution (Source A) and the new Weimar constitution.

2 Use the background information and all the Sources. Can you see any potential dangers for German democracy within the new constitution?

Opposition to Weimar Germany: part one

You have seen how the new constitution seemed to provide Germans with a democratic framework for conducting politics. However, democracy needs to have deep roots in society and the support of many people if it is to survive. The Weimar Republic faced opposition from many groups in German society.

Who opposed the Weimar Republic and why?

The democratic politicians of the new republic failed to take the opportunity presented to them by the 1918 revolution to remove from power those people who opposed the new system. The army, the police, the judiciary, the schools and the universities were all staffed by people who disliked, even hated, the democratic system. Many looked back longingly to the days before 1914 when the Kaiser was the unquestioned ruler and Germany was a first-rate power with an empire and a strong, growing economy. In those days, there was a feeling of certainty about living in Germany. Now, during the 1920s, there seemed to be nothing but uncertainty.

Even some politicians and their parties did not support the Weimar Republic. Although they took part in elections, they despised the democratic process. One such party was formed by Anton Drexler in 1919. It was called the German Workers' Party. Drexler was soon replaced as leader by Adolf Hitler, who renamed it the National Socialist German Workers' Party, or Nazi Party for short.

In this two-part investigation you will study evidence which will help you to understand the attitudes and beliefs of Germans who opposed Weimar democracy. The second part of the investigation looks specifically at the ideas and policies of the new Nazi Party.

Understanding attitudes and beliefs

During the 1920s the enemies of the Weimar Republic were very critical of the lack of 'strong' government. In some ways they were right: every single Weimar government was a coalition – usually an alliance of three political parties. These parties did not always agree; squabbling broke out and often coalitions broke up and new ones formed. The parties which featured most frequently in coalitions during the 1920s were the SPD (Social Democratic Party), the Centre Party and the DDP (German Democratic Party). Other political parties campaigned actively against the Republic. Even so, at election time, most Germans voted for parties which supported the Weimar democratic system.

Vote Communist! An election poster of the KPD shows the ghost of the murdered Communist, Karl Liebknecht, threatening his enemies.

SOURCE A

The main political parties in the Reichstag including those which formed the coalition governments during the 1920s. The parties are displayed left to right on the political spectrum.

PARTY	KPD (Communist Party, previously the Spartacists)	SPD (Social Democratic Party)	DDP (German Democratic Party)
SUPPORT	the working class	mostly from the industrial working class and some lower middle class	mostly middle class
POLICIES	against the Republic and in favour of a workers' revolution like the Russian model	supported the Republic; wanted social reforms to help working people and the less well-off	supported the Republi strong belief in individual freedom

SOURCE B

Percentage of the total vote won by the main parties in elections between 1919 and 1928.

	1919	1920	1924 May	1924 Dec	1928
Communists	—	2	12	9	11
Social Democratic Party	38	21	21	26	30
German Democratic Party	19	8	6	6	5
Centre Party	20	18	17	18	15
German People's Party	4	14	9	10	9
German Nationalist Party	10	15	19	21	14
Nazis	—	—	7	3	2
Minor Parties	9	22	9	7	14

SOURCE C

Growth of industrial production in Germany between 1880 and 1930.

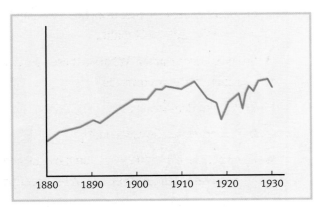

SOURCE D

From an interview with an officer of the Freikorps in 1919.

It really turned the stomachs of us old soldiers to see how quickly they got rid of the black-white-red flag of the old Empire. Under this flag thousands of soldiers lie buried in enemy territory. I don't hide the fact that I'm a monarchist. When you've served your Emperor for 30 years you can't just say: from tomorrow I'm a republican.

SOURCE E

This extract is taken from a report in a right-wing newspaper, Oletzkoer Zeitung, in August 1921. It comments on the assassination of Matthias Erzberger, a government minister and member of the Centre Party.

Erzberger, the man who is alone responsible for the humiliating armistice; Erzberger, the man who is responsible for the Versailles 'treaty of shame'; Erzberger has at last received the punishment suitable for a traitor.

Justice?

Judges were supposed to uphold the democratic laws in Germany fairly and justly. However, many of them gave lenient punishments to right-wingers who had committed violent political crimes while left-wingers were given harsh penalties. A communist called the Weimar state a 'robber's republic' and was sent to prison for four weeks. A right-winger who called it a 'Jews' republic' was only fined 70 marks.

Centre Party	DVP (German People's Party)	DNVP (German Nationalist Party)	NSDAP (National Socialist German Workers' Party, Nazi Party)
Roman Catholics from all classes	the wealthy middle class, especially the owners of businesses; led by Gustav Stresemann	middle and upper classes including some government officials and soldiers	nationalists and conservatives on the right of German politics including some Freikorps and lower middle-class people
supported the Republic and the interests of the Roman Catholic Church	really monarchists; came to accept the Republic with great reluctance; wanted government to support trade and industry	against the Republic; strongly nationalist; wanted strong central government to make Germany strong and powerful again	against the Republic; in favour of strong government

SOURCE F

„Sie kommen zu spät, meine Herren! — Er ist tot."

This cartoon was published in 1929, the year of Stresemann's death, in a German newspaper, Vorwärts. The nurse is saying 'You're too late, Stresemann is dead'. The Nazis following Hugenberg are carrying a stink bomb, a bucket of manure and posters saying 'Traitor' and 'Stresemann, rot in hell'. (Hugenberg became leader of the DNVP in 1928.)

SOURCE G

Political murders in Germany between 1919 and 1923.

	Murders by the extreme left	Murders by the extreme right
Number of murders	22	354
Number of murderers sentenced by the courts	38	24
Average length of prison sentence	15 years	4 months
Number of murderers executed	10	0

>> Activities

1 Study Sources A and B. Which political parties did not completely support the Weimar Republic? How much electoral support did these parties have during the 1920s?

2 Study Sources C, D and E. How would the author of Source D use evidence from Sources C and E to criticise the Weimar Republic?

3 Study Sources E and F. What do these Sources tell you about attitudes towards

   a Weimar democracy

   b Erzberger and Stresemann?

4 Use all the Sources and what you have learned so far about the Weimar Republic. Which groups of Germans appear not to have supported the Weimar Republic and what were the reasons for their opposition?

227

Opposition to Weimar Germany: part two

As you saw in the previous investigation, opposition to Weimar democracy came from many quarters. Some of Weimar's bitterest enemies were ex-soldiers, those who had fought and survived the Great War but came home to find revolution and their army careers ruined by the Treaty of Versailles. One of those most bitter about the defeat was a young army corporal named Adolf Hitler.

What were the ideas and policies of the Nazi Party?

Hitler was born in Braunau in Austria in 1889. Success at secondary school soon turned sour when he went to Vienna hoping to attend art school. Twice he applied for a place and twice he was rejected. His dreams of becoming a painter were shattered. For a few years he became a homeless drifter making a little money from his paintings. Then, when war broke out in 1914, Hitler's desperate years came to an end. His life took on new purpose. He went to Germany to join up and to contribute to a glorious victory – or so he thought.

As the war ended in 1918 so did Hitler's most 'unforgettable' experience as a corporal in the German army. He was twice rewarded for bravery with the Iron Cross. He had lived and breathed the team spirit of the trenches, seen Germans unite against a common enemy and sacrifice their lives for the Fatherland. Now that the war was over, what was he to do?

Hitler and the Nazi Party

In Munich, Hitler soon found work as a routine surveillance officer for the army. Many nationalist and racist groups had formed immediately after the war and Hitler was employed to spy on one of them: the German Workers' Party. Anton Drexler, the founder of the party, was so impressed by Hitler that in September 1919 he invited him to join the group as its fifty-fifth member and to become responsible for recruitment and propaganda. The ex-corporal relished the post. Hitler was such a good speaker at meetings that he

SOURCE A

This Nazi poster shows a worker smashing 'International High Finance' in the name of socialism. On other occasions, the Nazis stressed the 'national' elements of their programme to appeal to the business classes.

was chosen to launch the German Workers' Party programme on 24 February 1920. It contained 25 points and was partly written and edited by Hitler. He told his audience that the programme was 'unchangeable'. In the same speech, the new party name was announced: from now on it would be known as the National Socialist German Workers' Party or Nazi Party for short. (The term 'Nazi' is a shortened version of the German word 'nationalsozialistisch' meaning national socialist.)

SOURCE B

Extracts from the Nazi Party programme (1920).

1 We demand the union of all Germans into a greater Germany.

2 We demand that Germany be treated in the same way as other countries and we demand the annulling of the Treaty of Versailles.

3 We demand land for our growing population.

4 Only a fellow German can have right of citizenship. A fellow German can only be so if he is of German parentage. This excludes Jews.

6 Only German citizens shall have the right to vote; and they alone shall hold public office.

8 All immigration of non-Germans must stop immediately.

14 We demand that large industries share their profits with the workers.

15 We demand generous improvements in the old age pension system.

17 We demand a new law which would allow property to be confiscated without compensation if this is in the general interest of the nation.

24 We demand the freedom of religion in Germany so long as religion does not endanger the position of the state or the moral standards of the German race. The party opposes the Jewish religion for its love of wealth.

25 In order to achieve this programme, the party demands the setting up of a strong central government with complete authority for parliament over the whole country.

Later in the 1920s, Hitler amended point 17 of the Nazi Party programme which had allowed for the confiscation of certain private property without compensation. To woo middle-class voters, Hitler now said that the Party would only confiscate property owned by Jews.

SOURCE C

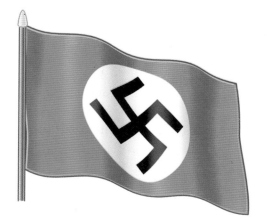

The Nazi Party flag.

SOURCE D

An extract from Mein Kampf *written by Adolf Hitler in 1924.*

As National Socialists we see our programme in our flag. In the red we see the social idea of the movement, in the white we see the nationalistic idea, and in the swastika we see our mission to achieve the victory of Aryan man.

Discussion point

> Which of the three colours in the Nazi Party flag received most attention in the 1920 programme?

Even at this early stage, membership of the Nazi Party was spread across all classes of Germans. Most members were lower middle class – shopkeepers and small businessmen, for example. It was they who set the tone of the organisation and its meetings: male-dominated, beer-swilling, authoritarian, anti-semitic and anti-intellectual. There were some members from the working class: craftworkers were particularly attracted to the Party. Some from the elite of German society also swelled Hitler's movement: managers, academics and university students.

>> Activities

Study Sources A, B, C and D.

1 Make a list of those Nazi policies which were 'nationalist' and those which were 'socialist'.

2 When he announced the Nazi Party programme in 1920, Hitler said it was 'unchangeable', yet later in the 1920s he did amend it. Does this mean that Source B is unreliable and cannot be used to investigate Hitler's attitudes and beliefs in the 1920s?

3 Why do you think the lower middle class were particularly attracted by Hitler, his policies and his movement?

1924–29: stabilisation and recovery?

Until recently the general picture of Germany in the period 1924–29 was one of stability and prosperity following the crises of 1918–23. With Gustav Stresemann as Chancellor in 1923 and as Foreign Minister between 1923 and 1929, the Weimar Republic recovered from its bad start. However, recent research in German archives has prompted a review of this interpretation.

To what extent did the Weimar Republic recover after 1923?

To begin with, the performance of the economy during this period has come in for close scrutiny. Some historians have pointed out that even though Germany recovered after 1923, her share of the world's industrial production between 1926 and 1929 was only 11.6% compared with 14.3% in 1913. This seems to throw doubt on the traditional picture historians have given of Germany between 1924 and 1929. Just how strong was this recovery in Germany? Did the loans from the Dawes Plan simply paper over cracks which would reappear later?

When Stresemann died through overwork in October 1929, it seemed to contemporaries that he had pulled Weimar democracy through its worst crises.

SOURCE A

An extract from Stresemann's obituary in The Times, *a British newspaper, 4 October 1929.*

By the death of Stresemann, Germany has lost her ablest statesman. He worked hard to rebuild his shattered country and for peace and co-operation abroad. In 1923 the French were in the Ruhr, the currency had collapsed, the reparations issue was unsolved. Germany seemed to be in ruins. Then he took over and under his leadership Germany is now orderly and prospering at home; in the affairs of Europe she has an important place.

THE TREATY OF LOCARNO

This treaty, signed by Stresemann in December 1925, helped restore Germany's pride. In spite of continuing problems over reparations payments, France and Britain began treating Germany less as a defeated enemy and more as an equal. Germany, France and Belgium agreed to maintain their western frontiers and to refrain from using force to alter them. Britain and Italy guaranteed the treaty.

Part of this debate depends upon how you interpret the word 'recovery'. Did Germany 'recover' its place in Europe as a respected nation and equal partner? Or did the economy 'recover' from its wartime dislocation, hyper-inflation and the burden of reparations?

SOURCE B

From A History of Germany, 1815–1945, *by William Carr, published in 1979.*

Gustav Stresemann contributed greatly to the stabilisation of the Weimar Republic. He was working for the speedy withdrawal of all foreign troops from German soil, for the removal of the moral shame of the war-guilt clause and for Germany's entry into the League of Nations.

By 1930, Germany was once again one of the world's great industrial nations. Her spectacular recovery was made possible by a huge amount of American investment; between 1924 and 1929, 25,000 million marks poured into Germany. By 1929 iron and steel, coal, chemicals and electrical products had all matched or beaten the 1913 production figures.

Up-to-date management techniques and more efficient methods of production brought about a tremendous increase in productivity; blast-furnaces, for example, trebled their output.

However, a number of scholars have found that the prosperity described by William Carr in Source B was neither secure nor widespread.

SOURCE C

This photo was taken during the negotiation of the Locarno Treaty in December 1925. From left to right: Gustav Stresemann, Sir Joseph Austen Chamberlain (Britain) and Aristide Briand (France).

SOURCE D

Table 1 shows the level of industrial production in Germany during the 1920s.

Table 2 shows the number of unemployed during the 1920s.

Table 1 *(1928 = 100)*

Year	Capital goods	Consumer goods
1920	56	51
1921	65	69
1922	70	74
1923	43	57
1924	65	81
1925	80	85
1926	77	80
1927	97	103
1928	100	100
1929	102	97
1930	84	91

Capital goods are machines used for making other goods. Consumer goods are things bought by consumers (i.e. finished products).
1928 = 100: this figure means that the standard against which all other years are measured is 100. Anything below 100 means worse, anything above means better.

Table 2

Year	No. (000s)	% of working population
1921	346	1.8
1922	215	1.1
1923	818	4.1
1924	927	4.9
1925	682	3.4
1926	2025	10.0
1927	1312	6.2
1928	1391	6.3
1929	1899	8.5
1930	3076	14.0

SOURCE E

From Hitler and Nazism *by Dick Geary, published in 1993.*

Germany's recovery had become dependent upon foreign loans. This meant that the country was very vulnerable to movements on the money markets and the level of confidence of overseas investors.

Agricultural prices which had been steady after the early 1920s were already falling by 1927 [...] The result was a debt crisis for farmers. Nor was everything rosy in the industrial sector in the mid-20s. Heavy industry (coal, iron and steel) was already experiencing problems making profits and even in the relatively prosperous year of 1927, German steel mills worked at no more than 70% of their capacity.

>> Activities

1 Using evidence drawn from the Sources in this investigation and your knowledge from previous chapters of this book, write two accounts of the Weimar Republic, 1924–29.

> Account **a** should explain how the period was one of stability, success and prosperity.

> Account **b** should explain how the period was one of instability, failure and severe economic problems.

2 Two recent historians have called this period: 'deceptive stability' and 'relative stability'. Why do you think these labels have been used? What use would these two historians make of the statistics in Source D?

The Nazi Party in the 1920s

Political power can be seized in many different ways. In Germany in the 1920s, those who wanted to take control did not all share the same ideas and values. Some were in favour of using violence, others wanted to use only democratic procedures.

Why did the Nazi Party have little real success before 1930?

To answer this question, this investigation looks at two issues:

> What tactics did the Nazis use to try and gain power?

> Why did they fail?

Using violence

In the years leading up to 1924, Hitler was convinced that using violence was the only way the Nazis would gain power. What he needed was his own private army. In 1921 he established the Sturmabteilung (SA) or Stormtroopers. Many of them were ex-soldiers but there were also younger men who felt they had missed out on the war. The SA was to be the 'battering ram' of the Nazi movement.

In November 1923 the timing seemed right to seize control in Munich, the capital of Bavaria. Inflation was out of control; the French were occupying the industrial Ruhr area to collect unpaid reparations; and Gustav Stresemann had called off passive resistance by German workers which had stopped production of coal and iron in the Ruhr. The government in Berlin appeared feeble.

Hitler's plan depended upon elements of the army betraying the government and coming over to his side. Only with military support could his strategy of force be successful.

Since the beginning of the Weimar Republic, Bavaria had been a hotbed of reactionary opposition. Many right-wing groups were openly hostile to democracy. The Bavarian government also opposed Berlin and its attempts to interfere in Bavarian affairs.

On the night of 8 November 1923, Gustav von Kahr, a member of the Bavarian government, went to a political meeting at a beer hall in Munich. He was to be the main speaker. Also attending were General von Lossow, who was in command of the army in Bavaria,

SOURCE A

A cartoon drawn at the end of Hitler's trial. It shows Ludendorff and Hitler shouting from Munich beer mugs that they are Germany's saviours. The judge below says 'Rubbish! The worst charge we can bring is breaking public entertainment by-laws!'

and Colonel von Seisser, head of the state police force. Some of Hitler's SA were present in the audience with concealed weapons.

Hitler's plan was to seize Lossow, Kahr and Seisser, persuade them to join the Nazis in sparking off a national uprising against the Berlin government, and to replace democracy with strong central government. Hitler's plan failed. He entered the beer hall, rounded up Kahr, Lossow and Seisser and tried to persuade them of his plan. At first they rejected it. Then, when Hitler told them that General Ludendorff was supporting the Nazis, they changed their minds. Ludendorff arrived at the scene to lend his support.

SOURCE B

There is some doubt as to how sincere Kahr and Lossow were in their support for Hitler. As soon as they left the beer hall they raised the alarm. The state police and army were put on alert. If Hitler was to succeed, he needed military support. It was not forthcoming. A march through the streets of Munich by Hitler and his supporters the following morning attracted much public support but a police cordon brought the Nazis to a halt. A shot was fired and a police officer killed. Mayhem ensued. Soon, 16 Nazis lay dead. Hitler was arrested shortly afterwards.

Found guilty of treason, Hitler was sentenced to five years. While in prison he wrote his autobiography called *Mein Kampf* (My Struggle). He dedicated it to the 16 men who had died on 9 November 1923.

SOURCE C

This is part of the evidence which Hitler gave at his trial. Kahr, Lossow and Seisser were chief witnesses for the prosecution.

If our putsch was high treason then Lossow, Kahr and Seisser must have been committing high treason along with us, for during all these weeks we talked of nothing but the aims of which we now stand accused.

I alone bear the responsibility for the putsch but I am not a criminal because of that. There is no such thing as high treason against the traitors of 1918. I only wanted what's best for the German people.

SOURCE D

This map of Germany shows the city of Munich and the state of Bavaria.

This cartoon appeared in the magazine Simplicissimus *on 17 March 1924. It shows Hitler sitting on the shoulders of von Lossow, who is in turn sitting on the shoulders of von Kahr. Hitler is setting light to the roof of the building but von Kahr calls out to a policeman, 'Officer, arrest that arsonist up there!'*

A change of strategy

SOURCE E

This is part of a conversation which took place between Kurt Ludecke and Adolf Hitler at Landsberg Castle in 1924. Hitler is speaking to Ludecke, who supports his aims.

When I resume active work, it will be necessary to pursue a new policy. Instead of working to achieve power by an armed coup, we will have to hold our noses and enter the Reichstag against Catholic and Communist members. If outvoting them takes longer than outshooting them, at least the result will be guaranteed by their own constitution. Sooner or later we shall have a majority and after that – Germany.

>> Activities

1 Use Sources A to D.

> To what extent do the cartoonists share the same attitude towards the putsch and Hitler?

> How would you find out if these cartoons were typical of German public opinion at the time?

> Which of the cartoons is most sympathetic to Hitler's view of the trial as expressed in Source C?

2 Use Source E. In what way did the failed putsch of 1923 alter Hitler's strategy to gain political power?

THE MUNICH PUTSCH: A TURNING POINT

Later in his life, Hitler was to call his failed putsch a turning point in his political career.

> His trial was headline news in the national press.

> He was able to defeat his rivals for the leadership of the Nazi Party by pointing out that it was he and not they who had shown strength and resolve in trying to take power by force.

> Finally, the Munich putsch enabled Hitler to pursue a democratic route to power and to take the party along with him because he had demonstrated to them that violence did not work as a strategy.

1924–29: success and failure

In December 1924, Hitler was released from Landsberg prison after serving only nine months of his five-year sentence. In his absence, the Nazi Party had split into various different factions. It was officially banned and so was its paper, the *Völkischer Beobachter* (German People's Observer). What was Hitler to do now?

For Hitler and the Nazi Party, the years 1924 to 1929 brought a mixture of success and failure. At election time the Nazis failed to make much impression on the voters, but the party gradually became better organised and Hitler's personal grip on its members tightened.

DEVELOPMENTS IN THE NAZI PARTY, 1924–29

1924: Brown shirts became the official Nazi Party uniform. The swastika was adopted as the party emblem. The Stormtroopers (SA) continued to recruit.

1925: In February, the ban on the Nazis was lifted. Hitler relaunched the party.

1926: Nazi organisations were established to try to appeal to certain interest groups: the Nazi Students' League, Teachers' League, Law Officers' League and Women's League. A Nazi Party rally was held at Weimar; this began the pattern of military-style parades.

In February, Hitler defeated Gregor Strasser in a party leadership contest.

1927: Membership stood at 108,000 compared with 27,000 in 1925. Hitler reorganised the party to make it more efficient. He created a national headquarters in Munich. He insisted on central control of finance and of admission to membership.

SOURCE F

Adolf Hitler with his private army, the Stormtroopers, at a rally during the 1920s.

In spite of these developments between 1924 and 1929, the Nazi Party performed badly at elections. In May 1924 they won 32 seats in the Reichstag; in December of the same year they won 14; and in May 1928 they captured only 12. Voters were not interested in Hitler's programme. Good times had returned to Germany thanks to the Dawes Plan of 1924. The moderate parties survived the crises of 1918–23 and seemed to be handling the recovery well. Weimar democracy appeared to be working: the necessities of life – food, clothing and housing – were in more plentiful supply, and most Germans had jobs. Hitler's policies seemed out of place and rather reckless to nearly all voters.

>> Activity

Use all the Sources and your knowledge of Germany's recovery after 1923.

Even though Hitler failed to seize power in 1923 he later called the Munich putsch a turning point in his career. Can you explain why?

Art and culture in the
Weimar Republic

During the 1920s, Germany replaced France as the cultural centre of Europe. German culture sparkled with creativity as artists experimented in photography, art, literature, cinema and architecture.

What were the cultural achievements of the Weimar period?

The term used to describe this remarkable cultural upheaval is 'Modernism'. Essentially, European artists and writers tried to break away from the artistic conventions of the 19th century to create new ways of seeing and interpreting the world. Not everything changed radically, however. Some trends continued from the years before 1914, such as the artistic movement known as Expressionism. Weimar culture was unique because, in a very short period, Germans experienced a multitude of avant-garde (experimental) movements and the rapid development of a 'mass culture' in the form of radio, cinema and the press.

Yet this rush to become 'modern' attracted bitter criticism from those, like the Nazis, who opposed the Republic. They condemned Modernism as being out of touch with the experience of ordinary Germans. For example, they disliked the new freedom in dress and social customs which women were now enjoying and blamed these on Jewish and Communist influences from the Soviet Union. In many ways it seemed that political and cultural developments were completely separate from and irrelevant to each other during the Weimar years. The liveliness and creativity of the cultural scene did little to win respect for the Republic as a political system or to stabilise it as a democracy.

American influences: music, cabaret and dance

In the 1920s, Germany opened up to foreign influences which had been kept out during the war years. American popular culture was welcomed; it was more 'democratic', more modern, and it celebrated living in the present rather than looking back to the past. Charlie Chaplin, black American cabaret groups, movies, jazz and boxing: all these were now part of the German cultural scene. The American dance, the Charleston, was the most popular dance in Germany in 1926. 'The Chocolate Kiddies' dance troupe performed in May 1925 and Josephine Baker, dancing nude to jazz music, was a smash hit with Berliners.

SOURCE A

Josephine Baker in the 1920s. Her cabaret performances were very popular in Germany.

SOURCE B

This poster appeared all over Berlin in 1921 to warn people about sexually transmitted diseases. It reads 'Berlin, stop and think! You are dancing with death!'

Literature

Some authors broke away from writing about traditional subjects. New novels dealt with topical themes such as the misery of urban life and, in the late Weimar period, the desperation felt by the unemployed. Novels were written on sexual themes and many contained bitter social comment. An example of the latter is the famous novel about the war written in 1929 and turned into a film the following year. *All Quiet on the Western Front* was written by Erich Maria Remarque and it contained a strong anti-war message. It was translated into 25 languages and it sold 3.5 million copies.

Architecture and design

In 1919, Walter Gropius founded the Bauhaus, a new school of architecture and design. It became famous for trying to break down the barriers between art and science. New and startling buildings were created and experimental designs were produced for furniture, lamps and pottery using different materials.

SOURCE C

The Einstein Tower near Potsdam. It was built in 1921 and was designed by one of the new architects, Erich Mendelsohn.

Cinema and photography

It is true that cinema had started to develop before the war, but it was during the 1920s that film-making and cinema-going really took off in Germany. Two million people went to the cinema every day; there were 2,300 film theatres in 1918 but 5,000 in 1930 (this was more than in any other European country); Germany produced more films than all the rest of Europe put together. Germany became famous for Expressionist fantasy films like Robert Wiene's *The Cabinet of Dr Caligari* (1920) and Fritz Lang's *Metropolis* (1926). American films were also shown and Charlie Chaplin was a particular favourite. Hollywood strengthened its commercial position when 'talkies' were introduced in 1928–29, but the German film industry responded and, in 1932, produced 127 sound films.

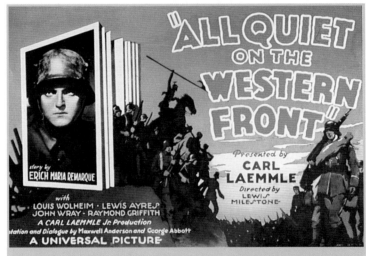

A poster for Hollywood's film version of Erich Maria Remarque's famous anti-war novel.

SOURCE D

This still is from The Cabinet of Dr Caligari, *directed by Robert Wiene in 1920. It shows Caligari's creature, Cesare, fleeing over nightmarish roof-tops with his victim in his arms.*

Radio

In 1923, the government gave permission for radio transmitters to be erected and for the manufacture of radio sets. This was a decisive turning point in public broadcasting. In 1924, nine radio companies covered the entire country. In April 1924 the number of listeners barely passed 10,000, but by April 1927 the total was 1.6 million and by April 1931 it had topped 3.7 million. In addition to music, listeners could hear radio plays and authors' readings.

SOURCE E

The Pillars of Society, *1926, by George Grosz criticises the leaders of Germany. This aggressive, modern style of painting was condemned by the Nazis. Compare it to the sentimental realism of the painting on page 54.*

Changes in attitudes and life-style

The 1920s saw significant developments in the mass media — radio, press and cinema. The consequences of this new technology affected the lives and the outlook of broad sections of the population. Old taboos were cast off: sexual matters were more openly discussed; new horizons opened for people through sport, hiking and the development of clubs.

German culture at this time was deeply divided. Modernism was not the only feature of the cultural scene. The new forms of art were not universally accepted and traditional forms were still influential. Nevertheless, the label often attached to Weimar culture is that of the 'golden twenties' and it is easy to see why.

>> Activities

Use all the Sources and your knowledge of the period.

1 Which of these cultural achievements would Hitler and the Nazis not have approved of? Why?

2 Choose one of the forms of culture that interests you and carry out some research. Find out what was typical in that form in the years before 1914. Were the 1920s a turning point in its development or merely a continuation of what had gone before?

Was the Weimar Republic doomed from the start?

It might seem strange to undertake a review of the Weimar Republic at this point (1930) rather than at the moment when Hitler assumed power in January 1933. But many historians see 1930 and not 1933 as the year when the Weimar Republic ceased to exist. Their argument is that from 1930, President Hindenburg used the emergency powers available to him under Article 48 of the constitution to rule Germany by decree. From that moment on the Reichstag became irrelevant and German democracy was dead.

This review of the Weimar Republic takes the form of a historical debate which still rages today.

Some historians argue that the Weimar Republic was doomed from the start.

> The Weimar constitution contained two fatal flaws. Firstly, the voting system of proportional representation produced weak coalition governments which were unable to provide Germany with strong central government. Secondly, Article 48 gave President Hindenburg the power to destroy democracy.

> Democracy is not just a piece of paper laying out rules and rights. It must have deep roots if it is to survive crises. The Weimar Republic was born out of defeat and revolution and never had the support of most Germans.

> Although the 1918 revolution had swept the Kaiser away, much stayed the same. Many Germans in the army, the civil service, the police, the judiciary and the universities and schools did not like what the revolution had done and opposed democracy and the Republic.

> Weimar politicians were burdened with problems which hampered their efforts to give the Republic a good name. Many Germans blamed them, rightly or wrongly, for 'stabbing the army in the back' by signing the Armistice in November 1918; for the punishing Treaty of Versailles (1919) and the ongoing reparations; for the terrifying inflation of 1922–23; and for Germany's dependence on loans from the United States through the Dawes Plan

Some historians argue that the Weimar Republic might have survived.

> The 1918 constitution was the best guarantee of individual liberties in Europe. Proportional representation is a voting system used in many countries today without problems; the same can be said of coalition governments. Furthermore, Article 48 was used successfully by President Ebert in dealing with the crises which arose in 1922–23.

> Democracy was nothing new in Germany in 1918. Under the old constitution, all males over 25 were allowed to vote for representatives in the parliament. The Social Democratic Party was established in 1875 and the Centre Party in 1870.

> The Weimar system and those politicians who had supported it had weathered all the crises between 1918 and 1923 and survived the taunts over their part in the Armistice and the Treaty of Versailles. If great German statesmen like Stresemann had still been alive, they could have rescued the Republic between 1930 and 1933.

> What destroyed the Weimar Republic was the crisis between 1930 and 1933. If the Depression had not hit Germany so severely and if the constitution had not been undermined, then the democracy established in 1918 could still be alive today.

The Depression, Nazi Germany and war

Germany, 1929–34: from democracy to dictatorship

These five years saw the death of the Weimar Republic and the establishment of Hitler's dictatorship, which was to last until his suicide in 1945.

Hitler was a political genius but he could not have been appointed Chancellor in January 1933 nor have established Nazi rule without help. In the difficult economic and social circumstances of the Great Depression, many longed for a return to strong authoritarian government similar to that provided by the Kaisers. Many people in Germany's political elite were looking around for someone to head this sort of government. Hitler was only one of several candidates, but the enormous success of the Nazi Party in elections during this period helped him to maintain a high political profile.

After several other Chancellors had been given a chance, President Hindenburg was persuaded to appoint Hitler. It was thought that he could be controlled; after all, his government contained only three Nazi ministers out of twelve. This was a serious miscalculation. Hitler took power with amazing speed. Within six months all organised forms of political opposition were destroyed. In the next six months he smashed what remained of the regional power of the Länder governments and in a further six months he had crushed opposition from within his own movement.

THE GREAT DEPRESSION 1929–33

By 1928, the economies of the world had become thoroughly integrated. The largest economy, that of the United States, was crucial in ensuring prosperity and jobs in Europe and other parts of the world. Germany, in particular, relied heavily on the United States after the Dawes Plan (1924). Huge loans helped restore the crisis-torn German economy and pay off reparations. While these loans lasted, most Germans had jobs and goods could be sold abroad. However, by 1928, the United States economy was starting to falter: the market for consumer goods had become saturated and factories were turning out products for which there was no demand. The Wall Street Crash in October 1929 worsened the situation; stocks and shares lost billions of dollars in value. Banks went bust as people drew out their money; companies and businesses who had lent money during the roaring 20s called in their loans. The loans to Germany had been short term and were called in quickly. Confidence evaporated overnight as factories shut down and businesses collapsed. It has been said that 'if America sneezes Europe catches a cold'. Germany's 'cold' was the worst in Europe. The Great Depression, which started in the United States, resulted in 6 million unemployed in Germany by 1933.

German children scavenge for food during the economic crisis of 1930.

Nazi Germany, 1934–39

Once in power, Hitler wanted all Germans to be one united national community and to cast aside the class, religious, political and regional differences which had characterised Weimar Germany. All aspects of life were co-ordinated to create this community around Nazi ideas and beliefs. Goebbels used propaganda to indoctrinate Germans; girls, boys, men and women all had their allotted place in the Nazi scheme of things. Of course, not every German was brainwashed. Many resisted in different ways. However, the changes Hitler made were popular: he got rid of the discredited parliamentary system; he provided strong rule; he gave Germans back their pride; and he reduced unemployment. It seemed he was their 'saviour'.

A poster celebrating Hitler's vision of Germany: 'One People, One Reich, One Leader'.

Hitler's second purpose was to deal with those who did not belong — in his eyes — to the national community of Germans. Many groups were persecuted throughout the 1930s. The Nazi view of race raised up the Aryan man and woman and damned everyone else.

Hitler's third purpose was to plan for war. He viewed war in global terms as a war between races (Aryan versus Slav) and considered war with the Soviet Union to be the inevitable final confrontation. The Slav race had been 'polluted' by the Jews, which is why the Soviet Union had 'fallen' to communism. Hitler saw communism as a 'Jewish disease'. In his mind there was bound to be a confrontation with the Soviet Union at some point, so Germany must be prepared for the conflict. Rearmament started; the armed forces grew in number and strength. The economy was stretched between two conflicting demands: preparing for war and satisfying the material needs of the German people.

Germany at war, 1939–45

Hitler's three aims were never explained in detail to the German people themselves. When war came, many feared the worst. After all, so much had been achieved peacefully. However, after early wartime successes in 1939–40, when much of Europe was in Nazi hands, Germans grew less fearful.

When the USA and the USSR joined the war in 1941 the tide turned against Hitler. Shortages hit many German households; accounts from the front undermined the propaganda that said all was well. Hitler was rarely seen in public after 1943 and his regime became unpopular. Attempts were made to assassinate him and to stop the war, but to no avail. With Soviet tanks crashing through the suburbs of Berlin in the spring of 1945, Hitler took his own life and Germany surrendered soon after. Hitler had said the Third Reich (the official Nazi name for their regime in Germany) would last a thousand years. In fact, it lasted only twelve, from 1933 to 1945.

Discussion points

> Why do you think Hitler only told the German people about his first two aims, but not the third?

> In what way was Hitler's rule different from that of the Weimar system?

Hitler comes to power

Since the Munich putsch in 1923 when Hitler failed to seize power by force, he had patiently bided his time. He reorganised the Nazi Party and followed the legal, democratic route to power. In 1933 his ten years of waiting came to an end: on 30 January he was appointed Chancellor. (This position is roughly equivalent to that of Prime Minister in Britain.)

Why did Hitler become Chancellor in 1933?

On one level, the answer to this question is easy: Hitler became Chancellor because President Hindenburg appointed him. But why is this not a satisfactory explanation? Firstly, it says nothing about why Hindenburg chose Hitler in preference to anyone else; secondly, it says nothing about Hindenburg's intentions and motives; thirdly, it says nothing about the beliefs and attitudes which shaped Hindenburg's intentions; and fourthly, it says nothing about why this event took place *when* it did. As you can see, 'why' questions in history can be complex.

In this investigation you will be looking at five questions. The answers, when put together, should give you a fairly complete explanation of Hitler's appointment, but first of all you need to have a clear picture of what happened in the fateful years, 1930–33.

President Hindenburg with Adolf Hitler in an open-top car during May Day celebrations in 1933.

GERMANY, 1930–33

In 1930 three important developments took place.

> Parliamentary government broke down and President Hindenburg ruled by decree, appointing and dismissing Chancellors as he wished.

> The Nazi Party became popular with the voters and was very successful in elections.

> Elite groups (army officers, owners of big business, the civil service and the big landowners) considered that their interests would best be served by a strong, authoritarian government rather than unstable coalition governments. In 1930, with the Depression deepening and the President acting alone, they were able to influence political decisions in ways which had not been possible before 1930.

A succession of Chancellors
President Hindenburg appointed Heinrich Brüning as Chancellor in 1930. Brüning did not need parliamentary support for his legislation, he simply needed Hindenburg to sign it. However, this system of rule by 'presidential cabinets' was always fragile. It depended upon the goodwill of Hindenburg and his advisers. Brüning's measures to try and deal with the effects of the Depression were unpopular and he resigned on 30 May 1932. The new Chancellor was Franz von Papen, a member of the Centre Party. Once again, unpopular laws were passed to cut back on welfare payments and von Papen too resigned.

A deal with Hitler
On 2 December 1932, von Schleicher became Chancellor. He tried to create some support for his government, but upset many groups by his discussions with trade union leaders. At this point, von Papen did a deal with Hitler: the Nazi leader would offer strong government with popular support (the many Nazi voters) and, in return, von Papen and his colleagues would form a majority of non-Nazis in the cabinet. Hindenburg was persuaded that in these circumstances Hitler could be controlled. Adolf Hitler was appointed Chancellor on 30 January 1933.

Question 1: What were Hitler's intentions?

From the time of the failed Munich putsch in 1923, Hitler's intention was to take power by any democratic method he could use. He wanted the position of Chancellor above all because only from that high office could he make decisions affecting the whole of Germany and have them enforced by authorities like the police, the army and his own SA.

Question 2: What were Hindenburg's intentions in appointing Hitler?

The evidence reveals that Hindenburg was hesitant about appointing Hitler as Chancellor. He had refused to appoint Hitler in August 1932 and again in November 1932, but he changed his mind only a few weeks later. In January 1933, Hindenburg was put under so much pressure that he agreed to appoint Hitler as long as his government contained a minority of Nazis. In this way Hitler could be tamed; or so he and von Papen thought.

Question 3: How did Hindenburg's beliefs and ideas shape his intentions and actions?

During the 1914–18 war Paul von Hindenburg had been joint head of the Supreme Command. In 1925 he was elected Reich President. He and some army friends deliberately set out to exploit the weaknesses in the procedure for forming parliamentary coalitions in order to build up the prestige and power of his own position as Reich President. He disliked democracy and considered that it led to weak government. His aim was to rewrite the Weimar constitution to make German government more authoritarian and less democratic. He blocked all attempts to pass laws to restrict the use of emergency powers under Article 48 of the constitution in order to keep a free hand for himself.

Question 4: What were the circumstances which made Hitler a suitable candidate for Chancellor?

A key factor here is the electoral success of the Nazi Party between 1930 and 1933. Indeed, it is easy to jump to the conclusion that this is why Hitler was appointed Chancellor. In fact, even if you look at the Nazi Party's best result in elections before Hitler took office, you will find that it only amounts to 37% of the vote. To put it another way, 63% of Germans voted for parties other than the Nazis even when they were at their most successful. Certainly, the Nazi Party did well but this only made Hitler one of several candidates for the post. Hindenburg did not have to appoint the leader of the most popular political party.

Nazi Party popularity stemmed from the issues they promoted in their propaganda. Speeches at impressive Nazi rallies, posters and leaflets played on themes such as nationalism and criticism of the Versailles treaty, and poured scorn on elements of left-wing politics: the KPD, SPD, the unions, labour law and welfare legislation.

SOURCE A

'We farmers are mucking out.' A Nationalist Socialist poster, 1932 election.

SOURCE B

This table shows the number of seats in the Reichstag won by the main parties in elections between 1928 and 1932.

	1928	1930	1932 July	1932 Nov.
Nazis	12	107	230	196
German Nationalist Party	73	41	37	52
German People's Party	45	30	7	11
Centre Party	62	68	75	70
German Democratic Party	25	20	4	2
Social Democratic Party	153	143	133	121
Communists	54	77	89	100
Other	67	91	33	32
Total	**491**	**577**	**608**	**584**

Unemployment

For other Germans, these issues were irrelevant in the context of their own desperate position as one of 6 million unemployed.

SOURCE C

Here are some grim calculations made by an employment exchange during 1931.

The average benefit paid to an unemployed man with a wife and a child was 51 marks a month. At least 32.50 marks went on rent, electricity, heating and other necessities. 18.50 marks remained to feed the family. Each person's daily rations consisted of six potatoes, five slices of bread, a handful of cabbage, a knob of margarine with a herring thrown in on three occasions during the month.

SOURCE D

This table shows the rising level of unemployment in Germany during the Depression.

Year	Number unemployed
1928	1,862,000
1929	2,850,000
1930	3,217,000
1931	4,886,000
1932	6,042,000

Question 5: How can the timing of Hitler's appointment be explained?

Between 1930 and 1933, the political and economic elites of German society were looking for an authoritarian replacement for the Weimar Republic. In this period, Hitler forged links with some of these leaders of business, industry and agriculture.

In November 1932 Hjalmar Schacht, a business leader, signed a petition to President Hindenburg requesting the appointment of Hitler as Chancellor. The President refused; he stuck by von Schleicher as his Chancellor. However, during the next few weeks, von Schleicher made some blunders which worried big business. Von Papen stepped in and liaised between big business, Schacht, the Nazi leadership and the group of advisers surrounding Hindenburg. The President finally agreed to appoint Hitler on the understanding that the government would be a conservative and not a Nazi one.

SOURCE E

An unemployed secretary advertises to passers-by: 'Hello, I'm looking for a job. I can do shorthand and typing. I can speak French and English and will accept any kind of household job...'

>> Activities

Use the Sources and the account of Germany, 1930–33.

1 Look again at questions **1** to **5**. Write an essay in two parts, answering these questions. What factors made it possible to appoint somebody like Hitler as Chancellor? What factors explain why Hitler was appointed on 30 January 1933?

2 In November 1932 the Social Democrats (SPD) and the Communists (KPD) together had more seats than the Nazis. Why didn't Hindenburg consider appointing someone from one of these parties to become Chancellor?

From democracy to dictatorship

It is astonishing how quickly Weimar democracy collapsed. Hitler took just 18 months, between February 1933 and August 1934, to establish his dictatorship. His first cabinet contained only three Nazis and, at the previous election in November 1932, the Nazi Party had managed to attract only 33% of the voters. So how and why was Hitler able to consolidate his position so quickly when he appeared to be so weak?

How did Hitler consolidate his power?

THE PATH TO DICTATORSHIP

1933

30 January	Hindenburg appoints Hitler as Chancellor.
27 February	The Reichstag building burns down.
28 February	Reichstag Fire Decree.
5 March	Reichstag election: Nazi Party gains 43.9% of the votes (288 seats), its coalition partners (the Nationalists) take 8%.
5–9 March	Nazis seize power in the Länder (German states).
20 March	Himmler establishes the first concentration camp at Dachau.
23 March	Reichstag passes the Enabling Act.
2 May	Trade unions are dissolved.
22 June	SPD banned; other parties dissolve themselves in the weeks which follow.
14 July	Legislation prohibits political parties other than the Nazi Party.
12 November	New 'election' to the Reichstag; the Nazi Party gains 92.2% of the vote.

1934

30 June	'Night of the Long Knives' – Ernst Röhm and other SA leaders and members of the conservative opposition are arrested and shot without trial.
2 August	President Hindenburg dies. The offices of President and Chancellor are combined. Hitler is now called Führer (leader). The army swears an oath of allegiance to Hitler.

These extraordinary events can be explained by a number of different factors:

FACTOR 1

Politicians underestimated the strength of Hitler's position and misread his intentions.

Although there were only two other Nazis in Hitler's cabinet, one of them, Göring, held the key position of Minister of the Interior for Prussia. As such, he was in control of the police in Germany's biggest and most important state. Hitler's position was further strengthened because cabinet colleagues shared his desire to destroy left-wing influences and end parliamentary government. Finally, Hitler's SA was now some 2.5 million strong and eager to be unleashed upon political opponents. Far from being in a weak position in a cabinet dominated by non-Nazis, Hitler was in fact very powerful.

Hitler with SA Brownshirts at a rally in Dortmund, 1933.

Even when the Enabling Act was passed, transferring power to the cabinet and freeing government from dependence on the Reichstag, von Papen and his colleagues were not concerned. This is what they wanted: strong central government to replace weak, fumbling parliamentary rule. Unfortunately, what they did not see was that Hitler meant to carry the process further by using the same emergency powers to free himself from dependence not only on the Reichstag, but also on the President, the cabinet, his coalition partners and their parties.

FACTOR 2

Hitler ruthlessly exploited every opportunity to consolidate his power.

Hitler called elections for 5 March 1933 in the hope of bolstering the Nazi Party and his own position as Chancellor. In the weeks leading up to the election, action was taken to destroy the left-wing parties. Hitler was ruthless. On 4 February a decree banned newspapers and public meetings from criticising Hitler's government. In the middle of the month, Göring let loose 50,000 Stormtroopers in Prussia; an orgy of violence against Socialists and Communists took place.

On 27 February, one week before election day, the Reichstag building went up in flames. A young Dutch Communist called Marinus van der Lubbe was caught at the scene in possession of firelighters. Under interrogation, he claimed he had acted alone. Historians debate this version of events. Most accept van der Lubbe's confession that he acted alone; a few argue that the Nazis set him up to take the blame for the fire which they themselves started. The truth may never be known but what is certain is that the Nazis used the incident in a propaganda

Van der Lubbe on trial, 1933.

campaign to whip up fears of a Communist uprising. Göring used it to justify the violent actions of the SA against political opponents, and concentration camps sprang up all over Germany.

The day after the fire, the Reichstag Fire Decree was introduced suspending all personal rights and freedoms. Political prisoners could now be held for unlimited periods without having to appear in court. By April, 25,000 were in custody in Prussia alone. The Enabling Act followed on 23 March. This allowed the government to pass laws without consulting the Reichstag and without the authority of President Hindenburg. Most Germans took the threat of a Communist uprising very seriously and accepted Hitler's drastic measures.

FACTOR 3

The Nazis made widespread use of violence to crush political opposition.

The Stormtroopers had long awaited their chance to settle old scores from previous street-battles with political enemies. Revenge and hatred fed their lust for violence against so-called German 'traitors' like Communists, Socialists, Jews, Catholic priests and journalists. Police often stood by and watched, quietly applauding the SA's brutality.

SOURCE A

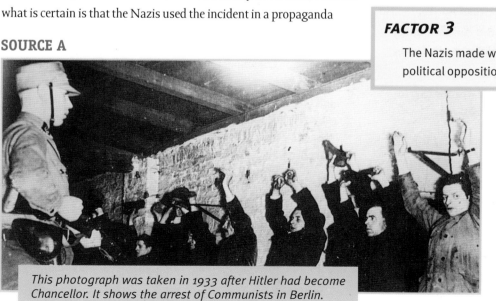

This photograph was taken in 1933 after Hitler had become Chancellor. It shows the arrest of Communists in Berlin.

FACTOR 4

Hitler dealt swiftly and efficiently with the threat to his own position from within the Nazi Party.

Hitler knew it would be dangerous to upset army leaders. They could become a focus for opposition. When they voiced their concerns about the SA as a threat to the army, Hitler showed himself ready to act ruthlessly. The 'bully boys' had outlived their usefulness to Hitler. Now he was in power their hooligan behaviour was unnecessary in creating an ordered Nazi state. Hitler struck swiftly. On 30 June 1934, SA leaders were arrested by the Gestapo and immediately shot. Ernst Röhm, the SA leader, was among the 85 victims. Hitler justified this 'Night of the Long Knives' on the grounds that Röhm was plotting to overthrow the government. Hindenburg said that Hitler had 'saved the nation'. The episode not only removed opposition within the Nazi movement, it also showed would-be opponents that the regime was absolutely ruthless in its use of force whenever it was threatened.

A few weeks later, following Hindenburg's death in August 1934, all soldiers swore an oath of loyalty to Hitler personally.

FACTOR 5

The opposition was so weak and divided that it could do nothing to stop Hitler.

Those organisations which could have opposed Hitler were stunned by the speed and surprise of the attacks upon them. The trade union movement, for example, was eliminated in March and April of 1933 in piecemeal fashion. First one town and then another saw their union buildings raided and closed down. Breslau, Dresden, Frankfurt and Hanover were picked off one at a time. No one could say when or where the next blow might be struck; no one knew when or how to make a stand.

In the city of Breslau the two opposition political parties – the KPD and the SPD – failed to join forces against the Nazis, a sad reflection of the bitterness between the two which had begun during the revolution in 1918.

SOURCE B

Ernst Röhm, the leader of the SA.

SOURCE C

This is part of a description of what happened in the city of Breslau on 31 January 1933. It is taken from a book called Life in the Third Reich *(1987), edited by the historian, Richard Bessel.*

The Communists reacted to the news of Hitler's appointment by arranging for a protest demonstration in the city centre at which a general strike was to be announced. At the appointed time when Communist supporters began to assemble, about 500 Stormtroopers decided to march through the square. The police kept about 500–600 Communist supporters out of the square while the SA paraded around; when the planned demonstration did start, the police quickly intervened to stop it. Police truncheons appeared and Communists scattered, some running up nearby streets and smashing the windows of shops selling Nazi uniforms. The SPD in Breslau had adopted a 'wait and see' attitude; they saw the results of the Communist demonstrations as justifying their own decision to do nothing.

FACTOR 6

The political elites co-operated with the Nazi regime.

Most members of the civil service felt at home with the nationalist, authoritarian style of Hitler's rule. They were prominent amongst those seeking to protect their positions and pensions by joining the Nazi Party. Similarly, most German judges and lawyers welcomed Hitler's strong, forceful government. The Reich Justice Minister, Franz Gürtner, was a conservative and not a Nazi, yet he was happy to back the illegal activities of the Nazis. He argued that they were necessary in very unusual circumstances.

You have already read about how other elites conspired to wreck Weimar democracy and replace it with a strong ruler. Now they had one: Adolf Hitler was a dictator within 18 months of being appointed Chancellor.

SOURCE D

Nazi Stormtroopers occupy trade union offices in Munich, 1933.

>> Activities

Study all the Sources and use your background knowledge.

1 Draw a table like this and fill it in for the period 1933–34, when Hitler consolidated his power.

Individual/ Group	Actions/ Decisions	Intentions/ Motives	Attitudes/ Beliefs
Hitler			
von Papen			
van der Lubbe			
Army			
Communists			
Social Democrats			
Trade unionists			
Civil servants			
Judges			

Which of the groups/individuals followed a course of action which had unintended consequences? Which of these was the most serious in allowing Hitler to consolidate his power?

Which of the groups/individuals could have prevented Hitler from consolidating his power? When and how could they have done so?

2 Using the information from the completed table and your answers to the other tasks, write an essay to explain why Hitler was able to consolidate his power so quickly. Structure it by referring to all the groups in the table and dividing them into those who supported Hitler and those who opposed him.

1930–34: Hitler's rise to power

PLANNING AND PREPARATION DURING THE 1920S

> Hitler tried and failed to take power by force so had to bide his time and use democratic methods.

> After he came out of prison, Hitler re-organised the Nazi Party and consolidated his leadership of it.

> He dropped the part of the Nazi Party programme which mentioned taking control of private property; from then on, it was only Jewish property which was in danger.

> He changed the Nazi Party from a small organisation to one which by 1928 was ready to be a mass party.

> Membership of the SA grew steadily.

WHY DID THE NAZIS GAIN POPULARITY BETWEEN 1930 AND 1933?

> The Great Depression created 6 million unemployed.

> Nazi propaganda from Goebbels worked effectively.

> Hitler had not been part of any Weimar government and could ask voters to give him a chance, as they had given the other parties.

> The Nazi Party was now receiving support from across the classes.

> The party received some financial support from industry.

However, Hitler and the Nazis were never supported by a majority of the German voters between 1930 and 1933. More people voted against the Nazis than in favour of them.

HOW WAS HITLER ABLE TO TAKE POWER IN 1933?

> Backstairs intrigue involving von Papen and Hindenburg.

> Political and economic elites wanted democracy to be shelved in favour of strong authoritarian government.

> Since 1930, democracy had already been killed off by President Hindenburg's use of emergency powers under Article 48 of the constitution, which allowed him to pass decrees without reference to the Reichstag.

WHY WEREN'T THE NAZIS POPULAR DURING THE 1920S?

> The government survived the crises of 1923 and, under statesmen like Stresemann, Germany seemed to be more stable.

> The huge loans given to Germany under the Dawes Plan in 1924 enabled the economy to recover from the hyper-inflation of 1922–23.

> Voters saw nothing in the Nazi programme which attracted them.

> Most Germans had the necessities of life (food, housing, etc.).

HOW WAS HITLER ABLE TO CONSOLIDATE POWER?

> Opposition was weak, split and badly organised.

> The SA ruled the streets with violence and terror.

> Many Germans actually approved of Hitler's strong leadership even if some minorities suffered.

> Hitler completely outmanoeuvred those in his non-Nazi cabinet who thought he could be controlled. He created a dictatorship under their noses.

> Hitler was careful not to upset the army, who could oppose him, but he was ruthless in eliminating the threat in his own ranks from Röhm and the Stormtroopers.

Prominent Nazis

Joseph Goebbels (1897–1945)

Born in 1897, Goebbels contracted polio as a child which left him with a club-foot. This deformity disqualified him from serving in the First World War. He studied history and literature at university and in 1922 he joined the Nazi Party.

In the Third Reich, Goebbels was Reich Minister of Propaganda between 1933 and 1945. He had control of all branches of the media and the arts. His aim was to mobilise Germans behind Hitler and his government. Goebbels was a brilliant speaker and his radio broadcasts reached into every German home. Propaganda became increasingly important during the war years when the Nazi regime had to prepare Germans to make huge sacrifices. Although Germany was losing the war, Goebbels remained loyal to Hitler right to the end. He died with his wife and family in Hitler's bunker in Berlin on 1 May 1945.

Hermann Göring (1893–1946)

Göring was born in Bavaria in 1893 and attended the military cadets' college at Karlsruhe. He joined the army in 1914 as an infantry lieutenant before being transferred to the airforce as a combat pilot. Göring was an ace pilot and won the Iron Cross (First Class) for exceptional bravery. After the war, Göring settled in Munich and met Hitler in 1922. He was appointed head of the SA (Stormtroopers) and led them from December 1922 until the Munich putsch. Göring was seriously wounded in the putsch but escaped abroad. In 1927 he rejoined the Nazi Party and was elected to the Reichstag in 1928. In 1932 he became first the Speaker and then the President of the Reichstag. In 1933 he was Prussian Minister of the Interior and played a key role in the seizure of power and the arrests of Communists and Socialists. He acted ruthlessly against Ernst Röhm and the SA in June 1934 in the Night of the Long Knives. In 1935 he was put in charge of the Air Force (the Luftwaffe) and in

1936 Hitler made him responsible for the Four Year Plan which laid down preparations for war. The failure of the Luftwaffe, the Allied bombing raids on Germany and Göring's own addiction to drugs resulted in his downfall. By 1945 he had lost all influence. At the Nuremberg Trials in 1945 he was condemned to death by hanging. He took poison in 1946 while awaiting execution.

Heinrich Himmler (1900–45)

Heinrich Himmler was an agricultural graduate and a poultry farmer. He had an obsession with detail and accuracy and during the Holocaust this revealed itself in his meticulous collection of statistics of murdered Jews. Early on in his political career he was involved in the Munich putsch of 1923. His loyalty to Hitler was rewarded: in 1929 he became head of Hitler's personal bodyguard, the SS. The SS became a racial elite with responsibility for killing the Jews. Himmler did more than any other single Nazi to carry out the 'Final Solution' by setting up the death camps in which millions of people were exterminated. He was arrested by the British on 23 May 1945 and took his own life.

Reinhard Heydrich (1904–42)

Reinhard Heydrich was Himmler's subordinate. He had the looks of an Aryan German and tried to keep secret the fact that he had Jewish ancestors. Heydrich joined the Nazi Party and, at the age of 27, became chief of the security services. Using spies, this organisation collected personal information on all of the leading Nazis and their opponents. When Hitler came to power, Heydrich was ready to cast his network of spies all over the country and his responsibilities included running the Gestapo under Himmler's overall command. In 1941 he was one of the foremost Nazis involved in organising the 'Final Solution'. He was assassinated in Prague by Czech freedom fighters in May 1942.

Coercion and consent

The previous investigation showed how some of the Nazis' political opponents were quickly dealt with: locked up in concentration camps, tortured, murdered, or exiled. It would be wrong, however, to exaggerate the extent of opposition to Hitler. Certainly, there was repression and coercion, but there was also consent for what Hitler was doing from many of the 66 million Germans. Who agreed with what Hitler was doing? Who opposed him? How were they treated?

How effectively did the Nazis deal with their political opponents?

Selective repression

Coercion and consent were the twin props of Hitler's power. Powerful groups such as industrialists, landowners and bankers were left alone. Jews were terrorised as were gypsies, homosexuals and beggars. Police harassment was concentrated in working-class rather than middle-class areas of big cities. There was no assault on farmers in the countryside. Nazi repression was aimed at the powerless and unpopular sections of society.

Communists, Socialists and trade unionists were unpopular with the German upper- and middle-classes, who were pleased to see Hitler break up the organisations and arrest their leaders. Levels of repression were not constant. After 1934–35, when organised opposition was violently crushed, there was a lull until 1937–39, when the persecution of the Jews and other 'undesirables' grew more savage. At this point, Hitler was busy preparing for war.

The Church and political opposition

In the early 1930s, the Catholic and Protestant Churches had co-operated with the Nazi state. Hitler had signed an agreement, known as a Concordat, with the Catholic Church in July 1933. This promised full religious freedom to Catholics in return for loyalty to the Nazi state. But the Nazis broke the agreement and responded to Catholic protests about Nazi interference in the life of the Church and violations of human rights by sending hundreds of clergy to concentration camps. The Nazi regime also persecuted Protestants who resisted state interference in Church matters. In 1937, 800 pastors were arrested and many were sent to concentration camps.

The price of resistance

Resistance from groups hostile to the Nazi regime never ceased. Thousands of people from all walks of life suffered persecution, imprisonment, and sometimes death, for defying the Nazis. Between 1933 and 1939, courts sentenced 225,000 people to a total of 600,000 years' imprisonment for political offences. Between 1933 and 1945, 3 million Germans were held at one time or another in prison or camps on political grounds or for active resistance.

SOURCE A

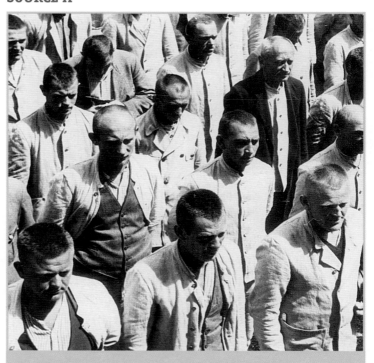

Political prisoners in Dachau concentration camp.

SOURCE B

From An Honourable Defeat, *a history book written in 1994 by Anton Gill.*

Otto Bauer, a 56-year-old businessman, said on a train in June 1942 that Germans only had two alternatives: to kill Hitler or be killed by him. He was overheard by a married couple who reported him. He was beheaded on 16 September 1943 for causing discontent and unrest.

Erich Deibel: on 29 April 1940 he drew the symbol of the SPD – three arrows – on the wall of the lavatory in his factory, adding the words: 'Hail Freedom!' On 22 July the following year he chalked up: 'Workers! Help Russia! Strike! Up with the Communist Party!' and drew the red star and the hammer and sickle. He also listened to broadcasts from the BBC. Accused of sabotage and treason, he was executed on 15 August 1942.

Nazi law enforcement

The SS (Schutz Staffel) was established in 1925 as a personal bodyguard for Hitler. Its duties were very similar to the SA during the 1920s. But in 1929, Heinrich Himmler took it over and built up numbers from 200 to 50,000. They acquired a black uniform to distinguish them from the SA. Initially they were subordinate to the SA, but this all changed after the Night of the Long Knives. As a reward for their services in purging the SA, Hitler made the SS an independent organisation inside the Nazi Party. In 1936, Hitler amalgamated all the separate police forces into one organisation and placed it under Himmler's control. This included an organisation called the Gestapo (Geheime Staatspolizei or secret police).

The Gestapo had been set up in 1933 by Göring. Its purpose was to discover the enemies of the Nazi state using whatever means they thought necessary; in other words they could break the law. Arrests late at night, interrogation, torture, internment and sometimes death: these were the hallmarks of the Gestapo operations. They instilled fear in those thinking of resistance. They were helped in their task by the Malicious Practices Act of 21 March 1933, which banned criticism of Hitler and the Nazi state. Denouncers and snoopers informed on their fellow citizens. Without the support of these 'loyal Germans' the capacity of the Gestapo to keep people under control would have been very much reduced.

SOURCE D

These statistics for three German cities in 1937 show the relatively low level of policing by the Nazis:

City	Population	Number of Gestapo officers
Düsseldorf	500,000	126
Essen	650,000	43
Würzburg	840,000	22

SOURCE E

Here are some statistics about the German population in 1933.

Total population: 66 million
Percentage of Jews: 1%
Percentage living in cities over 100,000: 30%
Percentage living in small rural communities of less than 2,000: 32%

SOURCE C

A recruiting poster for the Waffen SS, the military branch of the SS.

WAFFEN-SS
EINTRITT NACH VOLLENDETEM 17. LEBENSJAHR

>> Activities

Use all the Sources and your background knowledge.

1 What do the Sources suggest were the reasons why many Germans did not resist Hitler?

2 Using the statistical evidence from these Sources do you think Hitler relied more on coercion than consent or vice versa?

Propaganda

Terror and propaganda: these were the two weapons the Nazis used to control the German people. You studied Nazi terror in the previous investigation; propaganda is the focus of this one.

How did the Nazis use culture and the mass media to control the people?

Propaganda is not just telling lies to change ideas and attitudes; it is more complicated than that. Very often propaganda reinforces existing beliefs by giving them a sharper focus. Propaganda can be the outright lie, the half truth, or the truth taken out of its context, or indeed a mixture of all three. During the Nazi period both culture and the mass media were controlled to help build a unified national community based on Nazi values. How was this done? What were the propaganda messages?

The purposes of Nazi propaganda

For Hitler and Goebbels, propaganda had one prime function: to reshape people's beliefs, values and ideas along Nazi lines. Germans were told time and time again about 'racial purity'; the need to create 'national solidarity'; and the importance of trusting Hitler's leadership.

SOURCE A

This diagram shows the different purposes of Nazi propaganda and how they are linked together.

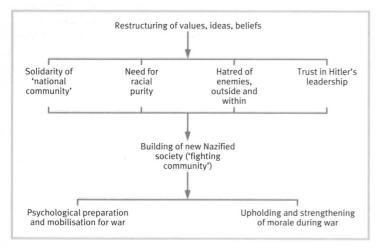

Controlling culture

Goebbels established the Reich Chamber of Culture and his Ministry for Propaganda in 1933. The Reich Chamber had sections dealing with newspapers, film, art, radio, literature, theatre and music. Germans wanting to work in any of these areas had to be members of the Chamber. Membership depended on supporting the Nazis: if you did not support the Nazis, your work could not be performed or published. Many creative people went abroad to work.

Censorship

Nazi versions of events were given to the public to read. Goebbels censored what newspapers could print and had shut down 1,600 newspapers by the end of 1934. Germany's 10,000 magazines and journals suffered too; half had disappeared by 1938.

Literature

The Nazis organised the burning of books whose authors were Jewish, unsympathetic to Nazi ideals, or both. In May 1933 Berlin students ceremonially set fire to a huge pile of 20,000 books which had been looted from libraries. In the pile were books by some of Germany's most famous authors. The works of over 2,500 writers were officially banned.

Radio

In 1932 there were 4.5 million radios in Germany. Ten years later there were over 16 million. A radio cost an average week's wages. Hitler made 50 broadcasts in his first year in office. Sets were placed in factories and cafés, and loudspeakers were installed in streets.

Music

The work of Jewish composers was banned and so was jazz because it was written by black Americans. Viennese music by Strauss was played most frequently along with the heroic German operas of Wagner.

'Yes! Leader we will follow you!' A propaganda poster intended to encourage mass support for Hitler.

This cartoon was published in the Westfälische Landeszeitung, a German newspaper, in January 1939. It shows two maps of Germany. The top one represents Weimar Germany, the bottom one, Nazi Germany.

Cinema

Cinema attendances topped 250 million in 1933. This figure quadrupled in the next ten years. The Nazi film industry produced about 100 films a year. About half were comedies and love stories and a quarter were musicals or thrillers. The remainder had historical, military or political themes or were films for the young. One of the best known was *Hitlerjunge Quex* (1933), which tells the story of a boy who broke away from a Communist family to join the Hitler Youth only to be murdered by the Communists.

>> Activities

1 Study Sources B and C. What messages are these images trying to communicate? (Use Source A to help you.)

2 Do Sources B and C contain **a** outright lies; **b** half truths; **c** truths taken out of context; or **d** a mixture of all three?

3 Given what you know about political opposition to the Nazis, how successful does Nazi propaganda appear to have been?

Nazi persecution

The Nazis began the persecution of minorities soon after they took power in 1933. Jews suffered the most and endured the greatest losses: over 6 million were systematically killed in what is known as the Holocaust. The Nazis planned to kill all the Jews they found so that they could create an 'Aryan' order in Europe. Other groups that suffered under the Nazis were gypsies, homosexuals, mentally and physically disabled people, Slavs, Jehovah's Witnesses, Socialists and Communists.

Why did the Nazis persecute different minority groups in Germany?

SOURCE A

A Nazi sculpture of the ideal Aryan.

Nazi ideas on race

Hitler believed not in the human race but in human races and the differences between them. The 'Aryan' race, in Hitler's mind, was superior to all other races in terms of physical strength, intelligence and cultural achievements. The ideal Aryan would be tall with blond hair and blue eyes. This was the ideal; it was obvious that not all Germans matched these features. Aryans were the most valuable race, and if they interbred with 'less valuable races' they were doomed to extinction. To prevent this from happening, the purity and health of the Aryan race had to be protected and improved. In practice, this would mean increasing the number of babies of 'Aryan stock' and reducing the number from 'inferior stock'. These ideas were not just Hitler's, nor were they new; plenty of ordinary Germans shared them.

The persecution of Jews

Anti-Semitism was commonplace in Europe during the 1920s. In 1922, Walter Rathenau, the Jewish German Foreign Minister, was murdered by racists. Between 1922 and 1933 there were 200 incidents in Nuremberg alone of Jewish

SOURCE B

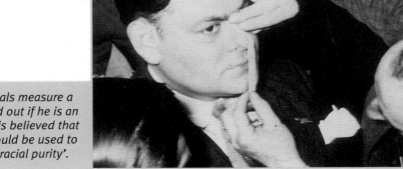

Government officials measure a man's nose to find out if he is an Aryan or not. Nazis believed that tests like these could be used to check a person's 'racial purity'.

graves being desecrated. *Der Stürmer*, the Nazi newspaper, was first published in 1923; its slogan was 'The Jews are our greatest misfortune'.

On coming to power, the Nazis at once set about excluding 'non-Aryans' (Jews) from public life. The Nazis defined 'non-Aryans' as persons with a Jewish parent or grandparent. Jews were banished from the civil service and from teaching in schools and universities, and barred from practising as doctors, dentists and judges. These measures were widely accepted by the majority of the German public. Jews were deprived of opportunities to work in the economy and to take part in German civic and cultural life. The main thrust of Nazi policy was to wage a legal war of attrition so as to make life so unbearable for Jews that they would leave Germany 'voluntarily'.

Many of Germany's 550,000 Jews did emigrate and more would have done so had other countries been more helpful. In July 1938, 33 governments were represented at the Evian Conference to discuss the refugee situation, but only a few agreed to accept more Jewish immigrants.

Once the war started in 1939, Nazi persecution of the Jews intensified. When the Nazis conquered Poland, Jews were herded into ghettos where they lived in the most appalling and dehumanising conditions. The Warsaw ghetto was the largest of all: half a million people were crammed into 1.3 square miles; the average room held seven people; and only one in every hundred flats had running water. Disease was rife.

March 1933	Department of Racial Hygiene established.
April 1933	Nationwide boycott of Jewish shops; laws passed to dismiss non-Aryans from public service and the professions.
1935 Nuremberg Laws	Jews lose their rights as German citizens. It became illegal for Jews to marry, or to have any relations with, Aryans. Jews were encouraged to leave Germany.
1938 Kristallnacht	Mass destruction of synagogues and shops; about a thousand Jews were murdered and many arrested.
1938	Jewish businesses taken over by Nazis.
1942–45	The Holocaust.

In June 1941 the Germans invaded the Soviet Union. A month later an order was signed by Goering to make the necessary preparations for a 'Final Solution to the Jewish problem'. The *Einsatzgruppen* (killing squads) went into action in the newly conquered Soviet territories. Sometimes, with the help of local volunteers, they killed local Jews and buried them in mass graves.

It soon became clear that the methods used by the *Einsatzgruppen* were unable to cope with the large numbers of people whom the Nazis deemed to be 'sub-human', so a more efficient method was found. At the Chelmo camp a mobile gas van was used to kill up to 40 people in one operation. Carbon monoxide from the exhaust pipes was pumped into the back of sealed vans. Over 200,000 Polish Jews were killed in this way as well as tens of thousands of Soviet prisoners.

In 1942 at the Wannsee Conference, leading Nazis agreed on a plan for the 'Final Solution to the Jewish problem'. The persecution of the Jews in Nazi Germany had now reached its last and most terrifying stage. By 1942, the Nazis had invaded many of the countries to which Jews had fled from Germany in the 1930s. The 'Final Solution' decided upon in 1942 was simple: when Jews were found, they were rounded up and then transported to death camps in the occupied countries. This applied to every single Jew in Europe. Many perished in the gas chambers at Auschwitz, where Zyklon B was used to poison them. Corpses were disposed of in large ovens

SOURCE C

From April 1933 Nazi Stormtroopers organised and enforced a boycott of all Jewish-owned shops and businesses.

which burned day and night to cope with the huge numbers. Historians estimate that between 5 and 6 million Jews were murdered. Hitler's role was central to the slaughter.

The persecution of the mentally and physically disabled

For many years this group of people was thought of as inferior by some scientists, zoologists and doctors. Euthanasia and sterilisation were two suggested 'remedies'. Many would have echoed the thoughts of Ernst Haeckel in Source D.

SOURCE D

From The Riddle of Life *written by German zoologist, Ernst Haeckel (1834–1919), in 1904.*

What profit does humanity gain from the thousands of cripples who are born each year, from the deaf and dumb, from cretins, from those with incurable hereditary defects who are kept alive artificially and then raised to adulthood? What a lot of pain they suffer! What a lot of money it costs to look after them! All of this could be avoided with a dose of morphine.

During the 1920s, debates about sterilisation resurfaced because the 1914–18 war had killed so many young men – those considered to be the 'most valuable' human stock. In 1923, the Zwickau District Health Officer announced that surgeons in his district were already sterilising mentally disabled people, illegally. During the Depression, governments cut spending on welfare, which included the care of the disabled. In July 1932 the Prussian state government had drafted a Sterilisation Law. Even before 1933, disabled people were already thought of as dispensable by some in German society.

January 1934	Law for the Prevention of Hereditarily Diseased Children – this law allowed sterilisation of diseased children. Over 360,000 sterilisations had been carried out by 1945.
October 1939	Euthanasia Order – its aim was to kill German mental patients. Special hospitals were established where disabled children were murdered usually by poison or starvation. Later, children who had malformed ears or who wet the bed were included. The killing of disabled adults soon followed.

SOURCE E

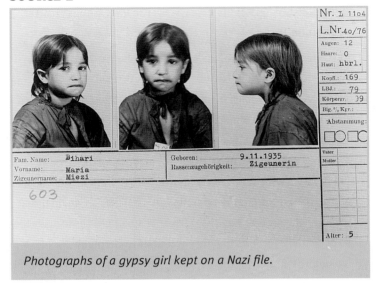

Photographs of a gypsy girl kept on a Nazi file.

The persecution of the Sinti and Roma (gypsies)

When the Nazis came to power they inherited Länder (state) laws which discriminated against the Sinti and Roma. The Bavarian authorities had kept a register of them from 1899, and from 1911 added fingerprints to it. In 1926 a new law enabled the police to send Sinti and Roma people to workhouses for two years if they did not have regular work. Under the Nazis, the Sinti and Roma were confined to designated sites after 1939. Those who tried to leave were sent to concentration camps where they were very badly treated.

1941 marked the change from persecution to extermination. 250,000 Sinti and Roma were shot in Russia, Poland and the Balkans. In December 1942 those living in Germany were sent to Auschwitz. Out of the 23,000 sent, 20,078 perished.

The persecution of homosexuals and black people

Homosexuals and black people were persecuted by the Nazis because they endangered the development of an 'Aryan order' in Europe. Homosexuals could not have children, and black people were close to Jews in the Nazi view of the 'human races'.

Laws against homosexuality had been in place since 1871, but during the Weimar period there were signs that persecution might end: a gay press flourished and in Berlin and Hamburg homosexuality was tolerated. Hitler brought these developments to an end. In February 1933 homosexual groups were banned. Large numbers of homosexuals were arrested towards the end of 1934 and in 1936 a law was passed to have all homosexuals sterilised.

In the 1920s many black soldiers came to an area of Germany called the Rhineland as part of the French army of occupation under the terms of the Treaty of Versailles. Many of the black soldiers from Senegal and Morocco formed relationships with local German women. The children born of these couples were called 'Rhineland bastards' by the Weimar press and then the Nazi regime. Instead of curbing the racist reactions of politicians and journalists, the Weimar authorities themselves collected information on the number, names and location of these children. In 1937 the Nazis used this information to track down and sterilise 385 children without them or their parents knowing what was going on.

>> Activities

1 What did the Nazis mean by 'Aryan race'? How can the Nazi vision of Germany's future help to explain their treatment of minorities?

2 Scientists (like Ernst Haeckel, Source D) and doctors suggested that some groups of people were more valuable than others.

   a How did these views help justify the actions of the persecutors?

   b Article 104 of the Weimar Constitution guaranteed equality before the law for all Germans, yet racism existed during the 1920s. Can you explain this contradiction?

3 Use the Sources and the timecharts to make a list of all the individuals and groups who appear to have treated Germans unequally. What does this tell you about the extent of racism in Germany?

4 '1933 was more a continuation of existing policy than a turning point in the way German authorities treated minorities.' To what extent do you agree with this?

Jesse Owens, a black American athlete, won four gold medals at the 1936 Berlin Olympic Games. His achievement undermined the Nazi belief in the superiority of Aryan athletes and Hitler refused to congratulate Owens.

Totalitarianism?

The term 'totalitarianism' was first coined in Italy in May 1923 as a term of abuse against Mussolini's Fascist government. In England in 1929 the term was used to describe both Fascist (Italy and later Germany) and Communist (Soviet Union) states.

Was Nazi Germany a totalitarian state?

After the purge of the SA in June 1934, there were three and a half years of political peace in Germany. This allowed the Nazis time to 're-model' German society according to their values and beliefs. In theory, all areas of German life had to be re-organised: no individual or group could avoid this process. German men and women were to be accountable for their thoughts and feelings as well as for their actions. The demands of the Nazi Party and the State were to be more important than the rights of the individual.

In practice, however, Nazi Germany turned out to be rather different:

> Until the outbreak of war, Germany was still open to visitors and foreign journalists – unlike the Soviet Union.

> The Nazis were sensitive to hostile comments from abroad: for example, foreign criticism of Nazi policy made Hitler stop those in the Party who wished to take extreme measures against the Churches.

> The ways in which the Nazis enforced their style of government changed dramatically after the outbreak of war. In 1939, for example, the number of prisoners in concentration camps was about 25,000 out of a total population of 66 million. A few years later, during the war, the number had increased to about 250,000.

> The Nazi government was not united. No one questioned Hitler's authority at the top, but there were fierce struggles for power in the ranks beneath him. Each government minister and Nazi Party official fought for their own interests and the favour of the Führer. This strengthened Hitler's own position but weakened the control of the Nazi government.

Carl Friedrich, a political thinker, described six features which totalitarian states possess:

> an official ideology (a fixed way of thinking)

> a single mass party

> police control based upon terror

> total control over the media

> total control over arms

> central control over the economy

THEY SALUTE WITH BOTH HANDS NOW.

There was no place for opposition in Nazi Germany. This 1934 cartoon by the British cartoonist David Low is a comment on the 'Night of the Long Knives' when the SA was eliminated.

>> Activity

Using Friedrich's six features of a totalitarian state and information you have obtained about Nazi Germany, make a list of those aspects of the Nazi state which were 'totalitarian' and make a second list of those aspects which were not. Was Nazi Germany a 'totalitarian' state or not?

Young people in Nazi Germany

In Hitler's eyes the young were particularly important. They had to be won over so that Hitler's policies could be implemented. To create a racial state, the Nazis had to indoctrinate children to believe in the superiority of the Aryan, the 'master race'. To fight a 'race war' against the Soviet Union, young men had to cherish the military ideals of discipline, sacrifice and obedience. Cementing together these two aims was the Führer: all young Germans were taught to see him as a father-figure who demanded and should receive unquestioning loyalty from his people.

How did young people react to the Nazi regime?

SOURCE A

SOURCE B

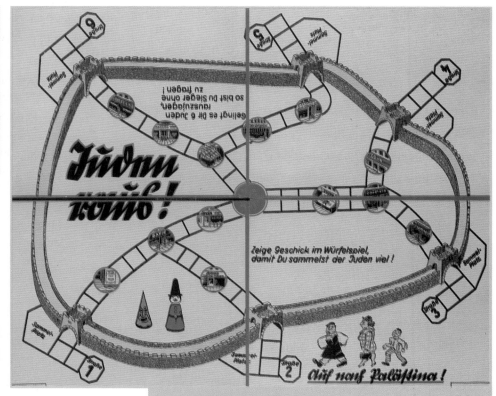

Hitler with a small boy dressed up as the SA mascot.

A children's board game called 'Get the Jews out'. The child who chased six Jews from their businesses and homes was the winner. The instructions read: 'Be skilful when you throw the dice and you'll gather Jews in a trice. If you succeed in throwing six Jews out, you're the winner without a doubt!' This game sold one million copies in 1938, the year that Nazi policy towards Jews encouraged emigration.

Education

At school young Germans were faced with a National Curriculum devised by the Nazis. The teaching of school subjects was changed to indoctrinate pupils. History was distorted to celebrate German victories during the Great War and to downplay the achievements of the Weimar Republic by teaching about the 'betrayal' of 1918, the humiliation of Versailles, and the inflation of 1923. All disasters were, of course, blamed on the Communists and the Jews. Biology lessons were devoted to studying the differences between races and maths problems contained facts and figures about looking after the disabled in ways which made them seem dispensable.

It would be wrong, however, to think that all young Germans were brainwashed and believed everything they were taught. Plenty did not. In practice, young people learned from lots of different influences both in and out of school. Some used Hitler Youth duties as an excuse to miss school and vice versa.

259

SOURCE C

This picture is from a children's book. It shows Jewish children being taken out of the school by their teacher. The 'Aryan' teacher stands watching in the background.

SOURCE D

This extract is taken from the memoirs of a German who was a student during the Nazi period.

No one in our class ever read *Mein Kampf.* I myself had only used the book for quotations. In general we didn't know much about Nazi ideas. Anti-Semitism wasn't mentioned much by teachers except through Richard Wagner's essay 'The Jews in Music'.

In spite of all the Nazis' best efforts through their National Curriculum, research seems to show that Nazi education had no universal effects on young Germans.

The Hitler Youth

This organisation had been running since 1925 and in the first few years after 1933 many young people joined voluntarily. It offered a variety of leisure pursuits. This was particularly welcomed in rural areas where the arrival of the Hitler Youth meant a first chance to join any kind of youth organisation. Boys and girls could now enjoy weekend trips, walking and sports. Indeed, the League of German Girls offered some the chance to break free from the female role model of child-care and devotion to family.

SOURCE F

This extract is from the memoirs of Marianne MacKinnon, a member of the League of German Girls.

I was not thinking of the Führer when I gave the Nazi salute, but of games, sports, hiking, singing, camping and other exciting activities. Many young people like me had a thirst for action and found it in the Hitler Youth. Almost everything took the form of competitions. Not only were there contests for the best performances in sport and at work, but each unit wanted to have the best-kept home, or the most interesting travel album.

SOURCE E

This table shows membership figures for the various sections of the Hitler Youth.

	HJ (boys aged 14–18)	DJ (boys aged 10–14)	BDM (girls aged 14–18)	JM (girls aged 10–14)	Total	Total population of 10–18 year-olds
End 1932	55,365	28,691	19,244	4,656	107,956	
End 1933	568,288	1,130,521	243,750	349,482	2,292,041	7,529,000
End 1934	786,000	1,457,304	471,944	862,317	3,577,565	7,682,000
End 1935	829,361	1,498,209	569,599	1,046,134	3,943,303	8,172,000
End 1936	1,168,734	1,785,424	873,127	1,610,316	5,437,601	8,656,000
End 1937	1,237,078	1,884,883	1,035,804	1,722,190	5,879,955	9,060,000
End 1938	1,663,305	2,064,538	1,448,264	1,855,119	7,031,226	9,109,000
Beg. 1939	1,723,886	2,137,594	1,502,571	1,923,419	7,287,470	8,870,000

Abbreviations: HJ, Hitler-Jugend (Hitler Youth); DJ, Deutsches Jungvolk (German Young People); BDM, Bund Deutscher Mädel (League of German Girls); JM, Jungmädelbund (League of Young Girls).

During the later 1930s, when membership became compulsory, the attractions of the Hitler Youth began to wane. When everyone was forced to join there were some who did not care and were not interested. Discipline was tightened and there was a greater emphasis on drill. This upset many members. Then, during the war years, the number of leisure activities was cut. Playing fields and youth club buildings were bombed and many Youth leaders were called up for the war. Thousands of young Germans now created their own youth gangs and culture in opposition to the Hitler Youth.

SOURCE G

HER ZU UNS!

Hinein in die Hitler-Jugend

A poster urging young people to join the Hitler Youth.

Opposition to the Hitler Youth

There were three main groups of young people who opposed the Hitler Youth: the 'Edelweiss Pirates', the 'Meuten' and the 'Swing Movement'. The Pirates got together in parks or on street corners. Each group had about a dozen boys and a few girls. At weekends they would go on trips to the countryside and meet up with other Pirates. Hitler Youth patrols were often taunted and sometimes beaten up by the Pirates. Such incidents attracted the attention of the authorities; some members were warned first and the next time they were rounded up. Barthel Schink, a 16-year-old leader of the Cologne Pirates, was hanged in November 1944.

The Meuten were similar to the Pirates, mostly working-class and based in Leipzig. All in all, there were 1,500 of them in various gangs.

The Swing Movement was founded by young middle-class Germans who shunned German nationalist music and preferred instead to listen to jazz and swing. Swing clubs sprang up in Hamburg, Kiel, Berlin, Frankfurt and Dresden. Their dancing appalled the authorities, who banned live performances.

>> Activities

1 How does Source A illustrate Hitler's attitudes towards youth?

2 How were Sources B and C meant to indoctrinate young people?

3 How would you investigate the impact of anti-Semitic propaganda such as that shown in Sources B and C?

4 How far was the image of the Hitler Youth in Source G matched by the experiences of young Germans who did join the Hitler Youth?

5 What was the range of responses to the Nazi regime from young people?

Women and the family

'Kinder, Kirche und Küche' – Children, Church and Kitchen: this sums up the Nazi attitude towards women. The Nazis assumed that there was a 'natural' distinction between the sexes. Men were the productive and creative sex in the big world of politics and war. Women were reproductive, and essentially passive in the little world of the family home. This meant that women should stick to their 'natural' occupations as wives or mothers. If they had to work, they should choose occupations which reflected their 'natural' talents, such as nursing or social work, which would not endanger their ability to have children.

How successful were Nazi policies towards women and the family?

From 1936, girls had to join the Hitler Youth. At 14 they went from the League of Young Girls to the League of German Girls (BDM). Between 18 and 21 they could join the Faith and Beauty organisation and thereafter the National Socialist Organisation of Women (NSF). Some women saw a career in these groups and a means of avoiding the authority of their parents and families. Others valued membership because it helped them develop self-confidence and hold positions of leadership and responsibility.

SOURCE B

These population statistics were produced by historians. They cover the period 1929–39. After 1937, all the figures cover not only Germany but also Austria (invaded 1938) and the Sudetenland (invaded March 1939).

Year	Marriages	Live births	Deaths
1929	589,600		
1931		1,047,775	734,165
1932	516,793	993,126	707,642
1933	638,573	971,174	737,877
1934	740,165	1,198,350	724,758
1935	651,435	1,263,976	792,018
1936	609,631	1,277,052	795,203
1937	620,265	1,277,046	794,367
1938	645,062	1,348,534	799,220
1939	772,106	1,407,490	853,410

SOURCE A

Familienbildnis, *painted by Wolfgang Willrich in the 1930s. It shows the ideal Nazi family.*

Creating a 'racially pure' society

Nazi policy towards the family focused particularly on women because they were worried about the falling birth-rate and the 'racial quality' of the population. The Nazis tried to tackle this problem in various different ways.

Not all German mothers 'benefited' from these measures. Women who
were socialist, pacifist, Sinti, Roma or Jewish were sterilised. So were
men. 320,000 people suffered in this way between 1934 and 1939, men
and women in equal numbers. In the three years 1934 to 1937, 80 men
and 400 women actually died during these operations. For the 'racially
useless', Nazi family policy meant not being allowed to have children.

SOURCE C

'You also belong to the Führer.' A propaganda
poster aimed at German girls.

Nazi policy towards women and the war

Once war preparations started in 1937, the Nazis reversed their
policies. Conscription and rearmament were gaining momentum
and as they did so, a labour shortage developed. Having praised the
virtues of motherhood and domesticity for so long, the Nazis now
had to find ways to lure women back into jobs. Women were
unimpressed. Dead-end, low-paid factory jobs were not attractive.
Kindergarten provision and maternity leave made little impact. The
number of women in paid employment only rose from 14.6 to 14.9
million between 1939 and 1944. This was not nearly enough to meet
the demands of a wartime economy. Ironically, it was the
government's emphasis upon the 'natural' roles of women in
peacetime that produced undesirable consequences during wartime.

>> Activities

Use all the Sources and the background
information.

1 What Nazi views of the family and of women are
  represented in the painting and the poster
  (Sources A and C)?

2 Study Source B. Between 1933 and 1939 how
  successful were the Nazis in

  a increasing the number of marriages?

  b increasing the number of births?

  Why do the statistics for the years after 1937
  have to be used very carefully?

  In 1933 the population of Germany was
  66,027,000. In 1937 it had reached 67,831,000. Is
  this evidence of success or failure for Nazi
  policies towards women and the family?

3 What evidence is there to suggest there were
  some contradictions in Nazi policies towards
  women and the family between 1933 and 1945?

A popular regime?

As you have seen, the Nazi regime was ruthless in its persecution of certain minority groups. But how was life under the Nazis for the majority of the German population?

Did most people in Germany benefit from Nazi rule?

The brief answer to this question is that it depends upon which period of Nazi rule you focus on, which particular group of Germans are being studied and how you define the term 'benefit'. Hitler was a popular leader with the majority of Germans until well into the Second World War. So, if his popularity is a litmus test, most Germans did consider they benefited from Nazi rule. But this does not mean that the Nazis were popular too. In this investigation you will study sources about groups of Germans who were not amongst the persecuted minorities.

Employment and the workers

Getting unemployment down was a priority for Hitler's government. The rearmament programme and conscription both took thousands off the unemployment register. The German Labour Front was set up to organise workers and direct them to jobs that needed doing. Public works such as afforestation projects, water conservation schemes and the building of houses, barracks and motorways got thousands of men back to work.

Once the Nazis were in power, Party membership shot up from 850,000 in 1933 to 2.5 million by 1935 and then to over 5 million at the outbreak of war in 1939. Party members were not just motivated by Nazi ideals. For many thousands of Nazi followers, their jobs, status and the necessities of life depended upon their commitment to the Party. Government organisations like the Labour Front were big employers too. By 1939 it was employing 44,500 paid officials. 'Jobs for the boys' benefited many Germans.

The economy and living standards

Not everyone benefited from Nazi interference in the economy and labour market, however. Small businessmen suffered because of the shortage of consumer goods which they sold for profit. They could not put their prices up to make up the shortfall because Nazi laws prevented them from so doing.

The Nazi regime also controlled food prices. In one way this was beneficial because there was no inflation. However, there were constant complaints about shortages of fats and about the poor quality of textiles and other goods which contained a high percentage of ersatz (substitute) materials in them. Wage rates were held down so workers did not experience an increase in their living standards. Since the destruction of their unions, they were in no position to bargain for improvements.

Leisure time

The Nazi organisation Strength through Joy (KDF) brought benefits to some people. It organised leisure activities for workers. Cheap holidays like cruises to the Canary Islands could be bought for just two weeks' wages. Although some workers did take advantage of this, places were mostly reserved for hardworking Nazi Party personnel.

People in the countryside

People in rural communities were pleased with benefits brought by the Labour Front, the Nazi organisations for women and young villagers, and the cheap holidays provided by KDF. Women benefited

SOURCE A

This graph shows the German unemployment figures for 1933–39.

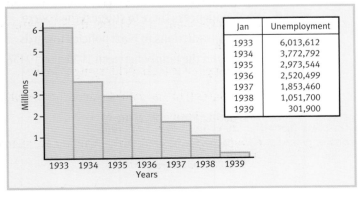

Jan	Unemployment
1933	6,013,612
1934	3,772,792
1935	2,973,544
1936	2,520,499
1937	1,853,460
1938	1,051,700
1939	301,900

'Hurrah, the butter is finished!' This picture by John Heartfield makes fun of a speech made by Hermann Goering when he said the choice for German people was 'guns or butter'.

A Strength through Joy poster, 1938.

particularly by being able to travel beyond the confines of the village. It brought them into contact with other women and allowed them to cross class boundaries. In many ways it actually liberated them from traditional village life. On the other hand, as war approached, demands on women increased. They were expected to combine the roles of mother, housewife and industrial worker.

Popular opinion in Nazi Germany

Hitler was popular. He had provided Germany with authoritarian leadership which is exactly what many Germans from all classes had wanted. He was successful in lowering unemployment and also in restoring German national honour through the Berlin Olympics in 1936, the re-occupation of the Rhineland in the same year, and the scrapping of the Versailles treaty. Instead of desperation and hopelessness, optimism and self-confidence reigned. All of this must have seemed a miracle to many Germans who had lived through the difficult times.

>> Activities

1 Did each of these groups benefit from Nazi rule: male workers; female workers; Nazi Party members; soldiers in the armed forces; small businessmen?

2 John Heartfield created Source B, which is a photomontage. He was a German Communist who left Germany in 1933 after the SA destroyed his work.

  a What point is Heartfield trying to make?

  b Is Source B of any value in investigating who benefited from Nazi rule?

  c Which groups of Germans would have shared Heartfield's attitude?

1939–45: Germany at war

In the years 1939–42 very little changed for most Germans. Many disliked being at war with England and France but Hitler's amazing military successes early on stifled some of the doubts people had about his policies. After 1942, the strains and stresses of running a war did have a profound impact on life in Germany. Who suffered and why during the war years?

How did the coming of war change life in Germany?

The effect of war on the German economy

Hitler knew that preparations for conflict had to be made and the German economy had been subject to a Four Year Plan between 1936 and 1940. In the early days of the war, the economy was little affected. The Nazis exploited the resources of the conquered territories: France paid Germany 1.75 billion Reichsmarks in 1940 and 5.55 billion in 1941, as well as being robbed of her raw materials. The German economy also benefited from foreign labour. By 1941, at the height of Nazi success in the war, just over 3 million foreign workers were labouring for the Germans.

However, as the tide of war turned against the Nazis, new pressures came to bear upon the German economy. Allied bombing raids were destroying factories and transport systems, and the running of the concentration camps in pursuit of the 'Final Solution' was draining resources away from the war effort. In spite of these problems, the Nazis succeeded in trebling armament production between 1942 and 1944. Once the Allied armies landed in Normandy in June 1944, however, and the Soviet armies rumbled towards Berlin, the Germany economy no longer had the resources of the occupied territories to fall back on. Shortages of fuel and food hit civilians hard and ever heavier air raids disrupted factory production.

SOURCE A

This table shows the number of bombs (in tons) dropped on Britain and Germany between 1940 and 1945.

	On Germany	On Britain
1940	10,000	36,844
1941	30,000	21,858
1942	40,000	3,260
1943	120,000	2,298
1944	650,000	9,151
1945	500,000	761

The effects of the Allied bombing raids

May 1943 saw the start of the heavy bombing of Germany by the British at night and the Americans by day. The results were devastating. In Hamburg, raids in July and August 1943 destroyed 60% of the city, wiped out 300,000 houses and killed between 60,000 and 100,000 people.

SOURCE B

This is taken from a diary by Mathilde Wolff-Monckeberg written in 1943. She was a housewife in Hamburg.

People here are curiously apathetic and dull. On their faces one can read despair, can sense wretchedness, irritation and exasperation wherever one happens to be: on the tram, in the post office, in the shops. Since the surrender of Stalingrad [January 1943] all is grey and still. Shop after shop has closed down, one tolerates discomforts, and forgets that life was ever different.

SOURCE C

'Black out! The enemy sees your lights.' A propaganda poster warning German civilians about British bombing raids.

The effects of terror bombing on morale are difficult to assess. The majority showed the usual signs of trauma: confusion, silence and blank gazes. A minority panicked; Germans were sometimes trampled to death in bunkers by other Germans. Some were able to master the situation and take appropriate action. Risking their lives, they fought flames to rescue those trapped in ruined buildings and defused unexploded bombs.

The effects of the war on German village life

Many rural communities had resisted outsiders, but from 1939 they had to accept evacuees and refugees from the bombings. Village populations rocketed but the available housing did not. Forced to share their homes and aware that they were losing the war, many villagers stopped supporting the Third Reich. From 1944 onwards some people openly defied Nazi officials by not declaring food they had produced. In a few cases villagers hid deserting soldiers.

Before 1939, agricultural work had been secure. Now people had to work in industry because of the demands of the war. The Nazis had promised to ensure the survival of rural German life; instead, they unleashed forces which effectively destroyed it.

Rationing

Morale on the home front depended on maintaining food supplies. The shortages at the end of the Great War had taught the Nazis that lesson. By and large Hitler's regime was successful in maintaining supplies; shortages never reached critical levels.

When war began, so did the rationing of items of daily diet. Ration-cards were distributed. In 1939 the meat ration was 700 grams per person per week; by 1945 it was 250 grams. During the winter of 1943 some Berliners enjoyed an unusual meat menu. Most of the city's zoo had been destroyed and many animals were killed. Berliners discovered that crocodile tail tasted like chicken if cooked long enough. Buffalo and antelope went down well and bear hams and sausages were much sought after. As ever in war, a black market flourished in food and items which were in short supply.

Evacuation

German parents sent their children out of the big cities to escape the Allied air raids. Austria and Bavaria were the main destinations. The Hitler Youth organised the evacuation programme and parents were encouraged to take up the offer with promises of a good education for their children. Many found separation from their families a terrible ordeal.

The Hitler Youth

Members of the Youth organisations found themselves doing all sorts of different jobs to help sustain the war effort on the domestic front. Boys helped the fire services, delivered post, distributed ration-cards and acted as guides during black-out. They also organised collections of metal, bones, kitchen waste, clothing and books.

Girls did their bit too. In kindergartens, old people's homes and hospitals they helped in whatever way they could. They brought coal and food for the homeless, war widows and refugees. They even formed choirs to entertain the sick and wounded.

SOURCE D

German refugees in the devastated centre of Berlin, 1945.

Women

The terrible human losses in the war and the labour shortage forced the Nazis to reverse their previous policy towards women. They tried to increase the birth-rate of Germans of 'pure stock' and tried to get women back to work. It was all to no avail. The incentives had little effect. Women's health was suffering. Indeed shortages of some foods, bombing raids, concerns over children's welfare, worries about loved ones at the front, and the disruption of the transport system all contributed to a serious deterioration of public health.

SOURCE E

This poster was designed to encourage women to work for the German railways during the war.

Resistance

During the war, opposition from youth groups grew stronger. News about concentration camps, about mass murder and the euthanasia programme leaked out and became widely known. In Berlin a group of young Jews led by Herbert Baum resorted to violence. They set fire to an anti-Soviet exhibition. The Gestapo arrested the whole group. Baum was tortured to death; the six others were beheaded on 18 August 1942. The families of those connected with the fire were immediately sent to Auschwitz, where they perished.

The 'White Rose' was a resistance group led by Hans and Sophie Scholl. Numbering about 15, they were mostly students at Munich University. On 18 February 1943 the Scholls were arrested while distributing leaflets encouraging young Germans to fight against the Nazi 'subhumans'. After three days' interrogation they were executed on 22 February 1943.

Hitler had opponents amongst upper-class Germans but they did not take any action until 1944 when they conspired to kill Hitler. They knew that they could get close to him by using their supporters in the German army. In July 1944, Claus von Stauffenberg, a senior army officer, left a bomb by a table in a conference room used by Hitler. The explosion killed four people but Hitler escaped serious injury. Those involved in the 'July Plot' were barbarically executed along with over 5,000 others connected with the conspirators.

>> Activities

Use all the Sources, the background information and your own knowledge.

1 How did the Allied air raids change people's morale from what it had been in the first few years of the war?

2 Compare the home front in Britain and in Germany. What were the similarities and differences in rationing and evacuation?

3 What changes did the war bring to the lives of

   a women

   b young people in Germany?

Review: what was it like living in Hitler's Germany?

MOST GERMANS WERE SATISFIED WITH HITLER'S LEADERSHIP

> Hitler restored national pride by flouting the Treaty of Versailles.

> He gave Germans strong, authoritarian government, which was what many wanted after the mess left by the Weimar politicians.

> He dealt ruthlessly with minorities who were unpopular anyway.

NAZI PERSECUTION

> Some Germans did resist Hitler and the Nazis, but those who opposed the Third Reich or who did not belong to the Aryan 'master race' were intimidated.

> The Gestapo and the SS rounded up suspects, tortured them and put them in camps.

> Many ordinary Germans helped the Gestapo by acting as informers.

> Concentration camps were set up early in Hitler's dictatorship.

> Minorities, especially Jews, were persecuted during the 1930s by laws intended to exclude them from German life. Many emigrated. After 1942, those that stayed were caught up in the Holocaust.

HOW DID PEOPLE REACT TO HITLER'S RULE?

> Young Germans were happy to join the Hitler Youth because of the range of outdoor activities offered to them. At school, lessons were deliberately used to indoctrinate children with Nazi values and beliefs: girls should grow up to be mothers, boys should learn to be soldiers.

> Workers lost rights when their trade unions were abolished, but benefited from the job opportunities in some of the public works started by Hitler.

> Rearming Germany and conscription helped to reduce unemployment and prepared the country for the war which Hitler wanted.

HOW DID THE WAR AFFECT THE GERMANS?

> The vast majority of Germans did not want war. Hitler's initial successes bolstered his popularity with the public. However, after losing the battle of Stalingrad against the Soviet Union in 1943, the tide of war turned against Germany and the Führer's popularity waned.

> Life was hard for German soldiers and civilians. Rationing, evacuation and shortages all took their toll, although the situation was not as severe as it had been in 1918.

> When Hitler committed suicide in 1945 his dream of a thousand-year-old Reich was left in ruins after just twelve years.

The surviving leaders of Hitler's Third Reich were put on trial for war crimes at the Nuremberg law courts. Twelve received death sentences.

Index